Due Return	Due Return
Date Date	Date Date

Jonson and the comic truth

Jonson

and the comic truth

JOHN J. ENCK

The University of Wisconsin Press

Madison, Milwaukee, and London: 1966

Published by The University of Wisconsin Press
Madison, Milwaukee, and London

U.S.A.: Box 1379, Madison, Wisconsin 53701
U.K.: 26-28 Hallam Street, London, W. 1

Printed in the United States of America
Library of Congress Catalog Card Number 57-9815

TO HARRY LEVIN

Acknowledgments

"I ha' such luck to spinne out these fine things still, and like a Silke-worme, out of my selfe." Not wanting to second John Littlewit's opening words in *Bartholomew Fair*, I am pleased by the opportunity to thank those who have aided me in writing this book. A fellowship from the President and Fellows of Harvard University for the summer of 1950 and a grant from the Research Committee of the Graduate School of the University of Wisconsin in the summer of 1952 both helped me to enlarge the scope of my doctoral dissertation into this study. I am grateful for the co-operation of the staffs in the libraries of the institutions where I worked: the University of Wisconsin, Harvard University (especially the Houghton Library), the Warburg Institute, and the British Museum.

During the preparation of the manuscript, Jonas A. Barish, from whose knowledge of Jonson I have always profited, pointed out lapses of information and judgment. William L. Hedges, generously taking time from his own research in a field remote from Elizabethan drama, read my first drafts and revisions; his incisive analyses of the speculative passages were particularly enlightening. My colleagues at the University of Wisconsin proved always sympathetic, and I owe special acknowledgments to Miss Helen C. White, Robert K. Presson, and Alvin Whitley. Suggestions by Gerald Eades Bentley, S. F. Johnson, and Ralph M. Sargent lessened the chore of clearing up the final copy. By the dedication I can at best try to repay part of the interest on a debt which has mounted for eight years.

Nevertheless, I was unable, or unwilling, to incorporate all comments. For example, several readers thought a preface would launch the book more gracefully. In the terms I projected for this study, I believe that, if it succeeds, no introduction is needed; should it fail, a few extra pages of explanation will make no difference. The decisions to exclude some fine things and to keep some perhaps less-than-fine ones have, obviously, like John Littlewit's pretty conceit, been spun by their respective authors.

John J. Enck

Madison, Wisconsin
9 January 1957

Contents

Jonson and the comic truth

Perdix

"**H**IS IMPRESSA was a Compass with one foot jn Center, the other Broken, the word. Deest qūod duceret orbem."[1] Jonson's emblem, reported by Drummond of Hawthornden, illustrates the complementary positives and negatives between which his addicted craftsmanship flourished. A joy in elegance and an anxiety about the shoddy always guided his writing. The reputation for thoroughness, contrived as skillfully as his comedies, after three centuries has a happy ending: posterity agrees that nearly alone among English authors he measured every syllable. One irony, which Jonson, connoisseur of all ironies, overlooked, blights his laurel: later generations have preferred comfortably incomplete compositions, which readers themselves can round out. In Scotland, on one of his infrequent journeys, he further confided to Drummond of Hawthornden, who jotted down conversational snippets, that he envisioned "tartars & turks Romans and Carthaginions" (I, p. 141) fighting battles around his great toe. Such idle phantasies do not disturb his lines. Wholeness forbids sentimental detours by writers or readers, and such accepted clichés as classical and pedantic are still used to describe his style. Jonson's editors suggest that the emblematic motto echoes a classic, Ovid's *Metamorphoses*, "altera pars staret, pars altera duceret orbem,"[2] in Daedalus' and Icarus' adventures. While the father buries his fallen son, a partridge beats its wings and whistles. A digression explains its curious delight. The bird is Daedalus' metamorphosed nephew, Perdix, the word for partridge in Greek and Latin. The boy's ingenuity in contriving a saw and a compass, thus the "altera . . . altera," made the uncle so jealous that he pushed his apprenticed relative from a wall of Minerva's temple. The favorably disposed goddess of wisdom snatched her young worshiper in air and, with capriciously divine charity, transfigured him into a partridge. Frightened by its traumatic plunge, that bird stays close to the ground and does not soar. Perhaps Jonson himself claims praise for being merely Daedalus' nephew, one saved by knowledge but, as a condition of this gift, unable to brave the irregular heights accessible to the winged cripple who symbolizes, at present, the artist.[3]

The twentieth century seldom grants him this distinction without quibbling. Possibly he invited his fate as the happy hunting ground of self-styled antiquaries, who, if they return, bear petrified trophies of his, and their, learning. Perhaps he earned his cramped niche in the Abbey and in memory while around both floats the jovial tag, "O Rare."[4] A number of prejudices have hampered the forming of opinions between the very general and quite special. For several decades critics and scholars have profitably reconsidered works by Jonson's contemporaries. When they come to him, most have admitted that he deserves recognition but that indelible flaws mar the achievements. Having perfunctorily rejected the heroic proportions which he bestowed on himself, they proceed to explain his limits by taking over the nineteenth-century criteria. The double view prevails that he is as good as possible and that his very manner betrayed him. Until these standards, which distort perspectives, are removed, he cannot take a place even as a modest Perdix.

Shakespeare is the first misconception. A usually drab literary history cannot resist the flamboyant contrasts which arise from pitting Jonson against Shakespeare. Everybody, except Jonson, wins in this fixed match where the seventeenth-century underdog emerges the all-time world champion. Obviously Jonson could never have written *Troilus and Cressida, King Lear, The Winter's Tale,* or *Titus Andronicus,* but he did not aspire to. The Elizabethan and Jacobean dramatists with whom Shakespeare may be contrasted more profitably, Kyd, Marlowe, Tourneur, and Webster, escape the Procrustean standard in part because Jonson's stature invites comparisons and mainly because his career nearly parallels Shakespeare's: literary coordinates are kept quaintly temporal. Apart from being contemporaries, the two have as little in common as artists practicing identical genres can. M. C. Bradbrook's survey of Elizabethan comedy starts with refreshing impartiality but soon tacks on qualifications.

> Among the great, Ben Jonson and Shakespeare stand so far above all competitors that they may well be called the creators of English drama . . . . But whereas 'Shakespeare's magic could not copied be', Jonson provided the succeeding age with a model which was only too acceptable. His influence might be compared with that of Milton on the subsequent writers of heroic verse. The 'Chinese wall' which he built against barbarism remained to divide Elizabethan from all subsequent drama; after Jonson nothing was quite the same again.[5]

Not, one cannot resist adding, until the nineteenth century; playwrights then made a shambles of that wall to rescue Shakespeare. And, while today Wycherley and Congreve enjoy revivals, only the realists who reacted against all poetic drama endure from the later period. Conversely, praying for Jonson need not posit imprecating Shakespeare. Until Jonson's achievements command a fairer evaluation, however, to be judicious one may ignore the works of the man whom he praised with keener warmth than did anyone else who, before 1623, thought the poet-entrepreneur from Stratford-upon-Avon merited a tribute.

The first mistaken approach swings too far beyond Jonson; the second ranges too widely within his own domains. A few English writers, notably Dryden and T. S. Eliot, have equaled his quality in scope and richness. Most essays on the two later poets content themselves with a single aspect, whereas Jonson's commentators gleefully play the field. Even excluding the drama, his variety demands a reader with a catholic taste. Among his poems he rated the epigrams highly. The neglected form will not enjoy a foreseeable revival, but this dearth of interest renders judgments quite hazardous. Who can pronounce how good Jonson's epigrams are, how much better than those of John Owen, the epigrammatist whose Latin exercises he summarily dismissed? The poetry encompasses a continent of metrics and subjects, most of them brilliantly exploited: lyrics, epistles, satires, and odes.[6] Of greater significance is the form he initiated and, simultaneously, perfected in English: the masque, over half of its surviving examples contrived by him.[7] As usual, the more courtly a genre in the past, the more academic the dust covering it in the twentieth century. Masques, as art, pass every test of endurance except one, the strength to be transplanted from the contexts for which they were created into foreign ones. In spite of well-meaning experimental groups who fitfully resurrect a specimen (and then usually they light on Milton's awkward *Comus*[8]), no one can today envision a full performance when royalty danced for nobility. They represent, with their ingenious *décors* and lavish costumes by Inigo Jones, awesome instances of late Renaissance creativity lavished on toys, Leonardo's mechanical lion or Michelangelo's snow statue. Whether or not Jonson lectured at Gresham College,[9] his random *aperçus*, titled *Timber*, penetrate their subject more trenchantly than does most of the Elizabethan "gallimaufry" which passes, in lieu of a neater term, for literary criticism.[10] The debt these reflections owe their eclectic sources does not vitiate their accuracy as evidence of insight.[11] A miscellany testifies to Jonson's diversified talents: translation, collaboration, a few surviving letters, and an English grammar. To appreciate any one of these achievements argues a highly cultivated taste in Jonson and in an audience. Although the collected works of other Elizabethans may bulk as large, none claims equal substance in every branch.

This unassertive excellence of composition tolerates a third error. The finality which he demanded in his script before printing asks unusually close attention from readers. To compensate for this thwarting of their imaginations, many have cut apart his plays and refashioned them into portraits of Jonson and his rivals. The most elusive passage will be tied down eventually to a reasonable number of possibilities for any given generation, but a dead writer's personality accommodates as many interpretations as interpreters. In this pursuit most have regarded Jonson as though he were the armed Prologue of *Poetaster*, hectoring his innocent associates. He presumably plagued from himself a labyrinth of libel, allusion, parody, and anagram, which the producers and audiences mistook for plays. Whatever conclusions psychologists and sociologists may reach by such investigations, for literary studies the double reflection from the page to author and back to the page distorts. When Jonson wrote about Shakespeare, "[Thou] art aliue still, while thy Booke doth liue, / And we haue wits to read, and praise to giue" (VIII, p. 391), he placed the emphasis where it should fall.

As if to counterbalance those who gaze through the works to discern the man Jonson, an equal number contend that he lacked individuality, his mind being a lumber room of fragments stolen from every writer under the European sun. Like schoolboys who cannot dismiss a master's superior learning, they presume a familiarity and call him Ben. Jonson was the first to acknowledge his sources. In *Timber* he defined his theories of borrowing with the qualification, "*One*, though hee be excellent, and the chiefe, is not to bee imitated alone. For never no Imitator, ever grew up to his *Author;* likenesse is alwayes on this side Truth. . . ." (VIII, p. 590) He considered his library a storehouse equivalent to those first lines which the gods sometimes bestow and for which, as Valéry observed,[12] the dedicated poet must contrive a second equally fine. The most meager talent will stumble across a winning touch here and there, if only through a typographical error. A true author blends every stroke into one single text. For this ability Jonson has no peers. Without wasteful research it is impossible to trace the borders of demarcation between where another's phrase stops and his own invention begins. A survey of how he adapted will indicate his standards and powers.

All his contemporaries played the same game with the same pack: doctoring old plots, lifting characters, devising sequels, and picking up lines. They avoid the strictures because, like Cibber, they can boast their ignorance of works in which the supposed thefts took place; wrongs against letters and society always invoke heavier pun-

ishments if they are premeditated. A plea in Jonson's defense cannot
cite any laws because the code governing attitudes toward plagiarism,
crime, the artistic temperament, and pardons takes erratic turns. (Jean
Genet supposedly made the acute observation that, after having been
sponsored by Cocteau, Jouvet, and Sartre, were he to be booked
again for robbery, everybody would dismiss it as kleptomania.) With
an author less honest about his pilferings, the imagination can resemble
a mental philosophers' stone and transform them into higher art.
Jonson, believing no more in psychic than physical alchemy, eschewed
apologetics. The casual echoes one hears in his lines mean that his
mind must have been fully stocked with phrases which he responded
to with as direct an awareness as do romantic sensibilities to the
countryside. A blind search for ornaments would not have unearthed
enough to permit his completing one play. A random passage in
Cynthia's Revels, singled out by two editors for praise, reveals how
casually the borrowings enter.

> In the lively description of Argurion in particular, as Gifford well
> remarks, 'the literal and metaphorical sense is so blended as to form
> a very distinct, though an amusing representation'. She is not only
> 'a *Nymph* of a most wandring and giddy disposition', but a symbol
> for money. 'Shee spreads as shee goes.... Your yong student (for the
> most part) shee affects not, only salutes him, and away. . . .'[13]

The selection merits the encomium. A fickle woman symbolizes
money and gains attendants as she proceeds in society, like a widow
with her gigolos. The touch, "shee spreads as shee goes," hits the right
note for both the woman's seeking more diversions and the expensive
tastes of the vulgar rich. While composing this, Jonson surely recalled
Virgil's phrase, "mobilitate viget."[14] In the *Aeneid*, however, it depicts the cumulative height of a monstrous rumor rushing from mouth
to mouth until the momentum suggests acceleration, whereas the force
of money lessens with distribution. Jonson unquestionably had encountered the passage, and this assertion does not have to presuppose
his familiarity with Latin literature. In *Poetaster*, the satire jerry-built
after *Cynthia's Revels*, Virgil himself figures among the dramatis
personae. At the end he reads aloud to the Emperor Augustus from

his Work in Progress; the chosen selection is the description of Rumor. Here, because Virgil embodies the ideal poet, opposed to the poetasters, the translation rings sternly, *"That mouing growes...."* (V. ii. 76)

As with brief borrowings, when Jonson reworked traditional concepts, he always kept a definite end in view which the direction of the verse itself shapes to the purpose.[15] A tirade from *Every Man out of His Humour* has Macilente complain of those who advance in station because of fawning rather than achievement.

> Who can endure to see blinde *Fortune* dote thus?
> To be enamour'd on this dustie turfe?
> This clod? a whorson puck-fist? O god, god, god, god, &c.
> I could runne wild with griefe now, to behold
> The ranknesse of her bounties, that doth breed
> Such bull-rushes; these mushrompe gentlemen,
> That shoot vp in a night to place, and worship. (I. ii. 157–63)

Blind Fortune and her wheel need no comment. Dust and inability fit together agreeably. The comparison of the pretentious climber lacking any real merit with a mushroom derives from English satirists, who did not have to search widely in Latin poetry to light on it. As part of a sequence of expletives, it describes fools appropriately and, furthermore, transforms a generalized locale into a specific setting. Fortune's blindness produces effects; she is a fickle woman like Argurion of *Cynthia's Revels*. When she dotes on what is dry and worthless, this lavishness causes the ground to push up rank growths indiscriminately. Bullrushes and mushrooms depict a lackluster flabbiness flourishing in moist wastes. The final line reinforces the comparison and returns with heavier disgust to blind Fortune, now equally strong in nature and society. *Every Man out of His Humour*, if comparatively early, already bears the identifying trademarks.

When several lines are retained, they blend with their context as smoothly as do the shorter phrases or traditional expressions. In a late play, *The Staple of News*, Peniboy Junior loves Lady Pecunia, who personifies aspects of money. Being an eager youth, he expresses his emotions in an agitated figure.

> P. Iv. My passion was cleare contrary, and doubtfull,
> I shooke for feare, and yet I danc'd for ioy,
> I had such motions as the Sunne-beames make
> Against a wall, or playing on a water,
> Or trembling vapour of a boyling pot—   (II. v. 63–67)

Part of this obviously derives from Virgil:

> sicut aquae tremulum labris ubi lumen aënis
> sole repercussum aut radiantis imagine lunae
> omnia pervolitat late loca iamque sub auras
> erigitur summique ferit laquearia tecti.[16]

The two deviate in tone; unlike the original, Peniboy Junior's figure lurches with rhapsodic clumsiness. Light does not leap upward to the ceiling but fumes away on the heavy pot. The miser Peniboy Senior parodies the already distorted image by substituting alchemical terminology more appropriate for an allegorical Lady Pecunia: "That's not so good, it should ha' bin a *Crucible*, / With molten mettall, she had vnderstood it." (II. v. 68–69)

A single source extended throughout several speeches achieves, likewise, the desired effects. *Epicene*, occupying the mid-point in Jonson's career, features husbands and wives, who see themselves growing old in loveless marriages. One metaphor on this condition sighs in a pensive prose.

> Hav. Besides, ladies should be mindfull of the approach of age, and
>   let no time want his due vse. The best of our daies passe first.
> Mav. We are riuers, that cannot be call'd backe, madame: shee that
>   now excludes her louers, may liue to lie a forsaken beldame,
>   in a frozen bed.   (IV. iii. 40–45)

The Virgilian "optima dies . . . prima fugit" requires neither documentation nor apology, although the connotation here renders the sentiment more gauche than elegiac. The second speech originates, as does much of *Epicene*, in Ovid, *Ars Amatoria*, but Jonson's English usually slants the translation along a satiric bias.

> Dum licet, et vernos etiamnum educitis annos,
>   Ludite: eunt anni more fluentis aquae;
>
> .   .   .   .
>
> Nec quae praeteriit, hora redire potest.[17]

The Latin lacks the pun on bed, the right harshness of the term beldame, and the overtone that the best days of spring age into sterile winter. Ovid elsewhere implied this aspect but with less economy of statement: "Tempus erit, quo tu, quae nunc excludis amantes, / Frigida deserta nocte iacebis anus. . . ."[18] Jonson prepared his dialogue carefully and compared a woman's accepting lovers with objects to anticipate the figure, "Is the *Thames* the lesse for the *dyers* water, mistris? . . . Or a torch, for lighting many torches?" (IV. iii. 34–36) Moreover, *Epicene* has two other images of frozen rivers, a condition uniquely appropriate for this play and seldom featured elsewhere.

Instances and examples might run on for pages, but the long demonstration would prove nothing new. If a borrowing clangs insistently, an extra fillip enhances it. This effect resembles a *trompe l'oeil* painting where, when one detects the trickery, the picture acquires an added depth of surface brilliance.[19] Just as the validity of this deceit requires the viewer to discover the virtuosity for himself, so part of the pleasure of Jonson arises from the unexpected turns famous lines take. These surprises intrude most often in *Epicene*. For the majority of comedies the inserted phrases belong to Jonson's regular mental process, and a reader need take no more cognizance of their origins than did the groundlings at a performance.

One last example of the mishmash resulting from too finicky an attribution of sources links Jonson, the nineteenth century, and a more recent writer. "The Second Coming" expresses in subject and diction a concentrated Yeatsian vision. Well known as it is, perhaps the first lines may be quoted again.

> Turning and turning in the widening gyre
> The falcon cannot hear the falconer;
> Things fall apart; the centre cannot hold;
> Mere anarchy is loosed upon the world,
> The blood-dimmed tide is loosed, and everywhere
> The ceremony of innocence is drowned;
> The best lack all conviction, while the worst
> Are full of passionate intensity.[20]

The independent images mount to the resoundingly ornate picture of disintegration, "passionate intensity." One would not expect to encounter this phrase in the prose of a poet for whom Yeats had qualified admiration. Nevertheless, Swinburne applied it to *Volpone* in his essays on Jonson.[21] Should one, then, read Yeats's "The Second Coming" with Swinburne's *Ben Jonson*, or Jonson's *Volpone*, or both the study and the play in mind? Or, since out of context the adjective-noun combination suggests, and may in fact have, a more remote source, should one go excavating elsewhere for the common ancestor? Or, since none of these nuggets appreciably enriches "The Second Coming," should one forget about the matter, except as one of those banal coincidences of literary history?

When willing to relegate marginal distractions such as his sources to their proper places, audiences and readers have genuinely appreciated Jonson. Throughout the seventeenth century his reputation appears to have been unexcelled,[22] and he held the stage in the eighteenth. With the nineteenth a decline started, and, while revivals have occurred now and then in the twentieth, praise falls short of enthusiasm. Enough critics whose opinions have instigated other revaluations have recommended him. T. S. Eliot's early essay found the plays congenial and modern.[23] John Crowe Ransom, in what has become the most publicized speculative comment on poetics for its decade, *The New Criticism*, glanced back at Eliot's conclusions.[24] Harry Levin edited a generous selection in the series of Nonesuch Press anthologies, and his preface analyzed the accomplishments persuasively.[25] Elizabeth Bowen saw fit to preserve a discerning review in a collection of articles.[26] Louis Kronenberger's gentle outline of English comedy recognized the obligation to credit Jonson with its inception.[27]

In all of these, however, the authors could touch points as they chose. For a more exhaustive enquiry, to gloss over topics generally considered essential may look irresponsible. The matter of borrowings, as has been seen, interposes no insurmountable barrier between the page and what it says. Similarly, for all practical purposes, the facts of Jonson's biography need not detain one unduly. The interrelations between a writer and his book throw a commentator on his own resources. In spite of a multiplicity of theories, the processes of artistic creation veer closer by their nature to the miraculous than to the demonstrable. With Jonson, especially, enough reports and rumors have been preserved to tempt one to easy explanations. The obvious data may be reviewed quickly.

He was born in 1571 or 1572, some months after his father's death. The circumstances scarcely predicted the kind of literature to which he later dedicated himself. His mother appears to have possessed the determined and domineering temperament that frequently drives a son to the arts when it does not first crush him. She remarried, and his stepfather, a bricklayer, attempted to induce the boy to enter his trade. Most critics mention this phase of his career with uneasy snobbishness or hearty fellowship, as though his poetry exemplifies a bricklayer's temperament versified: chunk cemented upon chunk. The comparison rings as true as analogies can, but his skill in construction, the craft of Perdix, requires no special attitudes when one has studied the results. Camden, an antiquary and schoolteacher, made Jonson his protégé and saw that the boy's education progressed as far as possible. Perhaps to escape a dull apprenticeship, he entered the army and served in Flanders with a degree of distinction. Subsequently, his early career in letters took the expected turns from acting with slight ability, to patching old plays, to composing his own, now lost, and looking for patrons.

Jonson lived a long time, longer than the majority of his contemporaries. In terms of literary activity, particularly for his kind of artistry, he enjoyed a surprisingly short span; in less than two decades all his memorable plays had appeared. Between 1598 and 1616 his talents for an authoritative innovation expanded with breath-taking sureness: he defined the comedy of humours, gave the English stage a unique tragedy, dedicated *Volpone* to Oxford and Cambridge, and issued the folio collection. From the initial entry of James I into London he assumed that he would serve as the royal entertainer. The coincidence of James and Jonson was an auspicious one. However unsatisfactorily the court may have functioned in governing the middle class, as patron of aristocratic arts it flourished for one of the rare times in British history without a parsimony that precluded grandeur. The feuding French and Spanish ambassadors may have stolen the show sometimes,[28] but James's royal celebrations represent a genuine expression of the baroque over which Jonson alone had the taste and energy to preside. With increasing patronage, his activities for the stage began to decline. The remainder of James's reign confirmed Jonson's triumphs, which culminated in a claim of being the poet laureate. The last years crumbled under misfortunes. He had to wheedle Charles I, nobles, the city of London, and theaters for money. He lost out at a court less kindly disposed toward him and expenditures. Illnesses troubled him until his death in 1637. His later plays were fiascoes, and not without justification. In the face of these defeats, an admirable confidence assured him of his powers and sustained him in his writing, the vocation to which he unflaggingly pledged himself.

The public career traces a decline from unqualified success to partial failure, but in personal affairs feuds troubled almost every year. The most famous episode involves the skirmishes between Jonson on one side against, at the very least, Marston and Dekker in opposition. This much may be affirmed. Whether the War of the Theaters encompassed other controversies, over how many plays it extended, who, if any, the other participants were, and what issues it indirectly included are problems still enlisting different partisans. Such conjectures bear directly upon one of Jonson's plays, *Poetaster*, and speculation about them can wait until the appropriate chapter. Jonson never shrank from battles, but he seldom won an undisputed victory. Inigo Jones, whose heavy decoration of the masques Jonson regarded as closer to decadence than vitality, managed to wrest most advantages away from him in their quarrels. Few associates escaped Jonson's spleen entirely. One shudders to think of the persuasions brought to bear on William Stansby in having him agree to publish an expensive folio without a precedent for its contents. In poems, masques, plays, and letters Jonson sprinkled his unflattering impressions of his printers and booksellers. The catalogue of names and trades could be extended on and on. The greatest enemy was the theater audience itself. If, however, his bluntness offended, it also retained friends. His association with Camden began when he was young and continued unbroken. Antiquaries and noblemen who shared his love of books and knowledge found his company congenial. Once he insisted on being imprisoned although no charges were brought against him, when his collaborators on *Eastward Ho* were in danger of being tried for offending the crown. A group of younger poets chose him their leader, and his popularity in the London taverns has been sufficiently publicized. Although friendship lasted long, enmity soon died down. Marston not only forgave him but dedicated *The Malcontent* to him and, along with Chapman, collaborated on *Eastward Ho*, which culminated in Jonson's gesture. Any insistence that the drive for alienation dominated over the motives of affection argues a vindictiveness more deeply embedded in his biographers than in Jonson himself.

Apart from friends and enemies, added conditions of his life may be chosen almost at random. He married a woman whom he mentioned seldom and bluntly. For a period he became a Catholic convert, but neither entering nor quitting that faith traced discernible allegiances across his writings. Brief travels and several prison sentences alone interrupted an unbroken residence as a citizen in or around London. Under Camden's guidance he collected books avidly, although losses by fire or by sale because of debts reduced a notable library. One might mention more characteristics, but the facts point toward few surprises. Even the improvisations of fictional biography cannot go far wrong when filling in spaces; several of them have been published,[29] and Edwin Arlington Robinson conjured a ghost to declaim a long monologue, "Ben Jonson Entertains a Man from Stratford."[30] From first to last the printed page itself attracted him, and to it he devoted all his energies. The traits in which his art was rooted provide the broadly relevant outlines; the rest is unprofitable conjecture. The merely personal detaches itself at once. Everything else derives from a sternly disciplined mentality which is peculiar only in the sense that few other writers have brought their faculties to an equal pitch of consciousness.

For literature Jonson cheerfully subjugated himself to every aspect of his task. Although bordering on anonymity, as true craftsmanship does, his penchant for completeness furnishes a positive foundation for all comments about him. The basic unit of his verse does not derive from the line but from the rhythm and orchestration of the whole to which it contributes a share. Citations from him do not flourish in books of quotations. His characters, likewise, resist being yanked out of their contexts and looming as myths or imagoes. They are reputedly "flat," possessors of one trait which they exhibit as part of their—the most damning consistency of all—humours. Complacent opinion keeps him a writer in spite of himself, one whose dull determination squeezed out invective beneath a study lamp against his better judgment.[31] A true appreciation begins with the consent to sustain the multiple details within a pattern rather than seizing a few touchstones. Taking a part for the whole still enjoys an unquestioned vogue in modern aesthetics; the reputations of the Niké of Samothrace, the Elgin Marbles, the Venus de Milo, and Samuel Taylor Coleridge would be rated proportionately lower if they suggested less picturesque ruins to the twentieth century.

A condition of wholeness in art relies, basically, upon survival. Here, again, Jonson wins a Pyrrhic victory. Although the stunning edition by C. H. Herford and Percy and Evelyn Simpson lists many variants, the majority of these tabulate Jonson's own emendations or his corrections of printers' errors.[32] Most of his extant plays, shortly after their productions, appeared in quartos which he himself saw through the presses. In 1616 a folio with all his writings up to that date which he chose to preserve marked an innovation in publication. The earlier plays had been thoroughly revised, although the degree of change differed. He gravely called this volume *Works;* unlike other English satirists, Pope and Max Beerbohm, who mockingly designated their youthful collections with this title, Jonson claimed distinction, a bit of pomposity on which contemporary caricature at once seized. Except for *Bartholomew Fair,* this folio contains all the important plays, some masques, but less of the poetry and no prose. He may have planned a second volume and supervised the proofreading of parts. Because of his failing health, it remained unfinished and was finally brought out posthumously. This attainment, nevertheless, surpasses any other dramatist's of the period in providing an authentic text. Because of the romantic assumption that mediocrity is brash and true genius indifferent, the precautions tell against him.

He devoted equal care to every genre in which he worked. All seems of a piece, and a harmony undoubtedly prevails through his total output. For the time being, however, to take up a single group will yield the most satisfactory results. The compositions for the theater comprise the bulk of his work and promise the greatest rewards. Omitting the poems and, except for incidental points, the prose will allow the plays to stand forth clearly. Similarly, the distraction of lingering glances at contemporaries to the right or left, behind or before, would only encourage a reliance on the same old preoccupations. To insist on this much does not presuppose Jonson peerless, but fresh comparisons will emerge only after an isolated revaluation. He had independence in literary and social manners, as when signing the dedication of *Cynthia's Revels* to the court, "Thy seruant, but not slaue." (IV, p. 33) Setting the plays off in a partial vacuum does not posit them in any wider sense *sui generis*. In constructing them Jonson obeyed the rules he laid down and was a slave to no other critic. Nevertheless, their own design remains obscure, a damaging oversight if one accepts Jonson as Perdix. After their individual proportions emerge, they may offer useful facts about the nature of comedy itself.

The text itself lays down the obvious foundation, signed as it is with Jonson's mark, "approved for posterity." Minutiae, such as act and scene divisions or typography, distinctly correspond to the individual plays. Anyone sufficiently skilled might analyze each one separately without knowing the author or any other work by him and emerge with a nearly adequate estimate. They do, however, give rise to each other, and the corpus transcends being the strict sum of its members. His arranging the folio in one way argues a purpose, and a chronological survey will simplify definitions of larger concepts. Out of this sequence may arise the tendencies of a general rationale which will refer back to and enhance single plays. Satirists, Swift and Evelyn Waugh, for example, do not as a rule command unlimited gifts; their success requires them to utilize each morsel of their talent. Jonson, although more vigorous, observed the same principle of conservation. He never repeated himself, and his ability in circumventing limitations has no equal. Viewing the plays in order of composition helps to explain why they mature in the pattern they do. This procedure supplies three complementary points of view, which do not claim the same importance throughout: the structure of the separate work, how each fits into a general pattern of change, and, finally, the unresolved elements which, dependent upon other factors, underlie otherwise puzzling insufficiencies. The humours will illustrate how this method of study can increase understanding. Far from being a cut and dried concept, they function with unsuspected vitality in places, decline in a curious manner, and in part contribute to the late failures.

Extracting a modern humor from the Renaissance humours establishes Jonson's profound awareness of the scope available to comedy. At the start of the sixteenth century another master craftsman depicted melancholia, one of the four humours, but Dürer envisioned a figure cursed with intellectual acedia. Erwin Panofsky, summoning his usual erudition, traced the medieval background of the design then described Dürer's refinements in terms of the Renaissance.

> Winged, yet cowering on the ground—wreathed, yet beclouded by shadows—equipped with the tools of art and science, yet brooding in idleness, she gives the impression of a creative being reduced to despair by an awareness of insurmountable barriers which separate her from a higher realm of thought. . . .
> In the light of this system Dürer's Melancholia, the "Artist's Melancholy," can in fact be classified as "Melencolia I." Moving as she does in the sphere of the "imagination"—which is, by definition, the sphere of spatial quantities—she typifies the first, or least exalted, form of human ingenuity. She can invent and build, and she can think, to quote Henry of Ghent, "as long as her imagination keeps step with her thought"; but she has no access to the metaphysical world. . . . Thus Dürer's Melancholia belongs in fact to those who "cannot extend their thought beyond the limits of space." Hers is the inertia of a being which renounces what it could reach because it cannot reach for what it longs.[33]

A willed acceptance of what he could reach permitted Jonson his expanding control over the comic truth, which eschews the Faustian ambitions of peering into hidden destinies. Rather, it revels in the knowable and disdains immoderate desire. Consequently, it can, within its designated sphere, promulgate a truth about human capacities and rejoice because all else must ultimately be vanity. The undertaking does not deny the existence of major truths but loftily admits that they lie beyond demonstration. Nevertheless, pushed far enough, comedy may embarrassingly discover that even rudimentary "facts" sometimes fail and that the simplest formulae yield results not covered by textbooks. (The multiple levels will define themselves more clearly in the ensuing chapters.) Resigned to its peculiarities, although comedy must judge, it suspects sweeping assertions because it knows how quickly truths may crumble as nonsense. It vigilantly summons any strength, if only to prove a weakness: ever conscious of how puny man's senses are, it probes them for whatever value they might, with luck, contain; always on the brink of melancholy, it thinks in secret so that publicly it may unmask logic as illogical; respectful of others' intuitions, it admits self-delusion never ends; fearful of passions, it plays the court jester to forestall what might otherwise drive them to tragedy. The truth of comedy, from children's masquerades to *Volpone*, happily guards its own prerogatives and seeks to annex no other. What raises Jonson to his eminent height is not just his grasp of such matters but the form in which he embodied them to bestow their enduring theatrical life.

What binds all considerations into one design is the language itself. Whatever else these dramas have, their poetry and prose, above all, proclaim their distinction. This wonderfully contrived stage speech, while never poetic in a commonly accepted sense, sweeps together wild declamations and rapid chatter into a sustained diction. In effects the style approaches two modern writers with whom Jonson shares much: James and Joyce. The language suits the purpose of each work, but it is not quite identical with it so that the disproportions add the abiding tensions which distinguish *The Wings of the Dove* and *Ulysses*. Appreciating this richness comes last in a recognition of Jonson's qualities. Because he designed his dialogues for the theater, they should be heard there. Opportunities to attend performances being as rare as they are, clumsy substitutes, like essays and explications, must serve, granted all their inadequacies.

This discussion should have cleared the ground. Other problems may be faced as they arise. If the sum total promises broader observations, this prospect does not grant permission to pass by what may seem slight topics or to take anything at face value. With a writer of Jonson's cumulative complexity, the assessing of the accomplishment follows after a slow journey, not upon a hasty beginning. The knowledge gathered along the way will, in the long run, furnish the most interesting conclusions. What must guide a fair consideration of any art is the simple desire for apprehending the practice of the creation itself, the triumph of the craftsman who performs his trade so surely that without ruses he translates dexterity into prestidigitation close to a practical magic. An exhilaration accompanies watching the freedom which sheer skill in executing the difficult engenders. An artist accepts the general rules, adds his own refinements of them, and obeys them faithfully, although thousands of short cuts exist. The formulation should apply to tragedy as well as comedy, but comedy, especially, stays close to a game which relies upon the limitations governing it. Jonson's command and authority derive from a critical awareness of the comic tradition and his rights to expand it. By sheer manipulation of the elements within a narrow compass he achieves overwhelming mastery of the knowable; compared with this attainment, any exciting flights of fancy are vulgar and crude. In a word, his implements are not the wax and feathers of Daedalus but the saw and compass of Perdix.

CHAPTER II

A Little Puffe of Scorne

No ATTENDING genius shook a wand above Jonson's cradle to bestow his precision and clarity instinctively; he purchased both piecemeal at prodigious cost. He had to prompt himself, always, that "if wee fetch the originall of our *Metaphore* from sea, and billowes; wee end not in flames and ashes. . . ." (VIII, pp. 624–25) His completed folio and the one partially proofread represent the bulk of his literary bequest; excavating fragments ignores the spirit of his testament. Nevertheless, unauthorized texts at the outset, *The Case Is Altered*, and toward the end, *The Sad Shepherd*,[1] offer new perspectives on official structures which by themselves look austerely self-sufficient. Two common assumptions about *The Case Is Altered*, that the script does not belong to Jonson[2] and that no similarities link it with the next play, *Every Man in His Humour*, often dismiss it as a trial run which failed. Such opinions, whose misconceptions reinforce each other, appear untenable after a review of the facts of its publication.

When Jonson brought out the folio *Works* in 1616, he led off the cycle with *Every Man in His Humour*, the inception, he claimed, of a new kind of comedy whose rules he thereafter obeyed. The notes to this volume exceed the information expected in printed drama at the time; pages before and after each play list data about time of first production, performing companies, the actors, etc. This camouflage has further protected *Every Man in His Humour*. Although given in 1598, it ranks as the discovery of his true métier, while *The Case Is Altered* remains a novice's indiscretion.[3] If Jonson's conscientiousness as an artist has been harped on, this is not to say he was absolutely honest, merely more honest than most of his contemporaries. In a choice between proving his own invariability and risking charges of improvisation, he was not above yielding to the temptation of stacking evidence for a hint at the more desirable, if undeserved, verdict. The background runs like this: during the last decade of the sixteenth century he had composed numerous plays, if one, perforce, trusts Meres's description of him in *Palladis Tamia* and Jonson's statement to Drummond of Hawthornden. All these juvenilia, except *The Case Is Altered*, have been lost. The first to enjoy general popularity was *Every Man in His Humour* on whose title he capitalized for *Every Man out of His Humour*. Although no one can now ascertain what the opening afternoons of these three plays actually presented, probably the remaining text of *The Case Is Altered* more closely approximates what was originally acted than do those of the two more famous. The first of them Jonson had printed in quarto was *Every Man out of His Humour*, which distended into a beetling book because, as the title page affirms and its inordinate length confirms, it was sold "*Containing more than hath been Publickely Spoken or Acted.*" (III, facing p. 418) The next year, 1601, appeared the earlier *Every Man in His Humour*, which may well have undergone a similar polishing; whether it did or not, tampering undeniably decked it out with the authority to head the folio. Pursuing the clues suggested by bibliography, a reading of the quarto *Every Man in His Humour* in the light of *The Case Is Altered* reveals more affinities between these two than between the two plays joined by a word. That *Every Man in His* and *Every Man out of His* are bracketed together because the term *Humour* handcuffs them illustrates how readily an assured writer can bully his audience. This line of reasoning leaves open the question why, since the author ignored the unwanted manuscript and was busy covering one set of his tracks, he permitted this offspring to emerge from the woods of oblivion at all.

A miraculous power attends the preservation of most Elizabethan plays: one possesses evidence of the event and believes it empirically, but its causes cannot scientifically be attributed to the usual machinery of the world. One can partially deduce why in 1609, over ten years after the first production, although there may have been interval revivals, a new firm of publishers, Bonian and Walley, secured *The Case Is Altered*. The few titles this partnership undertook indicate a shrewd perspicacity.[4] Probably wishing to add Jonson's name to their business, they obtained his permission to issue this old play when he had nothing else immediately available. Moreover, Jonson was planning his folio at this time, and he may have wished to test the possibilities of this script. The explanation looks satisfactory, but it is not incontrovertible. Obviously he had slight connection with the actual printing; he usually supervised both the format and correcting of his books. Indeed, *The Case Is Altered* did not claim anyone's attention. The title page has three variants, one of which lacks an author's name. It seems almost certain that Jonson's was added again after it had been inadvertently deleted to correct an error of the first setting.[5] If he refused to acknowledge the text with his usual care, the memory of it caused him no uneasiness. Into his copy of *Chorus Poetarum Classicorum Duplex; Sacrorum et Profanorum Lustratus Illustratus* he filled out correctly in longhand the cut or garbled passages of *Aulularia*, Plautus' comedy which he appropriated for *The Case Is Altered*. This anthology, published in 1616, must have come into his possession years after *The Case Is Altered* was acted on the stage, printed in quarto, and rejected for the folio.

As it stands, the script has a cogency. Brief sections which introduce Antonio Balladino and the description of an audience's bad manners in some "Utopian" theater are interpolations. Because remarks in a later scene prove that Balladino briefly usurps the function of another minor character and because Balladino probably parodies Anthony Munday, a poetaster with whom Jonson had not quarreled before 1600, his appearance may be dismissed as superfluous. The prose describing the Utopian stage progresses with a vigor Jonson had not yet mastered. By itself the best part of the play, it contributes nothing to the general themes. That two such patches can be conclusively isolated argues negatively the unity of the rest; more positively, the structural intricacies betray the talented novice so bent on achieving what he intends that he dare not glance aside or throw away a line.

Understandably this careful construction has gone unobserved. *The Case Is Altered* is usually labeled "romantic" in distinction to the (realistic? classic? satiric? humour?) folio comedies. The misleading factors are easily isolated. Jonson for the one time in his career stole two whole plots by transliterating *Captivi* and *Aulularia* out of Plautus' Latin into English. The story, obedient to this inherent cleavage, halves itself into the common Elizabethan double plot.[6] Commentators have therefore deduced a violation of Aristotelian unity and, lapsing into the easy either/or dichotomy, grouped it with the romantic.[7] Because five men want to marry a vapid ingénue, the assumption that love makes the action go round, whereas the comedies of humour banish it, is accepted. Because the setting is Milan and the satire is directed to less recognizably contemporary targets, spatial and temporal distance lends, of course, romantic enchantment. Because the verse and the prose wobble without mature fiber, a young poet sighs romantically. All such burgeonings of misinterpretation protrude when the play lies in a vacuum; placed in its rightful position, the very opposites of these opinions align its proportions more truly. Parallels and contrasts between the two parts dovetail squarely and quite transform what Plautus wrote. Rachel, sometimes elevated to a sketch for a girl worth ranking beside other supposedly romantic heroines,[8] functions as a cipher. The scene has as much to do with Milan as does Florence with the quarto *Every Man in His Humour:* that is, practically nothing. The follies ridiculed in both Milan and Florence are similar, and the methods of portraying them vary by technical refinements. If a more resourceful language paces the characters through *Every Man in His Humour* with freer agility than those in *The Case Is Altered*, the author sought no new effects; he embodied the same views more skillfully. On the strength of such observations the two earliest plays emphasize Jonson's inherent beliefs and heighten the really novel design he devised for satire in *Every Man out of His Humour*.

As a substitute for outlining the plots of *Captivi* and *Aulularia*, a brief summary of *The Case Is Altered* will lay the basis for noting what happens in Plautus and the major variations in Jonson. Count Terneze of Milan has two daughters, Aurelia and Phoenixella, and one son, Paulo. A second son, Camillo, had been lost as an infant during a military debacle at the hands of the French, whom the Milanese again are fighting. Paulo is taken by the enemy, who in turn lose the nobleman Chamont and his friend, a commoner, Gasper. On the day of battle these two, for no compelling reason, have exchanged names. Gasper, actually Chamont, returns to the French so that he may arrange Paulo's ransom for the price of Chamont's release. The ruse is revealed, but the real Chamont returns with Paulo in time to save Gasper from Terneze's rage at being tricked. It soon turns out that Gasper is Camillo, the lost son. So much derives approximately from *Captivi*. *Aulularia* supplies Jaques, a miser. Having stolen the gold and the daughter, called Rachel, of his French employer, he has emigrated to Milan. In seeking Terneze's aid when two servants, Juniper and Onion, rob him of his hoarded gold, he betrays himself into confessing his own crimes. Rachel, inevitably, proves herself to be Chamont's sister. This simplified outline provides the essential development, one no more unlikely than the revelations in *The Confidential Clerk*.

The leading, close to exclusive, concerns in *The Case Is Altered* turn on the oldest of dramatic themes: identity, recognition of the truth both about one's self and others. As fresh revelations dawn, the case is, of course, altered. The homilies for conduct stratify themselves into a series of precepts. In order to know one's self, one must not: be ignorant of one's family, appear better than one is, nor behave more meanly than one's appearance; in order to understand others, one must: sense true identity, unmask disguised evil, and perceive hidden virtue. The two trigrams of cautions combine in shifting negatives and positives to limit conduct. This code blithely assumes that goodness or vice exists in individuals as a self-contained chunk somewhat apart from what at any given moment they do or what surrounds them. The plot always turns on an aspect of comprehending personality; the figurative language refers repeatedly to it; from the outset the costumes reinforce it.

The death of Ferneze's wife, shortly before the action starts, occasions on a visual level the pervasive discussion of appearances. Neither of the sources hints at this topic. Were the invention gratuitous, an inexplicable pall would veil the scene, but mourning relates the disparate parts by costume. The play begins with Juniper, the familiar happy shoemaker, enlivening his work by a lurid song, an immediate attack on the popular stage and the broadside ballad, two institutions Jonson ridiculed constantly. Juniper leaves his shop when Onion presses him into service for the palace, where he will wear the prescribed black, "for now must I of a merry Cobler become ⟨a⟩ mourning creature." (I. i. 18–19)[9] Jonson, who always composed with the potentialities of his theater precisely in mind, thus merges by visual unity the two social levels. During the uncertainties of the second, third, and fourth acts the somber color spreads an atmosphere against which the rejoicing at the end glows more brightly. Numerous comments on the dreariness of the court underline the theme, and Ferneze's daughters frequently debate the necessity of this rite. The two are Jonson's own creation; their near monomania illustrates how undeviatingly he cultivated a thesis.

By the contrasting sister motif a sketchy characterization distinguishes Aurelia and Phoenixella; the differences between them substitute for individuality. They exist primarily by complementing each other; alone either would be more improbable. They agree chiefly that fashions can be pondered endlessly. When others are present they pointedly introduce the subject; when alone, they speculate on little else. Aurelia resents the restraints of mourning and, as an extension, of all curbs on spontaneity. When Phoenixella insists that the customs do not annoy her, Aurelia, judging by her own reactions, reproaches her for suppressing desires under the black. Phoenixella, in turn, accuses her sister of hypocrisy. These quaint disquisitions underline the theory behind the drama. Aurelia, in terms of this play, cannot be censured for subscribing to the doctrines of naturalism; her social role demands more sorrow than she can bring to it. Phoenixella, as a matter of fact, deserves no praise; she lavishes more denials than duty prescribes. Both are sentimental about themselves; their task involves self-recognition. At the end each, like water, finds her own level: Aurelia marries Chamont, and Phoenixella stays an avowed virgin. When they are not worrying about clothes, they discourse on men but betray no hint of passion. Gasper attracts Phoenixella Platonically because, she claims, he resembles her mother. The antique rationalization gains a thin piquancy because he is actually her lost brother. By concentrating on what might be exaggerated into spiritual values, Phoenixella has detected a true resemblance, although the source of her emotion eludes her. When Gasper is being punished for his impersonation, she continues her defense of him. Aurelia sensibly dismisses such tender sympathies as mere love, which in her temperament, concentrating upon surfaces and emotional responses, must blind. One reason why romance seldom enters the satires is that Jonson's ridicule exposes perverse delusions rather than dilemmas grounded on ambiguous forces. As part of the excessive duplication, two other men have courted the sisters, but this strand dangles unresolved.

The diametric temperaments of the daughters meet and clash in their father, Count Ferneze, whom all appearances confuse. When he corrects Aurelia, his attitudes contrast with Phoenixella's and sound nearly jocular: "Go to, my merry daughter, ô these lookes, / Agree well with your habit, do they not?" (I. vii. 74–75) Usually deceptions of any sort confound him; his entrance finds him complaining of insincere flatterers. Upon the discovery that he is the victim of Gasper's masquerade, his anger springs from an especially tender point. His diatribe draws a figure hastily from clothes with a self-conscious pun, "one left here / Of no descent, clad barely in his name" (IV. x. 15–16), but afterwards ranges through more subjects than does his daughters' vocabulary. His suspicion about deceit cannot be overcome entirely, no matter if his fears run counter to his desires. When, soon after his wife's death, he falls in love with Rachel, he asks in a soliloquy why he imagines, "in her sweet face / Gentry and noblenesse" (II. vi. 38–39), for her station as a beggar's daughter would deny her such qualities. Like Aurelia, he rejects the passion he feels. Like Phoenixella's, his intuitions, contrary to all evidence, urge a hidden kinship with

Gasper, so that, while his dagger moves to stab the pretender, the memory of his lost son paralyzes his hand. "What a child am I / To haue a child? Ay me, my son, my son." (V. ix. 28–29) However banal an echo this Biblical phrase may repeat, the weakness resides in the author's power of expression rather than in his judgment. The subdued recognition obeys the persistent philosophic assumptions, and the father's impotence at the prospect of punishing his son rests on a psychological truism. In the later plays, particularly *The New Inn*, revelations of family ties after years of separation induce corresponding emotions. Ferneze's Plautine prototype, the citizen Hegio, worries about none of these problems which beset Jonson's count, for standards of nobility permeate the English but not the Latin.

The courtly plot involves two significant sets of friendship between men, the one of Chamont and Gasper from Plautus, the other between Paulo and Angelo, Jonson's own. Just as Phoenixella and Aurelia embody two types of self-knowledge, and lack of it, so the men exemplify ways of understanding, or of incorrectly estimating, others. Neither of the sisters' contentions is correct, but with the four men one friendship preserves loyalty; the other breaks under treachery. Until the denouement Chamont does not know Gasper's parentage. Being noble himself, he believes that the commoner's worth, no more externally visible to him than it is to Phoenixella, equals his own. Chamont, unlike Ferneze, trusts himself and his own evaluations: "For natiue honour sparkles in thine [Gasper's] eyes." (IV. iv. 22) Trite and tedious though such protestations sound, they do not break with the tenets of experience as assumed throughout this play. Like their Latin models, the captive friends are loyal to each other but for different reasons; Plautus' youths are not patrician.

Jonson's reduplication, the friendship between Paulo and Angelo, culminates in betrayal. This and other perfidies mildly outrage most commentators, who overlook the qualification that nothing in the story exists by itself; every part balances against another. Angelo alone is the one intentionally wicked person among the courtiers; all the rest have sterling intentions which tarnish. Also, he alone advances the argument that surfaces determine values. Paulo uneasily suspects him, but causes for this repulsion elude the son as much as Rachel's attraction vexes the father. At one point Paulo protests to Angelo that goodness lies in conduct rather than in birth. Fortunately for the stability of the structure, this conjecture does not need to be pushed deeper. When, three acts later, he arrives home from the war just in time to prevent Rachel's abduction by Angelo, he promises to protect her from failings to which he has been more prone than she: "like an armed angell guard thee safe / From all th' assaults of couer'd villany." (V. viii. 54–55) All aspects of recognition are mirrored, if upside down and distorted, by the second plot.

Adaptations from *Aulularia* depart to a similar extent from their original meanings. Plautus presented Phaedria, who does not appear on stage, as Euclio's daughter through whose piety the family's lost gold is revealed to the father: both gold and daughter are his legally. Phaedria becomes Rachel who frequently appears, speaks seldom, and proves to be Chamont's kidnaped sister. Her innate goodness emerges faintly in a silhouette whose features her suitors' conjectures delimit. She expresses no opinion of her own on any subject; whether she impresses one as dull or demure depends on one's standards. Through five men—Ferneze, Paulo, Angelo, Onion, and, almost incidentally, Christophero, Ferneze's chamberlain—from the two social spheres, she links the two plots. An appreciation of her beauty does not require a keen insight; in spite of her low social position as a beggar's daughter she wears expensive clothes. Careful grooming, procured at no matter the extravagance in probability, must uniform virtue in the early comedies. The contradiction of economy and fashion could be dismissed by a playwright as one of those anomalies which he risks perpetrating without an explanation. Because style of dress does depict the major theme, a finicky attention to detail plausibly explains away Jaques' indulgence: it is either part of his comic sentimentality or a charitable gift from a stranger. The weakness of this central figure advances the chief contention that true worth cannot be hidden, for, no matter how meek, it secures proper surroundings, just as true viciousness cannot triumph, for it betrays itself in the long run.

Jaques incorporates many aspects of a man dominated by a humour who quickly lends himself to deception. The opposite of Angelo, he lives in quarters nastier than he might afford. His miser's traits have strengthened the supposition that he may be profitably measured against Euclio of *Aulularia* or Molière's *L'Avare*. When such comparisons have been made, a creature as minor as Jaques yields slim returns about himself or the others. All hoarders must share some habits; picking Jaques out of his specific context, a questionable procedure with any character, obscures rather than heightens his function in the comedy. One contrast between Latin and English will point up the important differences. Take the lines which one editor[10] suggests are expanded from "hoc quidem hercle, quoquo ibo, mecum erit, mecum feram, / neque isti id in tantis periclis umquam committam ut siet,"[11] into:

> Ile take no leaue, sweet Prince, great Emperour,
> But see thee euery minute. King of Kings,
> Ile not be rude to thee, and turne my backe,
> In going from thee, but go backward out,
> With my face toward thee, with humble curtesies.
> None is within. None ouerlookes my wall.
> To haue gold, and to haue it safe, is all.   (III. v. 22–28)

The two separate widely in portraying a compulsive attachment to property. Euclio's declaration vows to retain his money at all costs. Jaques' gold, on the other hand, possesses him. The sovereignty, and later divinity, which he attributes the treasure exceeds casual ownership. Despite his worshiping money, fear of its theft reduces him to degrading it, as he does himself, in a milieu less impressive than it could buy, less than it requires: "Ile hide and couer it with this horse-dung. . . ." (III. v. 13)

It remains for the groom Onion, accidentally spying on Jaques' burying the gold, to perceive more accurately: "The old prouerb's true, I see: gold is but mucke." (IV. ix. 20–21) It is true and not true. The context renders literal the figurative, but in terms of the play money does, and should, have other uses. Here, as elsewhere, a sense of fitness must determine policy. Onion's folk wisdom and mother wit soon desert him after he recalls the maxim. With his friend, the cobbler Juniper, he robs Jaques, and both promptly invest in sumptuous attire. Gold in their hands is squandered with the same ignorance which prompts Jaques to hoard it. As their betters try, with varying degrees of conviction, to control their mien, so Onion and Juniper are servants of their extreme clothes. In mourning Onion's vocabulary fails him: "S'wounds it has begun a seruingmans speech, euer since I belongd to the blew order: I know not how it may shew, now I am in blacke. . . ." (I. vii. 26–28) Once laced into his fashionable exterior, he notes that "aparel makes a man forget himself." (V. vi. 47–48) Onion and Juniper dazzle only themselves, and at court they are immediately spotted as "a sweet metamorphosis, a cupple of buzzards turn'd to a paire of peacocks." (V. vi. 4–5)

Action and language obey a thoroughgoing stratification, which aligns the principal characters and themes. Crammed as the plot is with variations, its elements seldom infuse one another; rather, they are parallel fibers, each moving separately. This perpendicularity shaping the earlier comedies contributes to the effect of marionettes which, it is claimed, Jonson's characters frequently produce. They respond dimly to another person, but their own egos are keenly stimulated by others' presence on the scene or just off it. The meaning demands this impression because at the heart of their problems lies their incompleteness as men and women, a deficiency either of sensitivity to classify information or of information to lend meaning to sensitivity. In *The Case Is Altered*, as in all the plays dedicated to the humours, the conflicts start from a lack (a negative) which with exercise breaks forth into rampant excesses. That Jonson had already hit on the predominant symbol of approbation which he retained throughout his life is moderately surprising. When a true ideal is named, the poetry automatically addresses itself to a circle, the icon which also shaped his emblem and its motto: friends are joined in the circle of each other's arms (IV. ii. 10–11), and souls are knitted together in spheres. (IV. iv. 5) Traditional as the sources of this configuration are, its pervasiveness argues a guiding principle. The crucial revelation springs from the concept embodied. Gasper proves himself Camillo, the lost son, by a medal; this part does not hark back to Plautus, and any identification might have served. That Jonson contrived this specific design stresses the enduring theme; it is a child's inscribed locket, "Vnder the figure of a siluer Globe: / *In minimo, mundus.*" (V. xii. 38–39) Mario Praz in his extensive survey of emblem books notes this one, but indicates no source from which it was copied in the publications of England or the Continent.[12] Whether or not one might be located has no self-sufficient importance; if the design were discovered elsewhere, it would not cancel the evidence that Jonson successfully invented or tracked down, for him the two processes being closely akin, devices which coincide with his purposes.

Were partial error about appearance and identity the sole standard in Milan, action strung along so flimsy a thread would break as unredeemable farce. All the early plays incorporate definite opinions about the cause of error. The unaided eye detects truth; it must survey surfaces and peer through them to what lies beneath until it uncovers data for evaluating discrepancies. Vision, when uncorrupted, cannot err. The voice transmits deceptions; at no time may the tongue be trusted. This crude division has some importance for Jonson's developing themes. In *The Case Is Altered* the embodiment of vocal idiocy is Juniper. His vocabulary rarely achieves the teetering threat to deviate into sense which distinguishes a distant sufferer, Mrs. Malaprop. His vices of speech happily disregard meaning. He shows a child's joy at hearing syllables combined into exotic patterns, lovely in themselves because nothing except his fancy restricts them. Truth for this play, if not naked, appears in simple trappings. Anyone has only to look at the world, to see it plainly, and understanding comes. Juniper and Onion, Jaques and Angelo, fool themselves by trying to deceive others, and the scorn one feels for them establishes, negatively, the suitability of social standards. The voice represents impossible subtleties, and, thus, in Juniper through ignorance and in Angelo through guile, it corrupts the eye. The rest of the action refines this outlook.

Guilty of unintentional or deliberate falsification, the voice cannot hide the truth. When an initial error of insight grows overwhelming, however, it can no longer cut through layers of selfish preoccupations. At the climax a thoroughly mathematical manipulation draws together the protagonists of the two plots, Ferneze, who distrusts himself, and Jaques, who distrusts others; the third with them is the somewhat neutral Christophero, whose love for Rachel seems to have been contrived chiefly to introduce this scene. Each of the three men wants a favor from one of the others, who cannot grant it. Because all are privately obsessed by a loss, no communication is possible. Jaques begs Ferneze's help in regaining his gold, Ferneze seeks Christophero's in ransoming his son Paulo, and Christophero asks Jaques' in finding Rachel. The three shouting men, blinded by their own anxieties, cannot comprehend what anyone else says, and these creatures behaving like fantoccini predict the conduct of humourists. In this part, too, a typically Jonsonian trick of a practical question's falling ineptly beside the mark undercuts the confusion of tongues. Christophero reproaches Jaques, "Who would haue thought you could haue beene so carelesse / To loose your onely daughter?" (V. xi. 13–14) Three centuries later Miss Prism confronts a similar question to resolve *The Importance of Being Earnest.*

In the fifth act of *Every Man in His Humour* during a trial the magistrate, Doctor Clement, decrees after certain testimony, "That alters the case." (V. iii. 27 a&b) [18] The implication that authority may err and that human nature can change matches precisely the rationale of Jonson's first and second plays. Although a more skilled technique guides the second, and a relaxing of parallels permits more freedom, it resembles *The Case Is Altered* in its assumptions, structure, verse, and tenor-vehicle relationships of metaphors.[14] The thorough pruning and grafting on the 1601 quarto for the 1616 folio have, nevertheless, been hailed as mature refinements which merely remove the foreign disguises of the original and expose the first humour comedy.[15] Recently, though, scholarship has analyzed its close kinship with typical Renaissance plays.[16] That its function as a link between Jonson's earliest and early styles long escaped recognition made a crippling oversight because misreading from outside its bounds has disfigured those bounds themselves. The best way to rectify a failure in method is to retrace more critically the steps in that method. Consequently, the basic text for comment will be the quarto with important folio deviations noted as they arise. Such an arrangement entails no inconveniences, except perhaps characters' unfamiliar Italian names; a table of both casts appears in note 13. Jonson revised from the printed copy of the quarto;[17] therefore, all alterations affect expression more than the design.

The basic prompting, motivation being perhaps too strong a term, in *The Case Is Altered* derives from mistaken identity; people try, or fail to try, to formulate a judicious estimate of the truth about themselves or others. This bent, with some shifts of accentuation, guides much of *Every Man in His Humour*. Basically the action stretches a loose frame from which episodes are suspended. This fluidity develops the impression of a structure akin to that of mobiles which the next plays create. A group of incidents swing about one another, but their unity refers to a multiple patterning rather than to what connects them in a single line of growth. Lorenzo Junior goes into Florence to visit his friend Prospero. His father, Lorenzo Senior, uneasy about his son's being corrupted by the city associates, follows. (Jonson unfortunately favored these senior-junior names; the excuse for retaining them is that any circumlocution would be cumbersome and any abbreviation silly.) The two young men trick three affected and stupid acquaintances: Matheo, who pretends to literary and social prowess, Bobadilla, dreaming of military fame as a conquering soldier, and Stephano, the expected bumpkin. Others, notably Prospero's relatives, Thorello and Giulliano, are likewise abused. Frisking along like a zany sheep dog to herd the pranks runs the Lorenzos' servant, Musco, who disguises himself as opportunities arise. Doctor Clement, a magistrate with a streak of determined whimsey, resolves the complications. In outline this plot sounds like the sort most calculated to set on edge the teeth of twentieth-century readers, but no synopsis of an Elizabethan play wholly avoids the ridiculous when deprived of its proportions, language, and stage.

Musco, who shares traits with the conventional English Vice and with the more traditional Italian Harlequin from the *commedia dell' arte*, stands forth here as a type for the first time in Jonson. Musco's delight in masquerading fits his nature, and he sees, not incorrectly, the progress of action as "the day of my *metamorphosis!*" (V. iii. 83–84 b) Through multiple disguises he becomes what he wears, capable of any alteration. His insouciance exempts him from the task of uniting surface with substance. He rejoices in a doctrine which in others would be heresy: "it holds for good policie to haue that outwardly in vilest estimation, that inwardly is most deare to vs. . . ." (II. i. 5–7 a&b)

The trickery bears authority because of its disinterest; the folio re-christens him Brainworm. If Musco acts on the edges of the law, his counterpart, Doctor Clement, is the law. Whereas *The Case Is Altered* culminates in the bickerings of three confused men, *Every Man in His Humour* allies the two impartial ones who have conquered their private confusions and can dispassionately chastise the distraught. Such reliance on an authority does not break with the first play; there the belief was that nonsense would eventually cancel itself out. Now, a recognized power, but of the slightest dimensions, intervenes.

Around this amorphous, if fixed, center revolve familiar figures. The three pretenders, Stephano, Matheo, and Bobadilla, temperamentally descend from Onion and Juniper. Lacking Musco's shrewdness, they affect solemn personalities so that they may appear what they are not. They valiantly pose to incorporate the models they have stolen. Stephano, the rural gull, an unpromising figure, copies with unconscious parody the already ridiculous mannerisms of the urban fools, Matheo and Bobadilla. He believes he will learn hawking from a book and pass for a city wit by wearing fashionable clothes. The one notoriety his dress brings him results from his arrest for stealing a cloak. He discovers sadly that he cannot shed his guilt like the garment. On the whole his follies are inept and ineffectual because they ape already seedy models. At the end he remains a sheep, lost and bleating.

Matheo and Bobadilla, while surely no wiser than Stephano, possess more information; their posturing strives awkwardly and vainly after originality. Matheo pretends to poetry; he flaunts plagiarized tags from faded titles as personal adornment, "for he vtters no thing but stolne remnants." (III. iv. 74–75 a&b) His offenses combine the gaucheries of Onion's wardrobe and Juniper's vocabulary. Bobadilla, who wishes he were a soldier, suggests many literary ancestors and progeny. The invocation of Plautus' *Miles Gloriosus* can hardly be avoided, but a braggart has never assumed these refined proportions. He is the first distinctively Jonsonian caricature. His pensive audacity expresses itself with appropriate flaccidity, but the patterned rhetoric saves itself from inanity. In lucid moments he recognizes his own situation, but he cannot resist spinning phantasies which swell from the first unlikely step with an inevitable logic to an improbability

grounded still in a corner of the actual. Bobadilla's gentleness of speech
contrasts with the extravagance of his daydreams. Later in the great
comedies this disproportion borders on a kind of horror, but the
impossibility of these schemes restricts them to gentler satire. Aided
by only nineteen men, he volunteers to defeat an entire army in individual combat, a certain number's being cut down each day by the
rules of dueling. The modest conclusion recognizes that the enemy
may hold chivalry more lightly: "and this will I venture my life to
performe: prouided there be no treason practised vpon vs." (IV. ii.
84–86 a&b) The satirist's handiest device, the *reductio ad absurdum*,
rarely has been employed for such subdued devastation. The folio,
however, drives the point deeper and amplifies it, "by faire, and dis-
creet manhood, that is, ciuilly by the sword." (IV. vii. 93–94 b) His
wistfulness furthers the ludicrous pretensions; Bobadilla aspires by
frequent oaths, which Stephano copies as a kind of badge, to pass for
a hero. At the end, while the volatile Musco triumphs, Bobadilla and
Matheo shrink down to what they are.

When these two, with Stephano, are hauled before Doctor
Clement, the justice, as charmed by costume as is Musco, calls for his
armor and sword in which to welcome the soldier. Upon seeing
Bobadilla, he drops these trappings. In the quarto their punishment
deflates the man of action and man of letters from their flattering
make-believe to a mocking reality: Bobadilla must wear a fool's motley and Matheo sackcloth sprinkled with ashes of his burnt poems.
They publicly sing a duet, words by Matheo, tune, "Who list to leade
and a souldiers life." Their punishment atones for their flaunted
fopperies, not, as Juniper's and Onion's, for a crime to which the folly
is incidental. In line with the relaxed sternness when the play was
revised, their sentences likewise grow lighter. They are dismissed as
"you signe o'the Souldier, and picture o' the *Poet* (but, both so false,
I will not ha' you hang'd out at my dore till midnight). . . ." (V. v.
49–51 b)

These three embody the more abiding aspects of the fools, and
concessions about their punishment tucked them satisfactorily into the
folio. The others, who more closely resemble the courtiers of *The
Case Is Altered*, needed more extensive modifications to blend with

the later rationale. In the main the 1616 version insists less rigorously upon the absolute validity of the wisdom which Doctor Clement cavalierly dispenses. Taking their key differences into consideration, one might reasonably place the time of rewriting soon after the composition of *Epicene*, 1609, somewhat past the date conventionally assigned, but not impossibly late, especially because it was then that Jonson started assembling his materials for the *Works*. What happens to the characters when transplanted from Florence to London reinforces this conjecture. If most of the deluded in *The Case Is Altered* may be forgiven because they carelessly deceive themselves about either verifiable facts or their nobler intuitions, too nice an introspection trips the relatively stable elements of *Every Man in His Humour*, where the major confusions impinge likewise upon incorrect judgment of others. Most of these misunderstandings hinge on opinions about the respectability of poetry and about jealousy, two topics of slight significance in the earlier play. Lorenzo Senior's efforts to protect his son from wasting his time on a literary life have warning examples in Elizabethan society, such as the losing struggle which killed off most professional journalists or, on another plane, the doomed young men in the *Three Parnassus Plays*.[18] A father's worrying about a profligate also repeats a favorite subject of Roman comedy. One need not debate which (or whether both or neither) influences the treatment because the script fully dramatizes the problem. Lorenzo Senior's pursuit of his son to Florence, and the ensuing gruff concern for his welfare, although almost vanishing for long stretches in the tumultuous auxiliary business, do get the action under way and through the servant Musco keep it in motion. It would be a flaw in the drama were the central thread loose or dangling by itself, a view sometimes put forth by those who reduce Elizabethan playwrights to children innocently tossing around the newly discovered toys of language in a public courtyard. Lorenzo Senior's harsh strictures on poetry revile it as a vice which blinds the practitioner to himself and the world.

> My selfe was once a *student*, and indeede
> Fed with the selfe-same humor he is now,
> Dreaming on nought but idle *Poetrie:*
> But since, Experience hath awakt my sprit's,

And reason taught them, how to comprehend
The soueraigne vse of study.   (I. i. 16–21 a)

In the folio the insertion of three lines and modification of the last
three make the accusations more concrete and the process of accumu-
lating wisdom less magisterial:

My selfe was once a student; and, indeed,
Fed with the selfe-same humour, he is now,
Dreaming on nought but idle *poetrie*,
That fruitlesse, and vnprofitable art,
Good vnto none, but least to the professors,
Which, then, I thought the mistresse of all knowledge:
But since, time, and the truth haue wak'd my iudgement,
And reason taught me better to distinguish,
The vaine, from th'vsefull learnings.   (I. i. 15–23 b)

Supposedly a qualification like this echoes Jonson's attaching a higher
value to the function of poetry.[19] Such an explanation considerably
oversimplifies the process. Aside from the question of whether an
author necessarily does, or can, intrude his opinions into a work without their being somewhat modified by the context, the folio refinements imply a conviction less charitable about human ambitions (including poetry) and an acceptance more nearly resigned toward
human failings (including poetry). When commentators have not
followed the first interpretation, the usual practice reads into it a
more realistic style of character portrayal.[20] The difficulties of defining
Jonson's realism may be postponed until later. The two opinions can
be defended, but both miss the main drift of the thought by seizing the
superficial. For example, Lorenzo Senior's long soliloquy on the mind
as supreme arbiter of rebellious matter disappears because it no longer
identifies adequately the *données* of the rationale; the one substituted
for it makes error a disease more than skin deep. With identical results,
an interchange between Lorenzo Senior and Doctor Clement is pared.
The father complains of a vacant mind's harboring worthless trifles,
and the justice consoles him, "Your cares are nothing; they are like my
cap, soone put on, and as soone put off." (III. iii. 132–33 a&b) Origi-

nally an equally persuasive answer permitted the two contentions to balance without immediately approving Clement's optimism. In the folio the rejoinder, let stand as an adequate answer, whereas dress elsewhere represents a fashionable whim, becomes sentimental. Such an objection may strain at a small point, but Jonson's fussy caution about snipping off loose ends, especially for his imagery, makes such lapses glaring. The three metaphors which equate light with knowledge are cut away in the folio (I. ii. 11–14 a; V. iii. 344–50 a; V. iii. 380–86 a). The folio, then, rates human ability to learn the meaning of its experiences with less assurance, and this awareness must expand tolerance.

If Lorenzo Senior's opinions of education are excised or modified, Lorenzo Junior's deification of poetry receives a more ruthless pruning. The skilled writer still is praised and a waste of talent deplored, but the long declamation on consecrated poetry, which exists eternally no matter how many vandals deface it, shifts its emphasis so that poets compete with an efficient official. "They are not borne euerie yeere, as an Alderman. There goes more to the making of a good *Poet*, then a Sheriffe, M^r. KITELY." (V. v. 38–40 b) More than a sheriff, true, but the folksy reassurance implies little more and lacks the stiff aspiration for an artifact, "fit to be seene / Of none but graue and consecrated eyes. . . ." (V. iii. 332–33 a)

Lorenzo Junior's friend, Prospero, through his relatives Thorello and Giulliano, starts the second theme, jealousy. The two older men contrast like Aurelia and Phoenixella or Ferneze split into his two contending halves. Thorello cannot trust surfaces and must probe out hidden intentions, which, being purely imaginary, grow monstrous. In contrast Giulliano puts all his faith into a rather too hasty seizure of the obvious. Both men constantly deceive themselves and fritter away resolution. Thorello loses his bearings in a maze of conjecture and Giulliano his temper in heights of anger. Thorello holds imaginary cross-examinations of his wife Biancha and servant Pizo until both loom as potential traitors. Fittingly, the later extensions of his speeches stress this regarding himself in impotent doubt. When in the quarto he fears being ridiculed, the folio highlights details: "mocke me all ouer, / From my flat cap, vnto my shining shooes. . . ." (II. i. 109–10 b) The adjectives particularly pin down this frozen mirror gazing which passes for introspection. Unfortunately for his peace of mind, and unlike many Jonsonian characters, not only is he unduly troubled by nuance, but he knows he is unduly troubled by nuance. Consequently, he both tries to spy out deceptions, and he regards himself, almost reprimandingly, spying out deceptions. He lucidly describes his own mind as an hourglass:

> And my imaginations like the sands,
> Runne dribling foorth to fill the mouth of time,
> Still chaung'd with turning in the ventricle.   (III. i. 43–45 a&b)

Capable of this detachment and irony, he can do nothing to heal his maladies. Giulliano holds down a minor part; it could not be otherwise because he explodes with rage a few minutes after any entrance.

Like the first play, this one has a few dispensable characters; in themselves they run through minor turns, but their presence contributes little to the drama itself. Into this category fall Cob, a waterman, and his wife, both having roles of tangential importance. The long diatribes spoken by Cob consist mostly of disgruntled observations about smoking and fasting days. He is a doltish creature, dear perhaps to the Elizabethan apprentices and the modern social historian, but his disquisitions add nothing to the major themes of poetry, vanity, and irrationality around which this play revolves. He also has views on the humours, and this quite marginal position shows how little the concept has to do with the play.

Thus *Every Man in His Humour* modifies but also repeats the patterns of *The Case Is Altered*. Although what originally were two plots tend to merge, the caricatured pretenders remain separate from the sensibly confused. In place of a passive Rachel who incites love, a volatile Musco prods idiosyncrasies. The difficulties and failures throughout resemble the ones besetting the nobility and commoners of Milan. If the plotting creaks less and the language flexes more sinews, neither exhibits the absolute rightness of later achievements. On the whole the accents in both are avuncular. They chide the deluded and recommend that affectations had better be eschewed:

> lest while you pretend
> To make a blaze of gentrie to the world

> A little puffe of scorne extinguish it,
> And you be left like an vnsauorie snuffe,
> Whose propertie is onely to offend.   (I. i. 69–73 a&b)

In contrast with the fierce demolition of poseurs and pretenders to follow, these are little puffs against petty follies. In a sense both prefigure *Every Man out of His Humour*, and by reading backward and forward one can watch the design emerging clearly. Since the term "comedy of humour" has been associated popularly with Jonson, calling for a change sounds irresponsible. The accepted term can apply, loosely, to all his earlier plays. For more precision, "humour comedy," to put the emphasis where it ought to fall, will be used to describe only the next three plays: *Every Man out of His Humour*, *Cynthia's Revels*, and *Poetaster*. On the title pages for the first of these in quarto and for all three in the folio Jonson invoked the description "comicall satyre." Oscar James Campbell has lucidly described how the concept harks back to the *vetus comoedia*, a kind of Aristophanic mockery. Late in the Elizabethan period authors resorted to it when the authorities banned satire because of a series of vehement exchanges embarrassing to the government. The attitude behind this veiled subterfuge intimately suits Jonson's definition of the humours.

The functions of the humours in both the first two plays, however, range through the same indeterminate scope. Cob's dialogue with Pizo about it, a passage which might have been tacked on later because it is not integral, attributes to the term a broad meaning. It implies little beyond whim or variability, a brief deviation which looks inconsistent, irrational, and therefore ridiculous, but only because it violates a pattern previously established by a character's behavior. *The Case Is Altered* depicts Ferneze in such a condition for the most detailed example.

> You know my father's wayward, and his humour
> Must not receiue a check, for then all obiects,
> Feede both his griefe and his impatience,
> And those affections in him, are like powder,
> Apt to enflame with euery little sparke,
> And blow vp reason, therefore *Angelo*, peace.   (I. vi. 85–90)

Although the term approaches a degree nearer consistency with

Every Man in His Humour, the casual way in which it occurs, compared with the genuine complexity it assumes in the next play, proves that Jonson had hardly begun working his way through its implications. Several passages foretell the ensuing connotations, but no one could isolate these were not the later enlargements available to verify their authenticity. It once is yoked with the water metaphor which most readily describes it in the humour comedies; Pizo declares, "Faith ile dreame no longer of this running humor, / For feare I sinke. ..." (III. i. 133–34 a&b) When Pizo and Cob hold their discourse upon the topic, in the quarto "(as tis generally receiued in these daies) it is a monster bred in a man by selfe loue, and affectation, and fed by folly." (III. i. 156–58 a) The folio refines it to the degree which fixes it in the vocabulary of the next three plays: "It is a gentleman-like monster, bred, in the speciall gallantrie of our time, by affectation; and fed by folly." (III. iv. 20–22 b) This explanation covers a superficially wide range and omits any psychological references. Only once does this play depict the exact force which humour later draws upon, when, however, it shows Thorello's jealousy:

> For like a pestilence it doth infect
> The houses of the braine: first it begins
> Solely to worke vpon the fantasie,
> Filling her seat with such pestiferous aire,
> As soone corrupts the iudgement, and from thence,
> Sends like contagion to the memorie,
> Still each of other catching the infection,
> Which as a searching vapor spreads it selfe
> Confusedly through euery sensiue part,
> Till not a thought or motion in the mind
> Be free from the blacke poison of suspect.   (I. iv. 207–17 a&b)

Jonson progressed steadily in his craft; he did not whip up "romantic" confections and then astound the world, and himself, by devising an unprecedented cracker bonbon. The humours were invented, not discovered, for dramatic functions. The standard of comedy which here begins to operate relies lightly on caricature. It takes unexceptionable individuals, shows how they carelessly allow themselves to become deluded, paces them through a series of amicable misunderstandings, and dismisses them as cured of their follies. The drift reassures one that no problem need be vast and no solution difficult. The tone has its darker moments, and cheerfulness stays uppermost only with resolute effort. Nevertheless, an obedience to the principles of a satire like the *vetus comoedia* wins ascendancy only in *Every Man out of His Humour*. Although on every level a difference separates the two earliest plays from the two following, it is one of degree rather than of kind, the distinction between scorn and contempt.

CHAPTER III

The Streame of Humour

WITH *Every Man out of His Humour* Jonson unveiled his decisive exercise in what a play with a singleness of purpose throughout ought to be. As such, it remains one of those focal points which reinforce all an author's undertakings. Its strengths, further refined, run as supports through most later achievements; its weaknesses may account for collapses where undue weight burdens a slight prop. The danger of taking the crucial work itself as a mere elevation from which to trace forth designs or of judging all ensuing plays by this single standard can be avoided once one recognizes the threat. All this apology does not champion the view that *Every Man out of His Humour* quite succeeds as drama.

Jonson took elaborate pains in preparing this, his first published volume, for the press. By it he bid to be both learned and popular, the diametric qualities which he strove to unite and which, even under his urgings, pulled always in opposite directions. The failures perplexed him. This time he undoubtedly went out of his way to dazzle readers by sprinkling claims of novelty over the title page. The drama is a "comicall satyre," the circumlocution for satire itself. The second bait, that of offering more than acted on the stage, may have stimulated literary curiosity.[1] The Latin motto seems a quaint flourish, but Jonson's example helped launch the practice later popular in printed drama.[2] The kinds of books most highly respected at the time served as models. For a dramatist to publish his script was infra dig; serious works, of course, deserved Latin mottoes, but not a popular playbook, which, among the literate, enjoyed a reputation not much higher than collections of comic strips command at present. Finally, the text is prefaced by a series of sketches setting forth attributes of the characters. Whatever indirect aspersions such portraits throw on the playwright's ability, they do exploit another vogue. The character sketch was a new genre in England, one to continue throughout the seventeenth century. These early ones list salient traits in perfunctory order. These paraphernalia on the title page, which booksellers tacked up on their stalls for advertisements, must have appeared insufferably pompous.

The decorations served as a prelude to the play itself, which has a prologue to explain the rationale, the humours. Much has rightly been made of them, but the context in which they place the action has been misunderstood or taken for granted. The humours describe precisely this play and *Cynthia's Revels;* by *Poetaster* they have already begun to wane. Extended too insistently into later plays, inflexible notions about them will mislead seriously. Mentioning this topic at all demands an apology. Jonson and his humours are among the most stifling subjects in literary history. The trouble, though, is that his concept has been misinterpreted and misapplied. Humours flow less pervasively throughout the plays than is commonly assumed, but in those where they dominate, no other psychology prevails. Dull as the topic may sound, through it alone one must approach these two plays.

In christening his psychology humours Jonson took over a term in common use for centuries with varying degrees of precision. Although modern theories of education disapprove of teaching any hocus-pocus except that having current credence, a few decades ago it was a schoolboy's cliché that Elizabethans believed the body contained four humours. Accepted as a kind of image, they continue at present in various arts and philosophies; in psychology Jung does not dismiss their usefulness as labels, and in music (and ballet) Hindemith (and Balanchine) based *Four Temperaments* upon them. Blood, phlegm, yellow bile, and black bile, or the hot and moist, cold and moist, hot and dry, and cold and dry, should blend equally in the body. When one gains ascendancy, physical and psychic diseases result. Much Elizabethan drama can be explained only by a belief in the reality of such distempers. Many commentators have misconstrued Marlowe's portrait of Tamburlaine because they forget the Asiatic conqueror displays a textbook fidelity to the symptoms of Melancholy Adust,[3] the most dreaded disturbance of the humours. Later Jacobean drama is puzzlingly pathological, if one discounts its origins in a physiological malady. Burton's *Anatomy of Melancholy* says the last word on the subject; by his time respectable medical knowledge already discounted the actuality of humours. Popular extensions of the term, as the original theory faded, mistook in the Restoration and eighteenth century any mild aberration for a humour. Jonson's working definition falls somewhat between the two extremes of theory and catchall; in his plays psychological manifestations turn into physical quirks. Although analogies often mislead, one might compare the range of meaning in *humours* with the usages of *neurosis* at the present time.[4]

The word neurosis has a reputable history and a fairly precise clinical definition. Recent extensions distort it. It becomes chic in the comment that " 'Thoreau as a neuro' sounded like a song by Cole Porter."[5] In fact, it crops up repeatedly in urban entertainments; the future play reviewer for the *New Yorker* entitled a collection of his essays, first published in that magazine, *Bed of Neuroses*. Intimate reviews on Broadway invoked it as a label of sophistication, e.g., the parody of love songs in *Lend an Ear*, "Neurotic Me and Psychopathic You," or *Small Wonder*, whose sketches were strung together by a twentieth-century everyman called The Normal Neurotic. Watered down, it has spread across many areas. In one sense of the word, neurosis has become the norm in the United States during its *Age of Anxiety* (poem [W. H. Auden], musical composition [Leonard Bernstein], and ballet [Jerome Robbins]). Positing that the denotations of *neurosis* in all these instances are identical would be foolish; presumably it does communicate similar connotations. Without arguing too fine a parallel, one may discern a similar variety, bordering on confusions, in the shades of meaning which the humours bore during the sixteenth and seventeenth centuries.

Jonson himself pledged the concept loyalties of different enthusiasms. As has been noted, in the first two plays it floated about mostly as a casual term which predominantly condemned eccentric behavior. For *Every Man out of His Humour, Cynthia's Revels,* and, partially, *Poetaster,* he did arbitrarily restrain its associations within a moderately confined range. From *Sejanus* through *The Alchemist* he improvised upon the definition without tying the term steadily to one point; afterwards, *The Magnetic Lady* notwithstanding, he became indifferent to both word and concept. For these two comedies, however, the humours must be understood in a rigorously Jonsonian sense. Other dramatists and satirists of the period,[6] notably Chapman, resorted to the same device, but one quotation from *An Humorous Day's Mirth* measures the discrepancy between the two authors' concepts: "The skie hangs full of humour, and I thinke we shall haue raine. . . . for we shall spend it with so humorous acquaintance, as raines nothing but humor al their life time."[7] Jonson was incapable of writing or of thinking anything which compares these two topics, atmospheric and human disturbances. For him humours never exist apart from the manifest behavior of the afflicted; stupidities spill out from an individual and cannot rain down upon him.

Humours, as Jonson fully expanded the term, have two extended meanings,[8] in addition to the nearly literal one of a fluid in the body. In its first enlargement a humour propels, helter-skelter, all one's endeavors in a single, and vain, direction. Time and again humour floods like a current of water, an association made casually before, or it resembles a flame but, unlike the explosion which unsettled Ferneze, spreads steadily on its victim until it has slowly consumed him. The traditional phrase, feed a humour, becomes thus literally true, but devourer and the devoured are identities. At first it resembles the indulgence of a minor vice which dominates the deluded in one aspect of his behavior. With practice, however, the stream of humour running through anyone cannot find sufficient outlet in an occasional exercise so that, like a raging river, it breaks forth and sweeps away all inhibitions. The partial eccentricity becomes a whole mania; it twists the powerless into freaks and the strong into tyrants. The spectacle of the minor's becoming the major must simultaneously appall and amuse any who can appreciate Jonsonian comedy.

> Cor. O, hee's a fellow of a strange nature. Now do's hee (in this calme of his humour) plot, and store vp a world of malicious thoughts in his braine, till hee is so full with 'hem, that you shall see the very torrent of his enuie breake forth like a land-floud: and, against the course of all their affections oppose it selfe so violently, that you will almost haue wonder to thinke, how 'tis possible the current of their dispositions shall receiue so quick, and strong an alteration.
>
> (IV. viii. 152–59)

Jonson wrote two endings for *Every Man out of His Humour;* in the one, humour is compared with a flame, in the other, with a current, but the results of visitation by holocaust or deluge are equally destructive. Such, then, is the full range of the first variation wrought upon the basic term. The second effect of humours is the affectation of a humour in speech. On the stream the word itself is nakedly released again and again, almost like flotsam on a wave, where it whirls about by itself until it loses any direction. This parody suits the satire, which is not only to show actual and copied humours in their manifestations but also "to giue these ignorant well-spoken dayes, / Some taste of their abuse of this word Humour." (Second Sounding, 79–80) The didactic and semantic elements cannot be separated.

While bandying the term loosely, the speakers, all unaware, exemplify their own humours. At the opening Sogliardo, a social pretender, mouths the word constantly: "Why, this fellowes discourse were nothing, but for the word Humour." (II. i. 56–57) From him it spreads like an epidemic to every character on the stage, including a dog. Therefore, by drawing upon three senses, a nearly traditional interpretation of distemper incurred with imbalance of the four fluids, the pampering of a humour, and, finally, the reduction of the word to jargon, Jonson fitted together a mordantly complex play. One is surprised after a careful reading that the levels blend into one another as nicely as they do. One might again think of a play about neurotics: those needing an analyst, those who are analysans because it is fashionable, and those sprinkling their conversation with Freudian clichés. If one protests that such a full-scale comedy would frequently be shocking or morbid in English (but hardly in French), the answer is that so was Jonson's until age softened the connotations. It was his biggest hit, nearly as popular, to judge by the book's sales,[9] as a Broadway review. Had Jonson regarded the four humours as absolutes in their control over men, he could not have considered them comic; if modern audiences took Freudian hypotheses quite literally, they would demand tragedies, not musical sketches, based on such material. Comedy utilizes its brand of truth when theories, e. g., of humours or the unconscious, have just been announced or have started to wane, or, as with the French attitude toward psychoanalysis, when one counts oneself in a group immune from foreign foolishness. At this level comedy exhibits possibilities falsely erected as idols to be worshiped in bondage. Multiplying the troubles which comedy must face, it cannot preach its truths but must dramatize them. Whatever caused the popularity of *Every Man out of His Humour*, the dialogue provides its vitality.

The language portrays eloquent thoughtlessness; the speech patterns echo manias. The stream of humour rushes like a river, carving a channel which, the more deeply cut, the more confining it is. If a later, comparatively sluggish style, the stream of consciousness, spreads everywhere to connect disparate associations, the stream of humour shoots toward only one end but in its course picks up much debris.[10] Meanwhile, the characters rant with a vigor which, whatever its peculiarities, obeys a pattern. All their thoughts force them back to one subject. No matter how far they roam, they inevitably return to their obsession. The preoccupation bulks most obviously in a long diatribe by the soldier Shift during which the phrase, "Sell my rapier?" (III. vi. 48–68), keeps intruding itself into a ramshackle monologue. Try as he will to drop the topic, he is dragged back to it. Another instance, of another sort, occurs when the miserly farmer, Sordido, chuckles with malicious joy that the almanac forecasts of innumerable days of rain, which he chants, will ruin all crops so that his hoarded stores will be worth more. Or, another, Fungoso and Fallace (a man and woman respectively) find different aspects of a fashionable courtier, Briske, so engrossing that, although they converse about him, they communicate nothing to each other because their attention can focus only on the single attraction which hypnotizes them. Similarly, at the end of the fourth act, and comparable with the three shouting men of *The Case Is Altered*, no one hears the requests of anyone else. The style fits this kind of affliction smoothly.

Jonson's proficiency with resemblance detaches one aspect, names it promptly, and moves on to a second object from which another single, and cognate, trait is selected. The process does not, as with the metaphysical poets, keep uncovering more and more connections between two items and continue probing further into their complex natures. Verse as compact as his needs constant neatness and clarity. Often, indeed, the underlying quality is not named, but incongruous objects, which share one resemblance, are reeled off in succession so ordered that the crucial part which links them gradually emerges. A related trick catalogues negatives for the same purpose, and by the elaboration of what it is not the silhouetted attribute emerges. Each syllable of this seeming babbling must be carefully constrained because the stratified levels of humour demand their distinctive sorts of verse or prose. For this task Jonson usually could modulate his effects as he wished. Although the characters are gripped by fixations and their discourse must be disjointed, the guiding reins never relax. Just as the stream of consciousness reveals by disguises and maskings, the stream of humour uncovers by distorted resemblance and false identity.

The most idle utterances have behind them a thorough logic within a demented pattern. Nevertheless, granted all Jonson's care with publication, with rationale, with characterization, and with language, the finished work fails to combine economically its fine parts and high standards. Aspects of this blemish may be blamed on the added sections which extravagantly distend the incidents beyond dramatic limits. Principally, though, no editing would rescue the ingenuity from its own caprices. The cause of the weakness boils down to one point: whatever else it may be, *Every Man out of His Humour* is hardly a play. To consider what it is predicates, at the same time, an understanding of what it is not. The plot resists condensation not because so much happens but because so little does, at least so little which coheres around traceable causes and effects.[11] This structural discontinuity does not mean that Jonson wanted the deftness to elaborate a plot; on the contrary, the overly ingenious design of *The Case Is Altered*, to say nothing of later plays, proves that contriving action was one area in which he unquestionably excelled. If this humour comedy lacks connections, they did not necessarily lie beyond the author's skill. His search for materials extracted richer effects elsewhere. Two axioms apply to all his writing: nothing is accidental, and deliberateness does not guarantee results.

The numerous characters, each of whom pursues his special fancy nearly in defiance of milieu, do not waste time considering others. As their paths cross, a kind of mutual recognition permits nodding disrespect based, however, not upon friendship or conflict but upon the struggle within themselves: either to keep the stream of humour within a semblance of control or to have it flow forcefully enough to gain recognition from society, the true humour and the affectations of humour. The major devices hark back to the two preceding plays, but they are here turned inside out. In place of Musco at the core of activity, a chorus, an approximation of classical models, stands to one side and comments on the menagerie of gulls who populate the scene. The resulting remoteness approaches the quality of an abstract ballet in which the pattern is supreme. One main thread of the story can be simply extracted. It concerns a farmer, Sordido, who has two children, Fallace and Fungoso. The father, being a miser, refuses to support Fungoso in town. In order to remain near his idol Briske, a dandy prancing on the court side lines, he seeks aid from his sister, Fallace, but she, also doting upon Briske's graces, refuses him. Her husband, Deliro, thoroughly devoted to his indifferent wife, becomes ridiculous through proffering her unwanted gifts. Sogliardo, Sordido's brother, also affecting city manners, is, as older generations are inclined to be, less knowledgeable in modish scandals and affairs. Singling out this feature does distort the play, just as, to a lesser extent, stressing the Lorenzo household does *Every Man in His Humour*. Outside groups in both frequently loom as more important; yet, the Sordido tribe's frantic drives compose a hunchbacked spine for the episodes. The five tell much of the humours. They form no family: no father named his sons Sordido and Sogliardo, nor did anyone, even if named Sordido, revenge himself by christening his daughter and son Fallace and Fungoso, nor did Fallace prolong the farce by marrying Deliro.[12] Their whole situation is a trenchant, almost distressing, parody of human disaffections, and it casts forth twisted supports from which the other characters dangle. At the end, unlike the Ferneze household, they cannot unite as a group in their family circle.

Around this grotesque clan the other characters clash or run off on their own tangents. The more important can be listed briefly. Macilente, the malcontent, whose role assumes most prominence, is the man whom nothing pleases and who ridicules all, hoping by railing to alleviate his envy. In these projects he is seconded by Buffone, whose pranks have less personal animus and aim at targets indiscriminately. Puntarvolo, a knight quixotically honoring the courtly decorum of a former age and boasting of his travels, and Saviolina, the determinedly smart court lady, round off the upper social reaches. Shift, like Bobadilla an impoverished soldier, who is always glad to earn a shilling by initiating outsiders into smoking and other arcana, completes the main hangers-on. The whole resembles a series of superior vaudeville skits by comedians who improvise on any theme. As such, if performed in a repertory company accustomed to ensemble playing before an audience able to appreciate nuances, the result might hit its targets.

Jonson left no doubt about what he meant. The care expended on the text relates to the central design. This labor includes a page devoted to "the names of the actors."[13] In the quarto the intended arrangement appears plainly, but in the folio, because of modifications for uniformity throughout the volume, the signs were somewhat blurred. Across the top of the quarto page are the names of Macilente, Saviolina, and Sordido. These three venerate their peculiarities most devotedly; their humours have cut so deeply that no escape from the confines of eccentricity exists. They have fed humours assiduously; the domination is total. Below them, those on the right represent townspeople or social climbers not wholly bereft of their wits, and on the left are rustics or those of no position trying to wedge a toehold on the fantastic ladder. This diagram further illustrates why the humours cannot indulge in a complicated plot; the afflicted are neither perceptive nor conceited enough to observe anything. Were anyone less obsessed present—a nightmare for him—he could establish no contact because no one is alive. The failures of *The Case Is Altered*, not recognizing the truth about one's self, predominate here; the saving grace of there being some sort of truth has disappeared. The dramatis personae are paired or balanced monsters who perform their tricks before any audience in the neighborhood. The plot does have a crab-like progression. It seeks to remove the characters from their humours, that is, to relieve the pressures of affectations. The emphasis on *in His Humour* stresses showing the behavior and on *out of His Humour* removing the excess, but the titles do not entirely suit the action. Here the equation, somewhat optimistically, permits the humours to cancel each other. Once they have nothing left on which to feed, they starve and presumably disappear. Jonson, whose aversion for puritanical capitalism increased, did not long harbor faith in so naïve a balance of trade.

The ways by which humours assert themselves depend, as usual, upon mistaken identity or the assumption that by mere appearance an underlying reality can be disguised, except that, a further irony, these shadows have no reality. The three most confirmed in humours have closed their minds upon all but the one force chaining them. Like the miser Jaques, Sordido seeks to hide his treasure, in this instance his grain, in the earth and to present himself to the world garbed in poverty. When the predicted floods do not blast the crops of less conniving farmers, he hangs himself. Several poor neighbors discover the suicide and cut him down. At the moment between life and death, the stream of humour continues to flow, and he protests that, if they had to rescue him, they might at least not have split the valuable halter on which he was dangling. This complaint is a last gasp; he decides arbitrarily to reform, but, as far as his performing personality goes, he may as well be dead. Saviolina, whose wit establishes her claim to be "the wonder of nations" (III. ix. 75), is demolished when she declares that Sogliardo, the farmer presented to her as a gentleman who, to test her, is masquerading in the guise of a rustic, must be a true gentleman. Such confusions of disguise proceed as far as they can here. Embarrassment because of this mistake does not work a permanent change on her: nothing could. Macilente, most venomous of all, vents indiscriminate hatred on whatever happens to be at hand. In this savoring of mischief he devises pranks to keep the action going. His images of loathing swell to cataclysmic proportions to become thoroughly impossible and, by this disproportion, comic.

> Would to heauen
> (In wreake of my misfortunes) I were turn'd
> To some faire water-*Nymph*, that (set vpon
> The deepest whirle-pit of the rau'nous seas,)
> My adamantine eyes might head-long hale
> This iron world to me, and drowne it all. (II. iv. 161–66)

As has frequently been observed, the ambitions of Renaissance man recognized no bounds. Just as Bobadilla's speeches keep a delicacy on the frontier of despair, so, too, Macilente in the progression of this resounding tirade would have the water nymph be, after all, fair. The stream of humour is not so deep that an idiosyncratic pebble cannot now and then ripple its surface. In spite of his affecting a melancholy black and protesting against the ostentations of others, he is not without vanity. He longs for a handsome face and, like Juniper and Onion, boasts that clothes will make him nearly a courtier. Humour so strong, for his is the stream only the Thames can check, requires a special destruction. In the original version Macilente was cured by the sight of Queen Elizabeth herself. If Jonson's tastes miss, they do not fall a little beside the mark. In the period when the English monarch was believed to possess a magic, medicinal touch, the fabulous denouement may have sounded less improbable. Fortunately cooler heads prevailed. A revised Macilente is righted because, all the other characters having been put out of their humours, his has nothing more upon which to feed. Nevertheless, Jonson, whose stubbornness sometimes drove him to fight battles long after the other participants had yawned and walked away, printed both endings in the folio.

Meanwhile, the minor characters run through traits observed

before, or new ones which vary familiar themes. The principle of selecting misconduct hinges upon consciousness of the ideal conditions of society. Briske, the courtier, lives beyond his means in order to lead the forefront with the latest novelty in dress, speech, behavior, and opinion. He possesses no innate characteristics of his own and seeks a personality by allying himself with the newest fad. In contrast with this bent toward modernity, Puntarvolo molds himself on older customs. When he returns to his own home, he pretends to be a lost, wandering knight; his wife shelters him as she would a stranger, with protestations of honorable conduct on both sides. The lines they speak to each other have a flat, stilted quality, the sort that did duty as discourse in *The Case Is Altered* but that here mocks it. Invariably a style which once implied conviction turns up later in parody, another example of how Jonson's talent, if limited, wasted nothing. Later Puntarvolo decides to tour, a pastime often ridiculed, and embarks upon a primitive scheme of travel insurance; the transaction is really betting with a number of people on the odds of returning alive with his wife and dog. Buffone represents, at further remove, Macilente, the man of at least rudimentary feeling who lacks judgment. His refusing any improvement makes his bluntness as affected as the aspirations for too much subtlety. Deliro and Fallace, the citizen and his wife, expound a more familiar dilemma. She seeks an affair with Briske, while her husband, perhaps the most deluded of all, tries to change nature itself, perfuming the house and grounds, to please her whim. These five, occupying the left column, are advancing ideals which, however wrongly applied, bear better pedigrees than those on the right, who copy the copies. Fungoso's doomed race to model himself on Briske always falls behind the whirlwind pace; by the time he has a suit duplicated his hero appears in a new one. The less glaring manifestations he never detects. His uncle, Sogliardo, does not achieve this level, and he stalks down amenities already discarded by the town as old-hat, such as smoking. The soldier Shift, like his name, will revert to any profession for money; of all chicanery he prefers parading himself as a brave fighter. A few minor figures complete the sketches.

All these eccentricities, improbable as they sound, in performance look more sinister than the self-indulgence of fools. The metaphoric strands begin to establish a pattern for criticizing conduct. Often desire for the recherché is linked with disease, "Plagu'd with an itching leprosie of wit" (Second Sounding, 68), so that it balloons in time as more than a quirk, an identification reinforced by the figurative feeding of humour and by the widespread translation of vanity into gluttony. A third condemnation through metaphor, the invective of animal names, a touch glancingly present in the first two plays, here emerges with a suggestion of the ferocity which turns *Volpone* into the snarling pit it is. In the image of the humours as a flood, on whatever level they are manifest, Jonson happened upon a device which, if one accepts Bergson, underlies most comedy: the mechanical. This term, within a range of meanings, has defined the comic from Dryden to the present. A stream of humour is, perhaps, the quickest explanation of the inability to adjust one's behavior. Taking his cue from this figure, a director might still gather together a troupe of comedians dedicated to their art who could subject themselves to the rigorous demands of this play and by stylization surmount its imperfections. If the suggestion sounds like armchair strategy, consider who would have seen in *Le chapeau de paille d'Italie* quite the comedy René Clair coaxed from the Labiche farce by converting the bourgeois into billiard balls bumping each other as they chase under the propulsion of their private drives.

The possibilities of Jonson's talent do not culminate at so easy a level; the very arrogance with which he shoved his plays before the public betrays uncertainty about their pedigrees. *Every Man out of His Humour* is scarcely a play, but that effect in itself may be not unintentional. The Elizabethan theater surely was less illusionistic than the picture-frame stage is; its very structure carried elements of abstraction which tended to push it toward allegory.[14] Jacobean dramatists thrashed around as tortuously to carry off a realistic representation of action as modern ones do to revive myth and symbol behind the proscenium arch. In the construction of the humour comedies the problem is to rule out cosmic overtones but to keep unobtrusively present the realization that these monsters are men. A chorus helps to mediate between the antitheses; it both creates the scene and believes in it. Unlike the Greek chorus, it does not suffer indirectly; unlike a Chinese stage manager, it does not control the plot. It is the function of the three men to comment on the bizarre behavior of those upon the stage. The give and take between the two groups is quite free. For example, the play begins with a discussion by the three, Mitis, Cordatus, and Asper. Asper himself, who rails heavily against audiences, becomes the actor playing Macilente, the principal humour figure. At the end of the play he rejoins the chorus in Macilente's garb but claims his identity as Asper. The theatrical impact of this doubling is obscure. An extended study of the considerable number of Elizabethan plays-within-plays and of the stage used as a stage ought to establish a more nearly just view of the drama beyond the crude interpretations based on only realistic representations.[15] Here, without worrying too nicely, one can distinguish several advantages which accrue to this shifting of stage effects. With the chorus Jonson tried to hold together the nearly footling pile. Rather than ignore this potential limitation, he capitalized upon it. Two characters named Clove and Orange once amble into view. Although they indulge themselves in some pretentious nonsense, nobody, thanks to his domination by the humours, hears them. They are explained by the chorus.

> Mit. What be these two, signior?
> Cor. Mary, a couple sir, that are meere strangers to the whole scope
> of our play; only come to walke a turne or two, i' this *Scene* of
> *Paules*, by chance.
> (III. i. 16–19)

One may safely assume that Jonson was not just filling up a page by the explanation. It has an ulterior purpose. The loose construction fits in with the rationale, indeed serves to point it up. Although it emerges strongly from the play itself, because it has so long been missed, an indication of the background may localize it more effectively. In spite of all that has been made of Jonson's reading, the really influential impact it made on his dramaturgy has been overlooked.

From a plethora of echoes one can deduce that Jonson was devoting not a little of his study to the works of Erasmus, chiefly *Moriae Encomium*, for *Every Man out of His Humour* and *Cynthia's Revels*. The sort of borrowing he did relies less on the type already swelling footnotes, that of lifting now and then a few lines or of adapting an extended scene, than of taking over a formal abstraction and giving it a human shape. For example, the setting of *Every Man out of His Humour* is the *Insula Fortunata*, a label usually read as a cipher for England. Folly, however, also claims the Fortunate Isles as her birthplace:

> Quod si locum quoque natalem requiritis, quandoquidem id hodie vel inprimis ad nobilitatem interesse putant, quo loco primos edideris vagitus, ego nec in erratica Delo, nec in undoso mari, nec ἐν σπέσσι γλαφυροῖσι sum edita, sed in ipsis insulis fortunatis, ubi ἄσπαρτα καὶ ἀνήροτα omnia proveniunt.[16]

Jonson's style might have copied the trick of piling on details from Erasmus' slyly mocking prose. Amplification as a rhetorical flourish distinguishes both high medieval and early Renaissance Latin; the influence cannot be isolated as distinctly Erasmian. One idea, however, seems to have fathered a direct descendant.

> Si quis histrionibus in scena fabulam agentibus personas detrahere conetur, ac spectatoribus veras nativasque facies ostendere, nonne is fabulam omnem perverterit, dignusque habeatur, quem omnes e theatro velut lymphatum saxis ejiciant? . . . Verum eum errorem tollere, est fabulam omnem perturbare. Illud ipsum figmentum et fucus est, quod spectatorum oculos detinet. Porro mortalium vita omnis quid aliud est, quam fabula quaepiam, in qua alii aliis obtecti personis procedunt, aguntque suas quisque partes, donec choragus educat e proscenio?[17]

These sentiments are voiced, of course, by Folly who, whatever her inconsistencies, always favors illusions. Jonson may have been trying by several ways, the diffuse plot, sardonically named characters, blatant chorus, and finally, an assumption comparable with Erasmus', to underline the fact that these humours, affectations though they may be, are, after all, but pretenses in themselves, shadows of shadows of deviations. Rather than weaken the mockery, the device emphasizes the sterility in folly. How the adult actors may have responded to this aspersion is not recorded, but the next plays, *Cynthia's Revels* and *Poetaster*, were performed by, and obviously written for, the Children of the Chapel. The differences suggest Jonson realized that, resolute as *Every Man out of His Humour* might be in its daring, its acrobatics stretch out the humour concept to dangerous limits. *Cynthia's Revels* has a modified and better integrated axis upon which its episodes turn.

Of all the 1616 folio comedies *Cynthia's Revels* probably pleases least any modern reader. Jonson's blatant exploitation of an experiment is borne out by the Prologue.

> In this alone, his Mvse her sweetnesse hath,
> Shee shunnes the print of any beaten path;
> And proues new wayes to come to learned eares:
> Pied ignorance she neither loues, nor feares.
> Nor hunts she after popular applause,
> Or fomie praise, that drops from common iawes. . . .
>
> (Prologue, 9–14)

His innovations might be recognized for what they are, had he polished them less. Instead, they incorporate a host of traditional materials along with the original so smoothly that they look less unusual than they are. For *Cynthia's Revels* he rearranged the whole stock of effects which stood him in good stead up to this time. The construction displays to advantage the ventures so far explored and, because circumstances unlocked different approaches for him, considerably advances his art. While lacking the exploratory vigor of *Every Man out of His Humour*, it combines episodes in a painstaking execution seldom congenial to novelties. Those commentators who have heeded the warning of the Prologue have failed to look beneath the immediate implications. They divide the action into three parts: the mythological business involving Cupid and Mercury, a static satire on the court, and the final masque. Properly understood, the play is as much of a piece as the other three. This is not to say that it is good, but its faults stem from flaws less superficial than those allowed it.

In reading any of Jonson's plays one must start from the Elizabethan stage itself. No matter how detailed might have been the preparation of the text for quarto publication and no matter how many emendations he may have appended to the folio, the stage itself first engaged him. The fact that he composed *Cynthia's Revels* with "*the* Children *of her* Maiesties Chappell"[18] in mind and that they first performed it, whereas the preceding two were by the Lord Chamberlain's men, bears directly on the interpretation. The arguments of the children in the Induction, which capitalizes on the arch precociousness of the boy actors, set the theme at once and are caught up by the opening with Cupid and Mercury, two young gods. All these prepare the way for accepting episodes involving human adults in miniature. Although it is hazardous to speculate on what Elizabethans themselves made of these children, Jonson, for his own taste, required special apologies to disguise them acceptably as adults. The Children also acted *The Case Is Altered* and *Epicene*. The former, probably, was not originally designed for them, but merely revived later. The second, though, has the same lightness of language and touch which marks *Cynthia's Revels*. *Poetaster*, also done by them, is in every sense an exceptional play. Lyly had earlier created a style suitable for the Children; one is always surprised by the felicity with which Jonson pursued and captured the most elusive forms of Elizabethan literature, such as masques and lyrics. In *Cynthia's Revels* the infants exploit adult failings; the "games" by which the bored courtiers kill time gain a sharper sting if one recalls that boys actually took part. The search for fragile social refinements underscores an immature, ephebic quality. The maskings and unmaskings again expound the theme with the added travesty of children in carnival dress. Just as *Every Man out of His Humour* has actors portraying people whose affectations make actors out of them, so the children become adults who behave like the young. The main problem of the satirist is fixing a point from which to gauge ridicule, a scale Jonson later abandoned by gliding, as does Swift in *A Tale of a Tub*, from improbability to improbability so gracefully that no pause exists outside the material for a critical evaluation. Here the children themselves furnish that center. Finally, by employing the boys Jonson apparently felt himself free to give women, whose roles they always performed, a more important function than in any earlier plays or in any later ones until *Epicene*.

The plot itself at first glance looks slighter than *Every Man out of His Humour;* it can hardly be traced. The scene is an imaginary kingdom, Gargaphie, specifically the court of a Queen Cynthia, a cipher, as she so often is, for Queen Elizabeth.[19] A group of false courtiers have somehow invaded her palace. Most of the action, if that term is not misleading, shows them waiting for water from the fountain of self-love and for an evening's entertainment, a masque. In the masque itself they impersonate the virtues whose opposing vices they embody. Cynthia discerns the deception and with a sternly maternal attitude punishes them. The affinities with *Every Man out of His Humour* are numerous, a hint again being furnished by the arrangement of the cast listings in the quarto. This time they are paired across the page by numbers: 3, 5, 7, etc., on the left and 2, 4, 6, etc., on the right.[20] Cynthia, as 1, centered on the page, heads both columns. They range downward from demigods, through the loyal courtiers, to the pretenders, and the mutes. An effort to keep the men on the left and women on the right almost succeeds. As before, appearance and social triumphs, those traits which began with the servant Onion and became a major preoccupation, carry the dominant theme. Juniper's vices of speech, rarefied and precious, are likewise scourged. In place of the chorus of *Every Man out of His Humour*, Crites, the maker of masques, and Arete, Cynthia's favorite, comment upon and eventually manipulate the episodes. Like a less assured Musco, Cupid and Mercury steer along the complications.

Having once restricted himself to all the limitations of a humour comedy, Jonson did not repeat himself. Perhaps the metaphor of humour as a stream proved too restricting. Whatever the reason, the images with which affectations are compared include more objects. Water recurs figuratively, but as the dedicatory letter to the court announces, it should be a source to refresh the land: "TO THE SPECIALL FOVNTAINE OF MANNERS: The Court. *THou art a bountifull, and braue spring: and waterest all the noble plants of this* Iland. *In thee, the whole Kingdome dresseth it selfe, and is ambitious to vse thee as her glasse.*" (Dedication, 1–8) A fountain literally introduces the play and figuratively sustains it. Instead of the humours' being dammed up and spilling over, the vice becomes self-love, which a narcissistic gazing must induce. The humours, properly mixed, fulfill their function, but otherwise they incite frantic activity; the fountain, comparably, nourishes self-respect, but it can become a stagnant pool for idleness. If the characters of *Every Man out of His Humour* often fail to observe others because they are so intent on themselves, those of *Cynthia's Revels*, because they are so intent on themselves, worry excessively about their impressions on others. Consequently, the voice, whose treachery has been assumed in all the plays since *The Case Is Altered,* increases its scope. Water and fire most frequently serve as the vehicles in metaphors for humours in *Every Man out of His Humour;* those of *Cynthia's Revels* also compare them to air and, sometimes, earth. Like nightingales, these people are *vox et praeterea nihil* or mere lumpish clods.[21] They exist as insubstantial pipings or as shapeless matter which tosses back a senseless echo. Within this concept Jonson's style, although not yet refined to its keenest resilience, achieves a convincing drive, a quality whose traits have been described in a wholly different satirist: "Mr. Connolly will invent a character—a Communist pansy, an arch young girl, the hero of an Aldous Huxley novel or a self-immolating member of a future totalitarian state—and allow it to possess him like a demon, carrying him away to lengths that are hilarious and a little hysterical."[22]

Jonson's symbols are rewarding once one investigates them; unfortunately, the most common assumption has simply been that they are so obvious that they require only a nodding glance. For example, after the Induction the story opens with a bit of mythology. Cupid and Mercury, while traveling together, free Echo from being bound to Narcissus. She curses the pool which destroyed him, and it becomes the fountain of self-love. As she fades away, the tourist Amorphus, on his way to Cynthia's court, enters. The belief has run that here Jonson merely indulged himself in a flight of clipped-wing fancy. Actually, by shaping traditional material to his own ends, he points the direction of what he is saying. The demigods do, of course, serve on one level to introduce the subject to the audience through the children, who already were quarreling in the Prologue. This explanation fails to mention why specifically the Echo-Narcissus story was selected; its suitability should be apparent from what has already been said about the water metaphors. One must look deeper to explain the other mythology in this scene: references to Actaeon, whom, when he burst upon Diana bathing in her pool, the shy goddess turned into a stag, and to Niobe, who with ineluctable feminine pride boasted herself superior to a goddess because she had fourteen children, while Leto had but two, and, in consequence, suffered having all her sons and daughters slain and herself turned to a constantly weeping stone.

One essay has defined aspects of this business.[23] Actaeon may, indeed, hint a parallel with Essex, who entered Queen Elizabeth's chamber before she was ready to receive him, and Niobe may, likewise, signal that insolence which defies sovereigns who rule by divine right. Analyzing the play and its literary backgrounds tells more about the reason for the choice of these myths than conjectures based on historical intrigues.

When Niobe's children were shot down, Diana (Artemis) and Apollo, the numerically smaller but militarily stronger children of the offended Leto, launched the arrows. In *Cynthia's Revels* Crites and Arete symbolically perform identical functions for Cynthia. Their association with these gods is pointed out directly. "Chiefe next DIANA, virgin, heauenly faire, / Admired ARETE" (V. v. 51–52); after this link Crites addresses his prayers for assistance in making the masque to Apollo, his patron. Presenting Echo also permits a rhetorical device, a reply made with the final syllables of the last word spoken. The trick derives from Ovid, "forte puer comitum seductus ab agmine fido / dixerat: 'ecquis adest?' et 'adest' responderat Echo."[24] This quickly wearisome trope had been well engrained into the English poetry of a period when crude ingenuity was too often prized for its own sake: Gascoigne, Sidney, Lodge, Heywood, Dekker, and Webster, all copying Ovid, indulged in it.[25] It achieves a pigeonhole in the rhetoricians' categories: Epanalepsis, or the Echo Sound, otherwise the Slow Return.[26] Jonson puts the device through its special paces. By itself this figure of speech could claim to be no more than a momentary flourish. There appear to have been several plays about Narcissus in English; at least one survives and extant notes describe another.[27] In both of these a hunting scene, reminiscent of Actaeon's chase, occurs. The combination boasts an honorable pedigree; in Ovid, just before the story of Echo and Narcissus, stands Actaeon's. Here again Jonson pulls together many divergent, but related, strands and shapes them for one coherent effect. The four mythological images at the beginning (Actaeon, Niobe, Echo and Narcissus, and Cupid and Mercury) balance with the four pairs of abstract virtues and vices in the masque of the fifth act, so that symbolic myths enclose the satire on the court of Gargaphie.

Structural coherence does not ensure achievement. The plot itself scarcely moves. What the play, under the new device, gains in unity, it loses in flexibility. After Cupid and Mercury dispatch Echo, they follow Amorphus to Cynthia's court. There the group, upon hearing of the powers of the newly cursed fountain of self-love, send a servant to bring them a sample of its water. It takes an unconscionably long time arriving. Meanwhile, because, Asotus apart, all the courtiers, whose names are adapted from the *Moriae Encomium*, have achieved whatever they wish, there is none of the frantic climbing which kept *Every Man out of His Humour* lively. The Echo-Narcissus theme further limits them; they display themselves in static attitudes until at the end they are unmasked. Moreover, in the folio text a number of dreary scenes are inserted so that whatever barbs the original had are weighted down by too many feathers.[28] Nevertheless, granting all this, one can isolate the design beyond the wastes of the nearly interminable character sketches of the original second act and the overwhelmingly stuffy "duello" interpolated into the last. The ingenious extension of the Echo-Narcissus story suggests best what Jonson had hoped to accomplish.

A common observation in the satire of the time assigned gulls the habit of repeating phrases. Chapman, for example, exaggerated in *An Humorous Day's Mirth*:

> *Le.* Marry thus sir, he will speake the very selfe same word, to a sillable after him of whome he takes acquaintance, as if I should say,
> I am marueilous glad of your acquaintance, He will reply,
> I am maruailous glad of your acquaintance,
> I haue heard much good of your rare parts & fine cariage,
> I haue heard much good of your rare parts & fine cariage,
> so long as the complements of a gentleman last, he is your complete ape.

(This prediction occurs with a bluntness as deafening to the ear as the preceding typography was flat to the eye.)

> *Le.* I shall be glad to be commanded by you.
> *Blan.* I shall be glad to be commanded by you.
> *Le.* I pray do not you say so.
> *Blan.* I pray do not you say so.[29]

Jonson modulated his passages considerably beyond this crude attack. Echo herself preserves the Ovidian trait; when she leaves, her repetitions are inherited by Amorphus.

> AMO. I am neither your *Minotaure,* nor your *Centaure,* nor your *Satyre,* nor your *Hyaena,* nor your *Babion,* but your mere trauailer, beleeue me.
> Ecc. Leaue me.   (I. iii. 4–7)

Such phrasing is pursued intentionally at court by Asotus, who eagerly allows Amorphus, the two being a "reciprocall brace of butter-flies" (I. iv. 77), to tutor him for social prominence. Initially he repeats the stilted lines, but if he forgets them, at a loss for words, he echoes himself. When he actually delivers himself of one of his foolish set pieces in public, circumstances suddenly intrude. "Now, by this watch (I marle how forward the day is) I doe vnfeignedly vow my selfe (s'light 'tis deeper then I tooke it, past fiue) yours entirely addicted, Madame." (IV. iii. 39–41) In preparing for a game of words, Substantives and Adjectives, an adumbration of Cadavre Exquis, Asotus becomes an echo with a short memory:

> AMO. Giue forth your *Adiectiue,* with the rest; as, prosperous, good, faire, sweet, well—
> HED. Any thing, that hath not beene spoken.
> Aso. Yes, sir: well-spoken, shall be mine.
>   (IV. iii. 101–4)

Thus the mythological and social, the figurative and literal, again join: the Slow Return.

Ridiculing sound without sense runs through all the acts, observable both by what characters say and by direct judgments. Echo is, literally, "meerely made of voice" (I. ii. 94), but Moria, whose imprecisions of expression match Juniper's and who as the oldest and silliest woman sets the pattern, is "a lady made all of voice, and aire, talkes any thing of any thing." (II. iv. 14–15) Another woman, Phantaste, is "of a most curious and elaborate straine, light, all motion, an *vbiquitarie,* shee is euery where. . . ." (II. iv. 99–101) Argurion, discussed on page 8 above, fits into this same pattern. Narcissism has wide implications for the false courtiers: "His eye and his rayment confer much together as he goes in the street . . . . and when he is most neat, and new, you shall strip him with commendations." (II. iii. 113–18) Both excesses grow from the pretenders' inability to feel any love for another person, as Echo complains in an elaborate conceit that had Narcissus bothered to regard her, rather than his pool, she would have wept so that, seeing himself in her tears, he would have caught his more nearly true reflection. This self-love extends further to match Niobe's boast: "what neede wee gaze on CYNTHIA, that haue our selfe to admire?" (V. x. 45–46) The subtle change from the humours, where most of the pretenders were affected so that they might become what they admired, to this, where they are wholly infected with self-love, marks the fine calibration of the Jonsonian scale on which differences of degree merge almost imperceptibly into those of kind. In *Every Man out of His Humour*, though not before, such elements were implicit in scattered expressions, similar to the echo trope. When Puntarvolo, pretending to be a lost knight, asks for the master of the house before his own home, the comment is that a mirror should be dropped down to him. One anticipation of the echo device shows Sogliardo, swept along by his humour, catching part of a word and immediately turning it into another:

CAR. You must talke much of your kinred, and allies.
SOG. Lies! no Signior, I shall not neede to doe so, I haue kinred i'the
city to talke of. . . .   (I. ii. 66–68)

Despite this careful patching into patterns, Jonson does not bring off the whole. *Cynthia's Revels* remains paralyzed while the characters seek praise from each other for doing nothing. Many comedies of manners display people inherently no brighter who are more amusing. The dogged refusal to allow the empty heads an iota's wit beyond their powers betrays the work, Jonson's only one which can be so blamed, into what one critic has termed the imitative fallacy. Effete boredom, despite the *reductio ad absurdum* to which it is pushed, produces, in general, boredom. The courtiers spend most of their time praising their past bons mots and devising fairly elaborate encounters in which their pathetic cleverness will become at best a tawdry adornment; many of these include improbably large casts to feed crucial cues. The projected interchanges, puerile as they are, never occur.

The discontinuity between the stream of humour and the fountain of self-love as sources of affectation leaves the motivation nearly inexplicable. The theory of the humours survives in the main. Crites, the good poet, possesses virtue because he is "a creature of a most perfect and diuine temper. One, in whom the humours and elements are peaceably met, without emulation of precedencie . . . ." (II. iii. 123–25) What actually does determine behavior fades into vagueness. The metaphoric reliance upon humours diminishes, but the fountain of self-love, which was the main title of the quarto version, cannot be substituted forcefully enough. The contradiction that all the cast already is quite intoxicated by self-love detracts from the principal line of what effects the waters may produce. For example, in the concluding masque[30] Philautia, standing for self-love, acts Storge, who is "*naturall Affection*, which giuen vs to procure our good, is somtime called Storge, & as euery one is neerest to himselfe, so this hand-maid of reason, *allowable selfe-loue*, as it is without harme, so are none without it . . . ." (V. vii. 26–30) Allowable self-love, if one can quite believe it, becomes analogous with the humours when they mix properly. Just as the humour characters have one kind of excess, which grows with feeding, so too these courtiers, inflated already with pride, can become only more monstrous by, literally and figuratively, drinking the water from Narcissus' fountain. When Cupid's shafts fail to penetrate them, the climax of a process operative at the start is realized.

Otherwise, the standard remains appearance, and the mistaken substitute the clothes for the wearer. The dangers of deception change; earlier, anyone not embroiled in his own preoccupations could detect disguises no matter how lavish the cloth. Unmasking interposes new difficulties. Amorphus promises to demonstrate "how cleerly I can refell that *paradox*, or rather *pseudodox*, of those, which hold the face to be the index of the mind, which (I assure you) is not so, in any politique creature . . . ." (II. iii. 12–15) The extended practice of this duplicity begins the process which, strictly controlled, leads to the great comedies and, when let wander at random, peters out as nearly inexplicable sentimentality. This complexity reverses the standard of *The Case Is Altered* and *Every Man in His Humour* where the leading characters were, in the main, capable of working their ways toward positive goals. In *Cynthia's Revels* each step confirms them more in their follies. The long sketches of the second act, incorporating character portraits like those prefixed to *Every Man out of His Humour*, often assume the allegorical strain necessary to connect creatures so attenuated with an atmosphere of playful indolence. The idly invented games, while unforgivable dramatically, have a mordant force when understood as ineffectual echoes of learning and manners. The final masque stresses that such temperaments depend upon continual outward change no matter what it embodies. The debilitating effects of travel are harshly ridiculed as another aspect of the desire for novelty. The humourists, at least, find satisfaction in being what they ape; the courtiers need, within their social playground, unending diversions to amuse themselves.

In spite of these darker intrusions, the whole effect produces a lighter comedy than *Every Man out of His Humour*, commensurate, perhaps, with the more delicate performances which the Children were capable of. For example, the pervasive animal metaphors which fill the great comedies and which begin tentatively in *Every Man in His Humour* here refer to brightly colored or harmless aspects. The rhythm of the prose itself slows down to explore lazy ingenuity. While the pretenders of the first humour comedy had to vent their manias and drives in vigorous assertions, the victims of self-love appreciate their own discourse and linger over it to shape it while speaking. Behind such bemusement a strong satiric drive prevents *Cynthia's Revels* from being a mere puppet show by children for relaxing adults. Bitter references to disease throughout the play remind one constantly that bodies are not air and voice, but that they sicken, wither, fail, and rot, just as Narcissus did and as a state governed by stupidity can.

Cynthia's role introduces a new force. She sweeps upon the scene as an absolute power, a ruler whose raised voice chastises or corrects. This sway repeats the one which she claimed at the first ending of *Every Man out of His Humour*. Jonson's motives in providing Elizabeth this function need not be questioned too persistently. Throughout his career he assigned kings a divine right, which might, under unhappy circumstances, be corrupted, but which, when united with a vigorous mind, bends to itself all possible strengths and virtues. He shared with his waning century a beautiful belief in a fallacy which an historian has described: "Skeptical as to the existence of unicorns and salamanders, the age of Machiavelli and Henry VIII found food for its credulity in the worship of that rare monster, the God-fearing Prince."[31]

For Jonson the homage transcended ulterior motives, however much royal favor voicing such a creed may have won him. The question was crucial for his art: on what did the authority of his position as poet and satirist ultimately rest? Beneath the surface of the earlier comedies a hesitancy mars the sure style with prosaic moralizing, which rings false, like a poet thinking officially against his better insights. No matter how much or how little he believed or wanted to believe the assertive declamations, they run to excessive lengths. First mere righteousness as common sense sufficed to correct; then a carefree magistrate cajoled the reluctant; finally the humours themselves canceled each other with the queen the final positive. Here, all virtue rests with Cynthia herself; she it is who orders the pseudoliturgical confession of secular sins at the end. The finicky tone throughout *Cynthia's Revels* hints that Jonson may have found the humours a bit too common, as does Crites' musing on man

> When, euen his best and vnderstanding part,
> (The crowne, and strength of all his faculties)
> Floates like a dead drown'd bodie, on the streame
> Of vulgar humour, mixt with commonst dregs.   (I. v. 36–39)

Perhaps it was well that at this point he had to catch himself up short. He ran the risk of abandoning dramatics for singing hymns to pure goodness.

CHAPTER IV

(Although no Paralel)

J ONSON, as inveterate critic of art and man, had this breed's
touching faith that censure of men, if made in conscience,
cannot miss its mark in art. It is a blind hope and bears rebuffs cheerfully so it may turn the other cheek in aggressions. One does, perhaps,
congratulate the optimism but must deplore the naïveté. With Jonson,
in whom nothing is proportionally life-size, the attack on poetasters
carried more invective than usual, and, it seems, he believed that chagrin would crush his detractors. As usual, too, when a writer risks
making his work à clef, he locks out whatever bestows permanence on
art, for the structure then rests on nothing more substantial than a
human personality, which, engrossing as it is as transitory scandal, becomes flatly dull when pressed into the printed page. *Poetaster*, then,
arose out of painfully personal circumstances; whether the achievement itself transcends these bickerings remains debatable. Were all
facts known, one might cheerfully dismiss it, but that saving solace is
denied. Because Jonson left one seemingly "incomplete" work, scholars and gossip mongers, two temperaments not always antithetical,

have flocked around to finish it. The entire effect, though, may be quite impersonal. The background of the quarrel out of which the play sprang repeats a familiar situation.

Among Elizabethan playwrights, not a notably friendly lot, reconstructed genial evenings in the Mermaid Tavern apart, Jonson had several detractors, headed by Marston and Dekker. The two factions apparently waged a feud for some months, and certain literary historians would involve every playwright and every play for nearly a decade. Hostilities culminated about the time of *Cynthia's Revels*. Probably Jonson heard of attacks planned against him, for obviously the London literary group at this time had many unreliable rumors but no secrets. He gained the initiative; before the Lord Chamberlain's men could present their comedy on a bookish poet, which became *Satiro-mastix* or *The Untrussing of the Humourous Poet*, he had prepared a reply, a story of some ineptly irresponsible Roman writers and their friends. He had this produced as *Poetaster* by the Children. The facts of its life are as simple as this outline, and one might assume that the episode has no bearing upon the worth of the play itself except obliquely to explain its shortcomings. Such deserved obscurity has been denied it by squeamish champions of dead causes in later centuries.[1] A dusty series of cryptic books and articles have split the shreds of evidence to try to determine who belongs in this anachronistic Hollywood column.[2]

Cooler heads have of late prevailed, and scholars have modified the wild guesses of the nineteenth century.[3] From background comment[4] to full critical study[5] to a word count of awesome proportions,[6] conclusions tend to agree that Jonson did not have Marston only in mind when he sketched Crispinus, although a remark to Drummond of Hawthornden suggests that parts may have reflected vices which centered conveniently in Marston. (I, p. 140) Recent arguments seek to tag new identifications,[7] but respect for human complexity should deter guessing at precise equivalents, unless one shares Jonson's Olympian assurance that one can, theoretically, detach the vices from the man, a conviction he championed with diminishing success.[8] Naturally, those less lofty might not suppress the feeling that they were what they said. Indeed, this theory of behavior was thoroughly engrained into Elizabethan psychology. Puttenham, for example, whose treatise Jonson certainly knew, since his own copy is extant and his borrowings are numerous, holds:

> Most men say that not any one point in all *Phisiognomy* is so certaine, as to iudge a mans manners by his eye: but more assuredly in mine opinion, by his dayly maner of speech and ordinary writing. For if the man be graue, his speech and stile is graue: if light-headed, his stile and language also light: if the minde be haughtie and hoate, the speech and stile is also vehement and stirring: if it be colde and temperate, the stile is also very modest: if it be humble, or base and meeke, so is also the language and stile.[9]

The first four of these attributes resemble the four humours in a general way. The opinion that the style and man are one further clarifies the humour comedies. Once afflicted, the men rant, and therefore live, only within the confines of drama. When out of their humours, they will presumably reform their speech. On the other hand, Jonson's prevailing belief that by observing countenances the eye sees the truth conflicts with Puttenham's opinion. The two standards, speech and voice, wage an undefined battle in *Poetaster* and weaken it. Before this play the humours incorporated a vice which generally could be eradicated without undue fretting; they were ridiculous because they were trivial. Here the former attitudes resound less patly. Whether Jonson was attacking particular men by the excesses of vocabulary they exploited or, as seems more likely, the abuses of speech he associated predominantly but not exclusively with these men, the fact remains that the objectives of the launched battles sought to demolish what he judged the enemies of the rules of grammar, rhetoric, and logic. Anything else is somewhat incidental. This line of conjecture follows what seems to have been Jonson's rationale; whether those attacked would be open to its persuasions remains doubtful. Borrowings enough from the classics decorate *Poetaster* to guarantee that a modicum of impersonality motivated its composition, but he was, for the period, a notoriously slow writer, and his hasty inventions betrayed him, from whatever causes, into uncommon ineptitudes.

So frequently has the play been a no man's land in the War of the Theaters, the Poetomachia, that few evaluations have appeared.[10]

Almost no one has tried putting it within a consistent frame. Under fire Jonson fell back on tactics which before had proved effective; improvisation when pressed cannot be counted his major skill. For the defense in *Poetaster* he mustered devices from the four preceding plays, simplified, bolstered, caricatured, and rearranged. Gone are experiments and, nearly, humours. Indeed, its episodic movement closely resembles the structure of *Every Man in His Humour*. In the two intervening works increased emphasis on shadings had exploited fewer kinds of situations. Language became codified within arbitrarily restricted limits. Cause and effect in plots dwindled to a minimum. Descriptions of static characters and ridicule of preciosity increased to proportions which rendered conflicts awkward. *Poetaster* has an ordinary structure; the actual plot derives from Roman history. Jonson dug up a situation which could be hammered nearly parallel to his own. It takes place at the court of the Emperor Augustus, whose power is as right as Cynthia's. Julia, Augustus' daughter, becomes the patroness for a moderately dissolute set of writers and pretenders, including Ovid Junior, who loves her; Crispinus, a poetaster; Demetrius, another of the species; Captain Tucca, a soldier living by his wits; citizens, scheming to crash the court circles; actors; and officials. In support of the Emperor stand Horace, the good poet, and Virgil, the impeccable poet. After episodic adventures Ovid Junior is banished for his part in the profane banquet when the participating guests pretend to be gods on a mortal spree, and Crispinus is forced to take an emetic which purges him of his "hard" words. Other strands of the plot may be separated as they emerge. All this seems a bit shoddy as history or drama, something James Anthony Froude or Gilbert and Sullivan might have spun out, but worth no more. Julia and her friends repeat the courtiers of Cynthia's kingdom, although the Romans have widely diversified types. The citizens might be mistaken for Fallace and Deliro from *Every Man out of His Humour*. Ovid Senior's deploring his son's poetic bent resembles Lorenzo Senior's in *Every Man in His Humour*. The duplications in action and gradation of vices obey a ruthless alignment unattempted since *The Case Is Altered*. Others embody the abiding traits of gulls with affectations. The one

standard which formerly held together such patches sinks into abeyance: a strict obedience to the workings of the humours.

Perhaps the deviations which the humours foster excuse too
mildly the Romans' rank stupidity. The word humour does occur in
contexts already familiar, but it carries less force than it had. Typical
of this change, the sea and water images diminish. No longer the limiting vehicle of humour metaphors, the sea itself swallows up all whims
with its somber strength:

> I will preferre for knowledge, none, but such
> As rule their liues by it, and can becalme
> All sea of humour, with the marble *trident*
> Of their strong spirits: Others fight below
> With gnats, and shaddowes, others nothing know.
>
> (IV. vi. 74-78)

Emotions link metaphorically with the four elements oftener than the
humours do, and thus Jonson revived his early style. These shifts of association lead to the inference that the failings transcend being a single
fault which may, through error, engross the mind and which one devastating stroke corrects. The emotions, being more complex than the
simplified humours, must also refer back to deeper sources. The conviction increases that initial misdemeanors will corrupt absolutely. At
least, this drift seems the main intention, although the play is contradictory enough to make the assertion less than unexceptionable.

The tone of *Poetaster* puzzles a reader. Perhaps a competent director could convince one about a single interpretation when it is performed, but, granted this point, one must also concede that a second
director, holding a diametric reading of the script, might evolve an
equally persuasive production. It seems unlikely, however, that opportunities for comparisons will be available; few revivals of *Poetaster*
have been presented, and, except as a curiosity, it will stay neglected.
This obscurity cannot be deplored. At times the tone rants with invective so bitter that one feels tempted to suspect that it parodies railing itself. When the Prologue Envy enters, her cry of dismay, even
if one remembers her supernatural nature, remains inexplicable.

> The *Scene* is, ha!
> ROME? ROME? and ROME? Cracke ey-strings, and your balles

Drop into earth; let me be euer blind.
I am preuented; all my hopes are crost,
Checkt, and abated; fie, a freezing sweate
Flowes forth at all my pores, my entrailes burne:
What should I doe? Rome? Rome?   (Second Sounding, 27–33)

The diatribe, at least, leaves no doubt about the setting. Envy, guardian of the poetasters, comes forth to censure and blame; upon reading
the three posters—Rome, Rome, and Rome—naming the locale, she
discovers that the satire will not be contemporary. The progress of
her discourse resembles the vexations of the humours when thought
twists back to a single word or phrase and bandies it about until it loses
all semblance of sense. In this instance the center is Rome, and all roads
which lead Envy from it lead her back to it. Opposites or variations,
instead of creating new concepts, as an oxymoron can at its best, stub-
bornly retreat to the original condition. With all this one might be
satisfied if, judged by her discourse, Envy were behaving ludicrously.
As her cajolery continues, and she bids detractors, with somber pleading, to eat the snakes adorning her neck, the malice cannot pass as pretense which may be checked or as a vice subject to exhaustion. A long
iconographic history assigns Envy the necklace of snakes;[11] the adornment may have been derived from several weighty authorities. Nor
can the tone of classical satire be invoked for defense; if one compares
the Latin poems from which Jonson borrowed and his own expansions, the greater invective always originated with him. Whereas Macilente's wish to be transfigured into a destructive mermaid was ridiculous, the discrepancies between the melancholy man and a Lorelei
being irreconcilable, Envy's injunctions probably are not.

Because of these uncertainties in diction, what tone and what
contrasts of tone modulate the play puzzle one. The choice of scene,
however, can be explained readily. From the fortress of learning he
had constructed over the years, Jonson hoped safely to repel Marston's
and Dekker's ignorant excesses with weapons which, if recognized
honestly, would render them powerless to rise in counterattacks. That
this genteel stratagem resembles Bobadilla's phantasy of defeating an
army of thousands by the rules of the duel seems not to have occurred

to Jonson, whose orderly processes of thought could betray him into a fallacious view of just how the world does operate.

His own fumbling for the detachment he wished is pointed up by the way in which the language gets out of hand and the, surely unintentional, gaucheries within the setting he himself elected. For example, after Ovid Junior has been sentenced to exile by the Emperor, his daughter Julia resents her father's highhanded discipline. As a descendant of the gods, she defends herself: "vertuous loue / Was neuer scandall to a Goddesse state." (IV. ix. 63–64) Since at this point she is being detained under guard, the assertion sounds unduly adolescent. When, remembering her father's anger, she adds, "But, hee's inflexible!" (IV. ix. 65) the condition repeats precisely that of the humour characters who, in their wildest flights, retain a small, unexpected link with the actual, like the sufferer from acrophobia who clutches a jacket button to confirm his sense of stability on a precipice. This mixing of the literal and the figurative becomes downright ludicrous when Ovid Junior cautions, "I heare thy father; hence, my *deitie*." (IV. ix. 97) In other contexts this disparity between the fancied and the real might satirize very young lovers, but, because claims for a traditional divinity have been advanced, it falls wide of any pertinent target. As a matter of fact, its freakish contradictions somewhat beguile one, but the suspicion persists that, for the good of the whole, it should not divert one in this way.

Sporadically the style succeeds. Captain Tucca stands out as the most wildly incongruous of temperaments in the Jonsonian gallery. His stuttering, repetitions, gusto, and schemes accompany a crudely analytic mind which twists situations to its own purposes and which no pretenses sway. So far, in other comedies fools busily deceived themselves about themselves and treated others as sounding boards or mirrors. Tucca, though swaggering and improbable, is the first knave to relish trickery for its own sake. Characters of this nature will replace the humourists, capitalize on their defects, and twist from them powers, all the more repulsive because within lunatic limits they enjoy self-control. Tucca's diametric energies dangle unintegrated so that his threat remains insubstantial and convincingly marks him as nervous, disorganized, opportunistic, and cunning. A comparable authority shapes no other figure. Tucca, significantly, has the least responsibility in setting forth any of the crowded themes. The effectiveness of other individual portraits varies, but in spite of the many mistakes a definite design shows through. Jonson's limited attainment surprises one all the more because, behind the imperfections, the blueprint of the plot looks promising.

The bases on which the plot rests combine approximately those of *The Case Is Altered* and *Every Man in His Humour*: the problems of how a human personality can appear constant with its material surroundings and of what a poet can achieve. In the two scornful comedies divisions formed along horizontal patterns; everyone possessed inherent worth, if he recognized himself and his place. In *Poetaster* the standards become vertical with absolute goodness at the top and villainy at the bottom, an intensification of the gradations in *Cynthia's Revels*. The preoccupations of the characters refer to social standards, as in the first play, and to literary decorum, as in the second. The two themes should support and infuse one another, but, unfortunately, they rarely do. The auxiliary business smothers the heart of the action, which is really the poet Ovid Junior's double ambition to achieve Julia's love and a writer's fame, two pursuits not separate because he names her his inspiration. Ovid Junior in many ways resembles Lorenzo Junior, except that whereas the latter defends poetry and is praised, Ovid Junior defends it, in practically identical terms, and is punished. Law no longer speaks through the bouncing Doctor Clement but becomes a strict study which Ovid Junior neglects for his undisciplined verses. Familiar attacks against professional writers permeate the first act with slurs more vehement than before. Defenses are fewer and less credited. Indirectly laudatory passages stumble over their excesses of turgid rhetoric: "What prophane violence, almost sacriledge, / Hath here beene offered thy [Poetry's] diuinities!" (I. ii. 233–34) Ovid Junior himself worships at profane shrines, or his impetuous blindness betrays him into elevating worldly objects as deities. The puerile scheme of rhyming the law is dismissed as impractical, but Ovid Junior does not stay crushed. His clumsy rapture rolls out to ally him with the humourists and poetasters:

In IVLIAS name; faire IVLIA: IVLIAS loue
Shall be a law, and that sweet law I'le studie,
The law, and art of sacred IVLIAS loue:
All other obiects will but abiects prooue.   (I. iii. 55–58)

The harping on a name, the retreating to the same subject, and the misunderstanding of values are telltale quirks; they repeat the zigzags of Envy's irritated maledictions. With more modulation this worship might depict a misguided intensity. As it stands, however, no reconciliation links Ovid Junior's two divergent predispositions: his hasty ambition and his not insensitive temperament. His most serious offense, comparable to the masque of Cynthia's false courtiers, commits an outrage not against poetics but society when he assumes leadership at the doubly sacrilegious banquet of the gods. Apparently this masquerading ought to shock one. Augustus, upon discovering it, exhibits the petulance only rulers who mistake a jest for treason can summon. The guests themselves have statures so trifling that one hardly cares very much; their chastisement resembles the all-powerful Cynthia sweeping spiders from her court. Inconsistently enough, Jonson's authority for the scene derives from an account by Suetonius,[12] but in the actual party the Emperor himself led the revelers, another indication that Jonson foraged far afield for his material, which he had, nevertheless, to distort.

Though poetic transports are stained with abuse, chaste (and chastened) poetry itself strides triumphant through the play and finally ascends to full majesty. In this theme of the plot the gradual defining of poetry pursues two directions after beginning with Ovid Junior, who loves it without understanding. In the third act the upper level justifies what poetry ought to be, and the lower debases it. Just as the first act contains a long translation from Ovid, so the third act incorporates most of the satire by Horace in which he encounters a Roman poetaster who torments him.[13] This insertion blends smoothly enough with the drama so that it does not call undue attention to itself. The confusions attendant on translating from one literary form into another, as well as from one language into another, involve more ingenuity than the result justifies. The victorious shrine of poetry is consecrated in the fifth act when Virgil, almost the *deus ex machina*, becomes poetic dictator, the arts wing of Augustus' puritanical phalanx, and declaims a portion of his epic. Logically for the action, he elects to present the description of Rumor, thereby rounding out at once the correct sentiments both philosophically and poetically. This scheme sounds feasible in outline, but at the climax adulation has become so solidified with wonder that dramatic movement itself lies frozen.

Poetry, however, takes a second, downward course from Ovid; lacking his misapplied devotion, it sinks. Crispinus, the poetaster, arrives to debase it, while Ovid Junior, whose reputation could not make him a spokesman for total ineptitude, wanders off for social desecrations. Crispinus, before turning poet, has recently busied himself with Ovid Junior's later pastimes, instructing the bourgeois in fashionable modes. For Crispinus, as for Matheo, the practice of poetry becomes a means of disguise; poetasters reduce to personal adornment what should be objective. He is, of course, the Bore of the Sacred Way whom Horace encounters. From this meeting, in which Crispinus tries to attach himself to Horace, rivalry grows and culminates in the fifth act with the false accusations brought against Horace. When the satirist's innocence is established, Virgil doubles as the judge, and Horace becomes the administrator of justice. Crispinus' punishment fits the crime, an emetic forcing him to cough up pet words which Jonson, as an Elizabethan authority, did not recognize. Thus, the theme of poetry and the damages it can inflict on society should unify the play, but so many incidents mar the progression of the story that the whole remains a jumble of intentions which crisscross ineffectually.

The language further highlights the disproportion, which the cumbersome translations from Ovid and Virgil help puff out, although these passages alone cannot bear the blame. The images concerning animals grow more ferocious than they had been before, some going so far that, like Envy's prologue, they may be interpreted as a kind of epic ridicule, perhaps, but others cannot be defended on these grounds. It is instructive to compare Horace's original satire on meeting the bore with its resurrection by the Horace of the dramatis personae. The stage speech by itself does not break in tone, but the English at every opportunity chooses a term projecting the maximum amount of vehemence. The animals named in the Latin are expanded with a concomitant harping on their stupidity. More than a dispassionate disdain selected the vocabulary in translating. Diseases, also, attain greater prominence as running images, and these lay a stress on physical details which derive from an animus none of the scenes themselves is strong enough to match by what it shows. The figurative language threatens throughout to burst apart, nearly escaping control. For Tucca, of course, this frenzy is suitable but elsewhere it is preposterous. The antics culminate with the actual emetic forced down Crispinus' throat and a count of the solecisms he figuratively spits out. Afterwards a diet of safe, tame authors is prescribed for his recuperation. Although precedents for this kind of horseplay exist, the gross concept offends one less than does the pseudo delicacy of presentation. No relief in the grim business, which extends to sadistic lengths, lessens the poetaster's embarrassment. Mincing apologies by Horace, who tenderly carries out Augustus' instructions, spread throughout the trial the bullying humility of a fifth-former beating his fag into conformity. Nor can the excesses of the scene be written off as an addition for the press beyond the limits of the stage; the hostility impelling Jonson did not allow him to waste time in polishing. The fact that the actors were children does not mitigate effectively in favor of their infantile revenges as it does in *Cynthia's Revels*. Throughout the play the charges mount with too lofty an insistence on how distasteful the subject is. The repeated desire for detachment finds an incongruous outlet in a mixture of bestiality and torment. Images of physical torture rarely occur in Jonson's plays, and more are present in this one than in any other. Their intrusions, as has been seen, cannot be written off against the sources. The last assurance of the author's withdrawn attitude scarcely wins one over to sympathy. Jonson will retire and watch poetasters

> like the barking students of Beares-Colledge,
> To swallow vp the garbadge of the time
> With greedy gullets, whilst my selfe sit by,
> Pleas'd, and yet tortur'd, with their beastly feeding.
>
> (Apologetical Dialogue, 45–48)

The emotions prerequisite for projecting this spectacle would under few circumstances induce composing Virgilian, Horatian, or Ovidian measures.

The language, then, when directed to satire breaks from its author's guidance. When it turns to praise poetry, it relies on pomposity instead of pleasure. Demands so priestly are invoked for the poet that the task of composition predicts a Mallarmé paralyzed by the brashness of transferring on to the white page the imperfect black lines of communication: "As if his mindes peece, which he stroue to to paint, / Could not with fleshly pencils haue her right." (V. i. 114–15) In itself this adulation of poetry frequently speaks with resolution, but it least resembles the better qualities of Jonsonian verse. The defense that this, after all, depicts Virgilian epic cannot make the attitudinizing more palatable. Both the embodied concept and the manner of regarding it curiously resemble a monumental metaphysical verse, certainly at wide variance with anything the *Aeneid* expresses, as when poetry is massively personified:

> Shee can so mould *Rome*, and her monuments,
> Within the liquid marble of her lines,
> That they shall stand fresh, and miraculous,
> Euen, when they mix with innouating dust;
> In her sweet streames shall our braue *Roman* spirits
> Chace, and swim after death, with their choise deeds
> Shining on their white shoulders; and therein
> Shall *Tyber*, and our famous riuers fall
> With such attraction, that th'ambitious line
> Of the round world shall to her center shrinke,
> To heare their musicke. . . .   (V. i. 21–31)

So high a function of art, so improbably expressed, enshrines it on a plane to which Jonson aspired and safely beyond assaults of Marston, Dekker, or other poetasters. Of course, in terms of the play the passage has almost no function except to say again that poetry as well as government must have dictators and both impose their laws profitably. Jonson's unfailing independence, however, necessarily creates authority in his own idealized and impersonal image, another instance of the warring indirections which pull askew any assertions in *Poetaster*.

The route Jonson has cleared to this point in his craft now appears plain. It takes its own coherent direction but not the inevitable one usually assigned it. Fond as he was of mocking humours, he freed

himself from all stock responses. From the outset he hit upon the basis
of what remains the *sine qua non* for comedy: in human beings the
invincibly consistent is ridiculous. Because tragedy must involve a discovery and a fall, the tragic hero varies from scene to scene and
experiences a range of situations drawing upon more emotions, from
himself and the audience, than a mere three hours' singularity conveys.
To the degree that this scope coheres within reconcilable differences, a
tragic figure satisfies his plot. Because comic characters must be a
single self, they reveal an incorrect notion of themselves or of the
places they inhabit, or of both. A man, nakedly himself and serving
no cause except his own ego's, is only comic; at least, periods which
have felt, rightly or wrongly, that man shapes his world believed it.
Moreover, less interesting eras, which assign an immediate material
determinism the more powerful weight, may have confused art with
life when they forced this domination into tragedy.

Although individually Jonson's five early pieces differ, in broader
terms they are consonant. In all of them those characters who allow
themselves to be swept away by what, given the frame of the play,
are irrational impulses earn the scorn of the stable. Being in this condition, they misunderstand what the qualifications for life are. Quite
obviously, when denied their eccentric behavior, they are not what
they were; all reverts to a norm, which, because it patiently subsumes
the excesses, cannot be dramatized. This standard, if presented obliquely, must be taken for granted; consequently, the extreme conduct
may be depicted extravagantly, for it has not a chance of prevailing. At
the same time, what lies outside the individual holds no complexity,
once he observes it properly. So that audiences will never doubt the
accepted principles, official spokesmen step forth to reinforce the
invisible codes. All this makes a sunny, if superficial, entertainment by
trifling exhibitions. Common sense will triumph because it must by
definition; otherwise it loses both its common and sensible qualities. It
draws up short of any extreme. A mediocre reasonableness closes the
connections between appearances, no matter how disparate, in order
to forestall inexplicable questions leading to the tragic fall. Jonson's
comedies in this vein have a tendency to be reassuring affairs. That is,
they begin and end at these points. In between, when the humourists

banish common sense, they speed with a fury to absurdity for its own sake, and, as has been seen, the rational touches become the more contradictory.

If the five plays share this broad definition of the comic, they apply it differently. In *The Case Is Altered* the mechanical errors occupy only a fraction of the character's being; a "better self" sporadically deplores conditions. At the end almost everyone shakes off his delusions and lives happily ever after. *Every Man in His Humour* splits between the majority, resembling those of the first play, and the three gulls, who are undiluted affectation so that at the end they perish entirely, and—the feeling should run—a good thing it is. *Every Man out of His Humour*, in its addiction to humours, employs only fools. *Cynthia's Revels* keeps the same pattern, but the end sweetly hints at a pseudoreligious conversion, part of the mysteries of Cynthia's powers. *Poetaster* tries to revert to *Every Man in His Humour* and, necessarily, fails to do so. In a surprisingly short time Jonson had explored and annexed two of the realms of comedy. The first traces misunderstandings into confusions which resolve themselves pleasantly in terms of the approved social standards. The second shifts the emphasis moderately so that the antisocial profits at the expense of the group's power. Indeed, mechanization may usurp all attention except for a slight bridge into and out of the arena of eccentricity. When the play burns those very bridges and mocks all standards, the result becomes *Volpone*.

Jonson's achievements on these two levels of comedy, and little goes beyond them, must rank very high for what they are. Within the concept of humours he developed a precise but flexible psychology and physiology to describe the comically creative impotence of the will without reason. By focusing on common foibles and end-stopping his characters, he reined the demented in the bounds of futility. This weaseling into and out of satiric modes served well enough through *Cynthia's Revels*. Had not the pressing problem of the poetasters' attack, which forced the defense of himself and his craft, brought a turning, the comedy might have matured later and more effectively than here, or it might have frittered itself away; the speculation is futile. The eye, however, would have gone on being the true instrument that it was; the voice would have woven its empty deceptions; stripping of affectations would have brought cures; and an uncritical subjugation before society would have taken care of the rest. The difficulty lay in the problem of how to square these views with those of the misinformed who refuse to heed the blandishments of common sense. In addition to the question of whether comedy can delight *and* instruct, Jonson now faced finding a way to reconcile his partially personal pique with his impersonal art. Something else had to be tried, but the remedy was not at hand. Unhappily for *Poetaster*, the heat of invention left him scant time for reflection.

Because of such indecisions he thrashes about in this satire. Chronically unable to break sharply with his own literary past, he did not, on the other hand, choose to repeat inadequate nostrums. Errors begin to penetrate more deeply than does a symbolic costume. Chloe, the citizen's wife of *Poetaster*, is pitifully old-fashioned in her outlook. She subscribes to the gulls' faith when she believes that her dress determines her position in society, that a man becomes a poet by trimming his hair,[14] and that shocking her betters establishes her wit and ingenuity. All these views would be proper and necessary for a humour figure, but here, in contrast, the main characters' failures exceed this comparative innocence. An official reprimand, even from a Cynthia, will not edit Crispinus' vocabulary, nor dissuade Julia and Ovid Junior from levity, nor improve any of the rest. Their punishments are meted out by a supreme judge whose power transcends a court for juvenile delinquents. He descends from an empyrean of pure authority and poetry. Presumably the truths he forces down offenders' throats derive from an ideal source, but *Poetaster* cannot dramatize it, nor does it seem that any comedy yet contrived could. Likewise, as the permanence of surfaces increases, how to spy out deceivers becomes more difficult. Earlier anyone in a drive of zeal might have mistaken, as does Lupus, a crown and scepter which are stage props for real ones. His misinterpreting an emblem is another matter. The subject of the allegory is hidden, and getting its precise equivalents demands intelligence not vouchsafed all.

At another point, however, Augustus declares, "Best matter, badly showne, shewes worse, then bad." (V. ii. 23) The gnomic line reinforces an assumption tacitly made all along, although it had to be partially suppressed. Desperate stratagems for keeping clear of it were invented: Rachel's fine clothes and the fearfully frigid diction of Cynthia. Here, when it comes to the surface as expression, that surface in itself gains importance; display, if difficult to define, accompanies grandeur. Hence, Virgil fears soiling the page with his imperfect lines. This moral sentiment, like all the heavily weighted ones, is delivered by Augustus, who brooks no questioning of his own infallibility. His authority harks back to an invisible force and rests solidly on his looking as noble as his titles, position, and uniform. This dictatorial assurance exists as an improbable code on which all else must depend, and, since the connections stay imperfect, the play itself collapses.

There remains, however, in *Poetaster* one difference from the earlier plays; it would seem to have promised more, but in execution it yields less. These people do respond to each other, not to a general stimulus. They regard friends and society as though more than a momentary impact upon them were possible. Julia and Ovid Junior are in love; if their behavior fails to show a convincing facsimile, this lack does not cancel the intention. Suspicions, likewise, permeate more fully through motivation. If the failures of language detract from what might pass for communication, they also make the atmosphere perplexed. Part of this style may be satirically intentional; mostly, though, it must be counted yet another of the curious indirections filling this play and making it less than understandable by itself and not pardonable when measured against the others. The exchanges fail to snap with any conversational elasticity. Because they must stand for more than monologues by people in the grip of a humour, however, this flabbiness further calls attention to itself. Assuming one knew nothing of the stage quarrel, but were familiar with Jonson's work, one would inevitably harbor the suspicion that outside pressures had produced the disjointedness.

Where, then, does this course of conjecture leave one in the question of what the play means, since it defies an explanation in its own terms? Several observations show through. To an extent Jonson must have honestly wanted to remove his attack and defense from a personal basis and to invoke abiding ideals. If he allied himself proudly

with the angels, his heaven was not exclusively for the elect. Crispinus'
purgation equals a purgatory; after being cured by the approved
authors, he would move up the ladder. Otherwise, the scene should
not have been Rome, and there would be no controversy about just
what personalities were satirized. At the same time, this haughtiness
exceeds a dispassionate, or reasonably impassioned, satire on the mis-
uses of poetry. If violations of decorum refer to others besides Marston
and Dekker, Jonson was aware of his own inability to encompass or to
ignore the personal scores he wished to settle dramatically. Thus, the
characters cannot stand objectively, and so they refer back to the men
for whom he had contempt. Possibly his experience in composing the
play forced him to realize a new emotion:

> Since our concern was speech, and speech impelled us
>> To purify the dialect of the tribe
>> And urge the mind to aftersight and foresight,
> Let me disclose the gifts reserved for age
>
> .   .   .   .
>
> Second, the conscious impotence of rage
>> At human folly, and the laceration
>> Of laughter at what ceases to amuse.[15]

The mastery of such bitterness may, in part, account for the greatness
of his next five achievements.

On the whole these first plays accept their universe; the comic
truth is pleasant: not only does it have the advantages of correctness
but also it presents man two profits, saving him from delusions and
putting him safely with society. Common sense rules supremely; denying it is self-evident folly. For Jonson the battle with the poetasters,
quite apart from the play, forced the maturing of his insight, as the
next works attest. Without denying the partial validity of standards in
which he had put his whole faith, he came to understand that some
knaves, those who thrive on further undermining the dialect of the
tribe, could not be put down by Aristophanes himself. One solution
might have been championing the old method again in defiance of experience, but such a policy would have made truth subservient to a
personal predilection. Another desperate escape would have renounced
the stage for other literary pursuits. Instead, Jonson chose to keep on

being amused in spite of all lacerations, to work more determinedly than ever with the truths of comedy. Ironically enough, this very vigor in exploration leads to the difficulties of appreciating his dramatic greatness. To the degree that he outstrips less daring plays, he resembles another writer.

> It is amusing to recall that this dream play, this "Government Specter," was treated as a skit on actual conditions in Russia. It is still more amusing to think that Gogol in his first dismal effort to check those dangerous revolutionary allusions to his play pointed out that there was at least one positive character in it: Laughter. . . . A bad play is more apt to be good comedy or good tragedy than the incredibly complicated creations. . . . In this sense Molière's stuff (for what it is worth) is "comedy" i. e. something as readily assimilated as a hot dog at a football game, something of one dimension and absolutely devoid of the huge, seething, prodigiously poetic background that makes true drama. And in the same sense O'Neill's *Mourning Becomes Electra* (for what *that* is worth) is, I suppose, a "tragedy."[16]

A further obstacle in grasping Jonson is that he declined to risk what he could not achieve. Refusing a complete break with his past, he chose to extend the truth from the ground already accurately surveyed. The great comedies remain based in the original starting point while pushing their assumptions more deeply.

Jonson's great ability lay in his power of abstracting one or two qualities which are essences, at least in making them appear so. When reduced to manipulating a complexity which lay within an object rather than between objects, he floundered with the equipment which had served him well until *Poetaster*. Consequently, the failure of this play becomes almost a necessity. His disclaiming of exact resemblances between his work and any living counterpart may be received as true in intention. Indicatively he insisted upon this disinterest within a parenthesis: "And by this line (although no *paralel*) / I hop'd at last they would sit downe, and blush." (Apological Dialogue, 106–7) The subordination indicates the beliefs taken for granted, but the pointedly offhand introduction of the remark implies that further refinement of thought might have added a desirable polish. The ambitious goal of objectivity is winning, but such a concession to fair play will not alter the final score: whoever may have won the real or imaginary pitched battles and skirmishes in the Poetomachia, Jonson, who had more to lose, came off defeated artistically in one play and with a reputation which aversely affected opinions of several others.

His ability, here as elsewhere, to grow and change has been too much obscured by his pride in a refusal to deviate. Few writers so cautiously dedicated have managed so many nearly inexplicable leaps. If he studied himself constantly, he invariably profited from his errors. Being wise long after the fact, one can see that the first plays helped shape *Every Man out of His Humour*, but nothing in them hints that a work fully realized, within its peculiar limits, was imminent. So, too, *Cynthia's Revels*, in the quarto, is as sure as *Poetaster* is floundering. Neither the strength nor the weakness of any would make the odds favorable on the appearance of a drama with the stature of *Sejanus*. True, it is aggressively Jonsonian, but without it would anyone be able to imagine the scope of this tragedy? The unpredictable reliability points to a faith in the efficacy of labor. Only someone with Jonson's capacity for filing painstakingly on each detail could have progressed as he did.

Defeated on his own battleground by his own handicaps, but still splendidly assured of his resources, he chose to withdraw for the heights of tragedy. Unrestricted by contemporary parallels, but proudly serving a classical plot, which he was free to interpret in generous bounds, he wrote *Sejanus*, a work displaying overpowering advances, almost worthy of the phrase which places itself in his mind when he bows out from defending himself at the end of the squabbling *Poetaster*:

> There's something come into my thought,
> That must, and shall be sung, high, and aloofe,
> Safe from the wolues black iaw, and the dull asses hoofe.
>
> (Apologetical Dialogue, 237–39)

CHAPTER V

The Shapes of Dangers

B Y WHAT is probably a fortuitous typographical arrangement in the folio, the leaf which follows Jonson's declaration to make his high, aloof song bears the title "SEIANVS HIS FALL."[1] These contrasting concepts provide the tragedy a kind of leitmotif, one obvious enough to engender multiple variations. *Sejanus* succeeds as none of the comedies yet has in weaving all its strands together for a brilliantly coherent and diversified drama. It is a particular sort of play and a particular kind of tragedy. Some of its strength springs undoubtedly from the position it enjoys in the Jonson canon; the inadequate assumptions which buckled under in *Poetaster* here are jettisoned or ridiculed. Decadence emerges in its own shapes as intrigue and violence which require no apology through the deforming humours. The unique Jonsonian attributes, the assumptions he accepted as *données* with the assurance that in time they would become archetypal, must be grasped before the tragedy can be appreciated. To the extent that its English singularities have been termed historical clichés, they have been oversimplified.

Jonson's scorn for other dramatists exceeded his pique with Marston and Dekker. Lack of standards in the contemporary theater roused his reformer's traits, and his reaction went to an opposite extreme. Just as he revered the classical rules of language profoundly enough to recreate and not to echo them, he adopted toward history an attitude of respect so intelligent that he could not readily imagine himself inhabiting any past. With him, refreshingly, the romantic practices of empathy and negative capability, which have widely been read back into Elizabethan poetry, cannot in any sense be applied. For *Sejanus*, then, he reconstructed a classical tragedy on a Roman theme. That some of the old rules defied obedience he admitted in a preface. The concessions are salutary. Tensions of the striving to keep a form and to justify the deviations from it simultaneously reinforce a single work which has more strength than partisanship to either temptation could have produced, at least in Jonson, who always is the uncomfortable traditionalist. He based *Sejanus* on numerous sources in Roman history.[2] Nevertheless, at crucial points their inadequacies forced him to draw upon his own resources and extend the facts. This further subservience to a guide which had to be surpassed provided the incentive for intermingling the known and the conjectural with each other. In the quarto the marginalia citing the sources from which this material was culled frame almost every page.[3] Enough animus against pretense, even on the stage itself, keeps the text from being a dated chronicle of disjointed episodes. Originally a collaborator had worked with him; from this double view another tautness may derive. His desire for uniformity led him to rewrite the first version. The script of the collaboration has vanished, and its author remains unknown.[4] So smoothly sealed off are these interruptions that one cannot hear where scenes by the second pen have been shifted. Jonson laboriously reshaped the entire work and recreated it in an organic form. Finally, although determined to compose the sort of play he favored and have it tower above detractors, he felt obligated to regain his damaged prestige after *Poetaster*. Such precautions directed him in publishing the text: commendatory verses preface the careful book; at least three copies on large paper survive. He tried to advance the drama on the stage by returning the English prodigal to its classical stepparent and on the page by raising the quality of the book to a higher level than the one usually accorded printed plays. Nevertheless, were *Sejanus* a mere collage of Roman and Renaissance drama, an antipasto of historical and personal imagination, an olio of collaboration and rewriting, and a mishmash of pretentious verse with careful printing, nothing could smooth over its patched origins. As it stands, it remains a work which, although sharing all these contradictory aspects, emerges tantalizingly complex in its own right.

The plot does not shrink from melodramatic twists. The Emperor Tiberius, growing old and bored with ruling, allows Sejanus, a man who has raised himself, a great share of authority to the consternation of nominally moral forces. Sejanus has Livia's husband, Drusus, a son of Augustus, killed and drives away Tiberius' nephews. The Emperor, yielding to his sybaritic tastes, retires to Capri for vacations and names Sejanus deputy when he absents himself from Rome. After Tiberius learns that Sejanus expects to marry his daughter, Livia, and to grasp for absolute power, he acts through Macro, a newly appointed lieutenant. In a long letter to the Senate he praises Sejanus at first but slyly changes tone so that, although feigning disinterest, he orders the Senate to condemn him. Macro, being a novice and therefore enthusiastic, directs Sejanus' destruction at the hands of a mob. The end does not prettily resolve the political dilemma. Corruption presides over a populace more addled than ever. Taking, then, the progress of deterioration, the plot fastens upon individuals whom a single ambition chains. They are less gullible than the humour figures, but, dealing with people of a limited scope, the tragedy does not concentrate upon the characters as important in themselves. It is the pattern of the Roman state in all aspects which impose images of terror. As the humours ran like a stream bearing away men, so here the passions obscenely taunt them upward onto impossible heights.

The characters must be conceived as superior to men. Their stature both physically and politically is equated with Atlas supporting the world on his shoulders, a figure named in none of the comedies. Sejanus flatters Tiberius by an icon of the demigod during the third act and at the end of the play thinks of himself in a similar fashion. Sejanus' enemies imagine themselves caryatids for him, "whom he [Tiberius] (vpon our low, and suffering necks) / Hath rais'd, from excrement, to side the gods. . . ." (IV. 405–6) The lines speak with the compact expression Jonson has mastered. Together the words, "low, and suffering," delimit precisely patrician pride brought down by Sejanus. An incident from history fits well with the picture. Tiberius was dining in a cave when it began to collapse; amid the ensuing confusion

> Only SEIANVS, with his knees, hands, face,
> Ore-hanging CAESAR, did oppose himselfe
> To the remayning ruines, and was found
> In that so labouring posture, by the souldiers
> That came to succour him.   (IV. 53–57)

Assessing all aspects which make this weird rescue appropriate would lead one far afield. Indicatively the "ore-hanging" and "so labouring" represent convincing details of great strength, but, at the same time, their tone of unemphatic understatement betrays an animal, gauche posture. For, although swaying ambition rules, it seems awkward and too heavy to support while it turns into a totem pole of snarling politicians. Sejanus resembles another sort of giant, a Colossus, who, from the statue at Rhodes, was pictured as bestriding objects. Here, however, while the Colossus is being described, the details scale him down to a figure of incongruously human size. Sejanus, referring to himself in the royal plural, dismissed portents:

> Or running of the cat, betwixt our legs,
> As we set forth vnto the *capitoll*,
> Were prodigies.   (V. 55–57)

The contrast sounds deliberate. Jonson borrowed this touch from Dio: καὶ προϊόντος αὐτοῦ ἐκ τῆς οἰκίας γαλῆ διὰ μέσων σφῶν διῆξεν."[5] The Greek animal is a weasel and, more to the point, it does not pass between his legs, and thus the iconographic resemblance to the Colossus is merely implied. Elsewhere, the monumental dimensions become part of the action with the raising of statues and the parallels drawn to the golden-age Romans.

   This repeated metaphor of size, of aspiring to a giant's stature, is everywhere sustained by an overwhelming number of images about the movements of going up and coming down. Some have to do with human aspirations, it is true, but many sound as overtones within other discussions. From the outset a contempt toward excessive ambition sets the key:

> We haue no shift of faces, no cleft tongues,
> No soft, and glutinous bodies, that can sticke,
> Like snailes, on painted walls; or, on our brests,
> Creepe vp, to fall, from that proud height, to which
> We did by slauerie, not by seruice, clime.   (I. 7–11)

Shift and *face*, baldly contemptuous terms, become more chilling when one recalls that two of the meaner characters in the comedies *Every Man out of His Humour* and *The Alchemist* bear these names. Afterwards the direction focuses on slugs with the pervasive snails moving slowly to proportionately mean heights. As the term humour swelled through the comedies, so here rising and falling tie together separate topics. Eudemus, a physician, brags to Livia of the joys which the elevation of marrying Sejanus will ensure:

> But, when they shall heare
> That, and the thunder of Seianvs meet,
> Seianvs, whose high name doth strike the starres,
> And rings about the concaue, great Seianvs,
> Whose glories, stile, and titles are himselfe,
> The often iterating of Seianvs. . . .   (II. 96–101)

The tone, a wonder of complexity beneath a surface simplicity, superficially resembles a Marlovian hero's when he dreams of world conquest. What Jonson christened Marlowe's mighty line here inverts itself for a dictatorial absurdity.[6] Whereas the conquering mania of the Elizabethan paranoiac generally soars outward, the narcissistic temperament, akin to the courtiers' in *Cynthia's Revels*, sees its own image encompassing the heavens, a sardonic adumbration of an Emersonian concept of history and nature. Moreover, the pattern exactly duplicates Ovid Junior's in *Poetaster*, when he praises Julia, but whereas his lover's raptures wobble with adolescent boasts, now the intoxication touches terror as the word rebounds. The whole passage bends oddly toward the final touch, the pleonasm of "often iterating." The language, which in the humour comedies ran the danger of abandoning all touches with its subject, chiefly because of its triteness and of wasting its effects in too fine details, is pared to essentials of the not inconsequential events. Although ambition motivates everybody in the play, the gradation of patterns modulates nicely on the scale of power. Tiberius, wily and indirect, betrays no hesitations. Macro, a busy acolyte in comparison with a secure Sejanus, at the outset of his service reassures himself with the commonplaces of tame fables and nostrums. Those critical of the vices, such as the speakers in the snail comparison, must participate in the crimes of power as silent accomplices. No one is spared; power corrupts all, and, because these men are demigods, it corrupts universally.

This vertigo of rising and falling is conventional in theme, having behind it the *ubi sunt* laments, wheel of fortune, the *Mirror for Magistrates*, and Elizabethan tragedy from *Gorboduc*. As a persistent metaphor, it here serves a definite purpose. *Catiline*, a tragedy with related subjects and setting, employs the figure incidentally. Unlike most other plays about conquest in the period, *Sejanus* does not set the highest premium on the physical pleasures which wealth can buy. Authority enchants because it is a desirable good in itself. No explanation justifies this motivation; Sejanus' first step must be accepted as a gratuitous act, after which everything evolves with a single emphasis upon the drive to rise amplified by a dread of falling so compulsive that success changes to a migraine of acrophobia, whipping the sufferer ever higher. Unlike the humourists, the Romans do not wink toward audiences with touching reassurances by their lapses into the reasonable. If the humour figures are ridiculous because they cannot impress their surroundings, those of *Sejanus* are terrifying because, boasting no more wisdom, if greater authority in cunning, they may ruin permanently the society which they govern.

Along with the metaphor of upward and downward, light, which resembles imperfect darkness, flares like sulphur across the scene. In the comedies light has often been equated with knowledge, but now it summons no resources to check a positive night. Indeed, books themselves are burned to prevent the truth's being revealed, flames whose embers are blackness. In the last act the approaching destruction turns to murky smoke belching from Sejanus' statue, and light sinks in the flash of a meteor. Man himself outdoes nature, when Sejanus takes

command: " 'Tis he / Makes vs our day, or night. ...." (I. 206–7) One
has become accustomed to these shadow-clashing melodramatics in
Milton, the eighteenth-century seekers of the sublime, the nineteenth-
century satanists from whom they reverberate with the calculated
thud of a crash box in the wings, and the divine business of the classics.
If one sloughs off such tarnished memories, Jonson's verse sounds particularly right, for the supernatural relates directly to the human
situation. The drama never needs to emphasize these swelling effects
for their own sake because they always inform the larger designs.

Contrary to popular opinion, Jonson could, when he put his
mind, if not his sensibilities, to it, incorporate observations drawn from
outdoors with his poetry. Because the men of the early plays cannot
care about such phenomena, since they are cut off from any direct
experience of the country by their materialistic desires, rural references
have no place in the humour comedies. Even as contrasts they would
invoke possibilities Jonson had to rule out. When the geographical
frame functions as part of the whole which corruption threatens, the
concepts of growth and fruition have an intrinsic meaning and explain
the metaphors accordingly. These figures vary from incisive references
to set declamations in which men are compared with trees. Sejanus
becomes, in a further extension, like the sun. Because, in the struggle
between him and Tiberius, the Emperor always retains the upper hand,
the association linking Sejanus and a strong object tends to imply a
balance of matched contestants. The Roman sun, however, shines with
no benevolence, and its rays fall for destruction:

> Then LIVIA triumphs in her proper spheare,
> When shee, and her SEIANVS shall diuide
> The name of CAESAR; and AVGVSTA's starre
> Be dimm'd with glorie of a brighter beame:
> When AGRIPPINA's fires are quite extinct,
> And the scarce-seene TIBERIVS borrowes all
> His little light from vs, whose folded armes
> Shall make one perfect orbe.   (II. 38–45)

The insight is unfailing; as the ultimate touch, after the wounded
brightness, the "perfect orbe" of imperfect parts rings with a flat disgust. So far all these plays have referred to a circle to represent com-

pleteness; the lovers of *The Case Is Altered* receive their benediction in just these terms. *Sejanus* ruthlessly tests every metaphor, while standard after standard is inverted or perverted from its accustomed ends. Similarly, the picture of an impure stream's being swallowed up by a larger body of pure water, the cure Elizabeth wrought on Macilente for *Every Man out of His Humour,* in Tiberius' mouth becomes blatant hypocrisy, as a detractor's scoffing aside points up. Two happy coincidences in the sources extend the contrasting light and dark. The historical account of Sejanus' day of downfall compares him to the sun, and Tiberius reputedly had the ability to see by night. Again Jonson tracked down the literal conditions to suit the patterns of figurative language.

The verse of *Sejanus* is both tight and compact. Separating the images into figures by subject matter impoverishes them. Nevertheless, the condensations here employed are almost requisite; any other system leads to useless repetitions. With comparisons drawn from animals, Jonson realized his fullest scope. In all the great comedies animals are variously summoned for effects. The cumulative view becomes as terrifying as Baudelaire's menagerie, from which only one monster is notably lacking in Jonson's: "ce monstre délicat, l'ennui."[7] The animal images heighten aspects of senseless activity and casual cruelty. Because they interlock smoothly with the rest of the verse, extracting some of them will point up their outstanding qualities: "dull camell" (I. 568); "wolues do change their haire, but not their harts" (II. 273); "a world of wolfe-turn'd men" (III. 251); "Excellent wolfe! / Now he is full, he howles" (III. 347–48); "The *Roman* race most wretched, that should liue / Betweene so slow iawes, and so long a bruising" (III. 486–87); "But, greatnesse hath his cankers. Wormes, and moaths / Breed out of too fit matter" (III. 689–90); "Gods! how the spunges open, and take in! / And shut againe!" (V. 506–7); "claw his subtle elbow, or with a buzze / Fly-blow his eares" (V. 510–11);

>   reare
> Their forces, like seene snakes, that else would lye
> Rould in their circles, close; (II. 255–57)

>   We that know the euill,
> Should hunt the Palace-rattes, or giue them bane;

Fright hence these worse then rauens, that deuoure
The quicke, where they but prey vpon the dead;   (I. 426-29)

"Then thinke the gods, like flies, / Are to be taken with the steame
of flesh" (V. 75-76); "Two of SEIANVS bloud-hounds, whom he
breeds / With humane flesh, to bay at citizens" (III. 376-77); "This
asses fortitude doth tyre vs all" (IV. 156); "The prey to greedie
vultures, and vile spies" (IV. 140); "And not a beast of all the herd
demands, / What was his crime?" (V. 793-94) Grouped together, the
images sometimes sound flat or routine, a grab bag of clichés, proverbs,
maxims, and generalizations. One of the specialities in Jonson's versifying takes such lines and gives them a sting. No matter how ponderously
thought and expression weigh, they sing together with a grave music.
They claim their intensity through multiple abstractions, which raise
one point and prepare for the next. Within this strong unit great
modulations are subtly effected so that a single word well placed
reverberates with prolonged overtones back through the meaning of
preceding lines as well as influencing those to come. The simplicity of
the diction affects the strength of the whole, and from the harmony of
the generalizations a definite quality emerges. A common trope begins
with a brief comparison, then allows the aspect compared to drop, but
by the bent of the ensuing lines continues the vehicle in a suppressed
metaphor. This delicacy is elusive and demands the fullest attention.
For example, the following extensive quotation depicts the hunt, but
its inherent elements of cruelty, cunning, and domination of animal by
animal are not directly scored so that when the figure shifts, the hunt's
sadistic sport grows. (A group of Sejanus' opponents are huddled
together and note spies outside the house.)

> HOw is it, that these beagles haunt the house
> Of AGRIPPINA? ARR. O, they hunt, they hunt.
> There is some game here lodg'd, which they must rouse,
> To make the great-ones sport. COR. Did you obserue
> How they inueigh'd 'gainst CAESAR? ARR. I, baytes, baytes,
> For vs to bite at: would I haue my flesh
> Torne by the publique hooke, these qualified hang-men
> Should be my company.   (II. 410-17)

From the outset the animal comparisons portend a primitive

force within the atmosphere. As the pace increases, the actual animals, off stage, achieve an archaic dignity lacking in man. Thus, when the innocent Silius kills himself, his body is thrown into the river; his dog jumps after its master and drowns. The deed does not predict a pretty Victorian homily about a dog's faithfulness, but it rather points up how much more treacherous men are, since the dog by its act, dumb though it was, was "vpbraiding all vs *Romanes.*" (IV. 285) When the mob moves toward destroying Sejanus, it is suggested ironically, although not improbably, that if Sejanus' statues are pulled down and the wheels of his chariot broken, then the legs of the innocently assisting horses may as well be cracked too. A human capacity for bestial deformity reaches such proportions that the supernatural chimera of a portent scares less than does its counterpart among men:

> there leap't out
> A great, and monstrous serpent! SEI. Monstrous! why?
> Had it a beard? and hornes? no heart? a tongue
> Forked as flatterie? look'd it of the hue,
> To such as liue in great mens bosomes? was
> The spirit of it MACRO's?   (V. 36–41)

The echo of the forked tongues and fawning on chests catches up the initial comparison, here more terrifying since men are no longer repulsively weak snails. Finally, a senseless cruelty spreads to madden all Roman citizens, who, like a composite beast, devour Sejanus:

> A thousand heads,
> A thousand hands, ten thousand tongues, and voyces,
> Employ'd at once in seuerall acts of malice!   (V. 811–13)

The hyperbolic vagueness does not number strictly the animal parts in terms of the human anatomies composing the monster and makes the understated "seuerall acts" amorphous and strikingly malicious. Insanity rages like an epidemic, not like a single mad creature to be hunted down and destroyed.

Like bestial ferocity, sexual vices are castigated with an aggressive disdain. The humour plays, by innuendo and allusion of language, by behavior and temperament of characters, made explicit the aberrations.[8] Because the comic intent always had to keep the deformities pseudointellectual, a cure by the humour theory being more readily effected then, it was impossible to have the desires spread to more complex emotions, such as any passionate love. On the authority of Juvenal and Petronius, charges of perversions and homosexuality are lodged openly against the politically corrupt leaders. Sejanus is a self-made man:

> ARR. A seruing boy?
> I knew him, at CAIVS trencher, when for hyre,
> He prostituted his abused body
> To that great gourmond, fat APICIVS;
> And was the noted *pathick* of the time. (I. 212–16)

Tiberius is "an Emp'rour, only in his lusts" (IV. 376), and he withdraws to Capri where he hides and practices "new-commented lusts, / For which wise nature hath not left a name." (IV. 400–401) In one of the most coldly contemptuous images by Jonson, or any other writer, the ruler of Rome is depicted with savage outrage,

> As (dead to vertue) he permits himselfe
> Be carried like a pitcher, by the eares,
> To euery act of vice. . . . (I. 416–18)

These aspects of immorality are not singled out for special criticism. They take an expected place with other evils of degeneracy. Jonson at his best allows no innocent intentions. Corruption, whatever form it takes, must be absolute and nothing escapes. Nor, as has been pointed out, does it confine itself to a few; it reaches all. Even the mean hangman, charged with executing Sejanus' quite uninvolved son and daughter, first rapes the girl because no virgin may be put to death. This insistence upon the positive force of evil does not overwhelm the poetry into bombast or the maudlin. The firm tone of the verse always keeps the reported horrors restrained. The classical precedent, which prompted Jonson to reduce to a minimum acts of violence on the stage, forbids, of course, sensational effects for their own sake. The one exception, as will be seen, provides an indispensable turning point in the story.

The tragic implications of *Sejanus* have frequently been undervalued because of discrepancies between stage action and the manner

of expression. Jonson does not, after all, reproduce a Senecan report of
gore. The dialogue proceeds with turns appropriate for its subject and
its style, although conflict itself may seem, on the superficial surface,
held to its lowest degree. To push a wax museum of criminals on the
stage would concentrate on the individuals, and the spread of ruin
through Roman society would carry less horror. For example, the
old melodramatic device of a letter for revelation takes a fresh turn.
Tiberius' seemingly static communication sent from Capri dramatizes
the extent of the Empire on the stage itself.[9] As for the final fate of
Sejanus, that audiences unleash waves of sympathy with the fallen man
does not circumscribe the primary intent. The benediction at the end
of so many classical tragedies, that only the dead are happy, while
echoed formally, has no significance here.[10] That defeated Sejanus
be counted a warning to mankind matters less than the collapse of the
nation into chaos. At the end the rabble mixes him in the rubble he
helped bring down. For the comedies of humour the landscape and
society lay beyond assaults; Macilente could never become a mermaid
and drown the world. In *Sejanus* all political institutions must be felt
as the suffering antagonists. The tragedy, in spite of all these quieter
qualities, does adopt a Senecan tone in its refusal to stay always sober
on the important matters. Such scenes, while by no stretch of the term
comic relief, have further confused ordinarily perceptive critics; even
one as generous as Dryden condemned the passages between Livia
and Sejanus because to him they seemed out of place.[11]

The scene in which Livia calmly connives with Sejanus to dispose
of her husband Drusus occurs while her physician-cosmetician, the
dual trade itself a commentary upon health, treats her. Roman cruelty,
which for political and civil acts can only be described, becomes part
of the visual structure and undercuts, if that Jamesian term is not too
tame, the ruthlessness off stage. Although recent literature has exploited the discrepancies between a quest for artificial beauty and the
physically or psychically stunted seekers, ranging from Thomas
Mann's *Der Tod in Venedig* to Eudora Welty's "The Petrified Man,"
in its period the episode carries a unique force which has not been quite
reproduced since. The intelligently cool tone of both Livia and her
physician as they glide from make-up to love to murder without any

noticeable transition of attitude contrasts strangely while it blends with steady logic:

> Evd. Lend me your scarlet, lady. 'Tis the sunne
> Hath giu'n some little taint vnto the *ceruse*,
> You should haue vs'd of the white oyle I gaue you.
> Seianvs, for your loue! his very name
> Commandeth aboue Cvpid, or his shafts—
>   (Liv. Nay, now yo'haue made it worse. Evd. I'le helpe it straight.)
> And, but pronounc'd, is a sufficient charme
> Against all rumour; and of absolute power
> To satisfie for any ladies honour.
>
>   (II. 62–70)

By the close of the scene Sejanus becomes no more than another aid to Livia's complexion against the ravages of monotony and time. She emerges the one power which Sejanus' ambition cannot rise superior to, partly because their desires do not compete in the same area. He must regard her as an equal. Their interview, in the middle of the attentive application of cosmetics, comments adequately upon their relationship, one frankly grounded on disguises and duplicity.

Such an activity, with its sardonic undercurrent, does not diverge from the tragic rationale, which draws upon decidedly mixed tendencies. Much of the dialogue has a bite of self-awareness antithetical to commoner tragedies. If the tragic principle involves a moment of self-discovery by a man until that crisis unaware, though suspicious, of his weakness, then *Sejanus* cannot rank very high inside this genre. The characters are surprisingly candid, and, in the madness of their climb to power, they do not pause for any disarmingly personal doubts and pangs of conscience. Their lucidity about the rules of the game and of self, and the ways of cheating both, rarely has been bestowed by any author. The Romans fix their attention upon only one end which rules out all else, so that their logic, impeccable in itself, fails to ascertain all the facts. Theirs is, of course, the humourous temperament for trifles made intelligent for the consequential. Lacking, then, any stigmata of a soul, they can fasten upon effective action with the same doggedness which misled the humour figures. The characters of *Sejanus* are basically as "mechanical" as those of the comedies, but the latter had to be crushed by their society, and at no point did they have a chance of controlling it. The danger from Tiberius, Sejanus, Macro, and the rest lies in their attaining positions powerful enough to channel all external streams of action into their own demented designs. Contrariwise, the world takes little notice of the men of humours, who are comic and unimportant. Whereas those in authority, being the center of attention, cannot fall without bringing down all about them. The characters' awareness, their importance, and their fearlessness tend to ally them with the malcontents of Jacobean drama, a type becoming a stock figure. The malcontents, however, generally chose to deprecate entirely both themselves and whatever they did; the politicians in *Sejanus* are detached and engaged while they recklessly exploit themselves. In a word, they are not for a moment sentimental, but this surface disinterest does not preclude a belief in the necessity for action. To stay still is to perish. They whip themselves into masochistic intrigues with a determination which no arguments can deter. Were they to deviate for an instant, they would collapse as the humour characters do when the stream dries up or the fire burns out. Just as the comic figures keep a last grip on the probable in which they anchor their most fantastic plots, so these men hold onto their human meanness while they become giants. The rulers of *Sejanus* have scrutinized themselves, but, in spite of that, understand the world imperfectly enough so they can fall.

Furthermore, the humour figures were amusing, if distressing, because they knew little. These Romans are frightening because they may know much. The courtiers of *Cynthia's Revels* have nothing under their children's artificial faces and elaborate clothes. Beneath Livia's cosmetics and the men's tunics lurk, or may lurk, many concealed plans. The uncertainty increases the torment. The difference indicates a major shift of emphasis. Since the happy assumptions about the availability of truth in *The Case Is Altered*, the eye, of course, has been praised as the instrument for detecting disguises. Here its abilities shrink. Not one among the Romans understands the whole imbroglio; the most vigilant are liable to error. The voice deceives as much as ever when—another function of Tiberius' letter—from Capri the Emperor's accents sound in the Roman Senate with the complete assurance of winning what they desire. Deprived thus of reliable allies, reason must become a hit-or-miss game of chance in which no throw of the dice can be final until the last, catastrophic cast. This mode fits with the tragic theme of Fortune's wheel twirling in lottery princes and peoples, although fortune lives in the population and not as a goddess apart. Direct references stress these plottings, for example: "steepes his wordes, / When he would kill, in artificiall teares" (II. 422–23); "Their faces runne like shittles, they are weauing / Some curious cobweb to catch flyes" (III. 23–24); "For, night hath many eies, / Whereof, though most doe sleepe, yet some are spies." (V. 169–70) The trickery, blending well with the darkness, animal cunning, portents, and cosmetics, runs throughout and bolsters the dramatic themes. Suitably, for tragedy Jonson abandoned the clarity of the comic truth and by action and imagery summoned darker forces. Even here, contributing to the special tone of this complex work, he does not analyze psychological drives but keeps to what can be observed. This thorough grasp of surfaces ensures the tragedy its firm, if limited, outlook.

In construction *Sejanus* towers notably above its predecessors, which, indeed, as the revised versions of the folio indicate, could be stretched without losing much effectiveness. Because the comedies depict essentially static figures, who must repeat themselves, they could extend, theoretically, forever, at least for as long as new actions are contrivable. The obedience to a close unity of time in *Every Man in His Humour* and *Cynthia's Revels* fills no indispensable function; it serves to hold the matter conventionally within bounds. Although usually an acceleration of tempo marks the last acts, the stressing of such accentuation depends almost as largely upon the performance as upon the script. *Sejanus*, covering considerably more than twenty-four hours, gathers cumulative force throughout its five acts; nothing need be added and little could profitably have been removed. Each episode has a definite force; this is not to say that the humour comedies wanted structure, but that *Sejanus* has one more organically realized. To ascertain with information now available just what the Elizabethans, playwrights and audiences, made of their dramatic conventions presents moderate difficulties. Of the many documents brought to bear on this subject—and Jonson's own testimony is not lacking—the statements say less than one wishes to learn and fail to account for the finer touches which grace the best dramatizations.[12] The rhythm of *Sejanus* beats slowly, almost regally, toward increasing clarification of the inevitable fall. The acts themselves break irregularly, but the divisions appear more than a printer's convention; at least, at the end of each a chorus of musicians is called for. The second and fourth, of nearly equal length, are the shortest, the first nearly one-fifth again as long as either of these, the third nearly one-fourth again of the first, and the last almost double the shortest.

From the outset the dialogue betrays no nervousness to gloss over details lightly. Not until one-third of the first act has passed does Sejanus appear. The matters of exposition, being about conditions in Rome, have referred to him predominantly. Almost as soon as he enters, he interviews Eudemus, Livia's physician, who seeks to purchase a tribune's position, proof of Sejanus' political power; it further prepares the way for the assignation with Livia. The large cast weighs inconclusively the importance of Sejanus' influence. As rumors of his waxing strength continue to circulate, the extended dialogue with Eudemus, which proceeds by corrupt winking and indirect questioning, relates Sejanus to duplicity and disguise, summed up by the cosmetician's trade. Both men are bothered by the innuendoes, exemplified in Sejanus' strangely reversed prayer, "Prosper it, PALLAS, thou, that betterst wit; / For VENVS hath the smallest share in it." (I. 373–74) Drusus, Livia's husband, appears with Tiberius and receives Sejanus' flattery, while the opposition, led by Arruntius, grumbles on the side and preserves an impotent semblance of criticism. Tiberius' overly pompous speeches, a fault the Emperor himself indirectly acknowledges they have, ramble emptily onward. The duties of his office have grown so arduous that he has decided to retire and put Sejanus in command; furthermore, to recognize his services, Sejanus will have a statue erected. As the group leaves, Sejanus steps before Drusus, who reminds him of his inferior position. This insult brings to a head the latent feud. Thus, the first act fully describes the situation, but always in terms of the conflicts themselves. One is not told any truth but many opinions.

The next act belongs to Sejanus as a swellingly triumphant figure.

It presents the scene between Livia and Eudemus, interrupted by Sejanus, while they plan Drusus' assassination with complete composure. The next step requires that Sejanus seek out Tiberius with whom further murders are plotted to secure their power in the state. In neither of these situations does Sejanus enjoy sole control. He remains subservient to Tiberius, and Livia, always an independent force, might well change her mind. The outcome remains indecisive; one never knows how clever, or lazy, Tiberius is. When the scene shifts to the opposition, Sabinus, Arruntius, and Cordus, they have gone into hiding, a contrast with the openness of the first act, where they were divided from the Emperor, but at least outspoken in their censure. Afer, who will conduct the trial in the next act, appears and is stamped untrustworthy. Meanwhile, those members of the royal family who disagree with Sejanus also gather. The fragmentation of the society has started, a condition which the announcement of Drusus' murder at the end of the act breaks apart.

The third act picks up the consequences of the scheming of the second: the trials and Tiberius' retirement. The scene occurs in the Senate, and, although it poses nearly insurmountable problems of staging, an insidious complexity protrudes everywhere from the multiple intrigues. Tiberius turns his nephews over to the care of the Senate and announces his withdrawal. Arruntius grumbles sardonically about the proceedings, but he is a potential victim, unlike the immune chorus of *Every Man out of His Humour*. Following the Emperor's decision, the next plan, accusing Silius of treason against the state, although his greatest crime was disagreeing with Sejanus, culminates in his choice of suicide rather than false imprisonment. This deed is the only violence shown on the stage, and as such it gains effectiveness. It graphically represents the culmination of Sejanus' triumph, and it simultaneously frightens Tiberius sufficiently to arouse his qualms about the extent of Sejanus' ambitions. It looms later as one of those divine warnings which foretell that the high point of success has been reached. After Silius, Cremutius Cordus is brought to trial; he is a scholar and historian. His defense of his devotion to understanding past events, no matter how their implications distress the present, rings bravely in contrasting corrupt Rome and a nobler history. His being set free does not score a defeat for Sejanus; the order to burn his books blots out a brief triumph. Sejanus' downfall has, nevertheless, already begun; any further heights will merely make the crash more rapid. Tiberius, partially aroused, is further distressed when Sejanus asks consent to marry Livia; in a soliloquy he reveals that he plans to raise Macro to check Sejanus. The ensuing interview between the old master and fresh novice proceeds with less innuendo than does that of Tiberius and Sejanus. Macro is unskilled, and Tiberius deliberately refrains from naming his functions.

Act IV indeterminately sways between Sejanus' victory and downfall with nothing clear-cut except the creeping deterioration. Sejanus, on the whole, faces reduced obstacles and enjoys greater favor than ever with Tiberius, especially after the rescue in the collapsing grotto. Macro, uncertain of his duties, promises no effective threat. Every motive and all evidence look suspect; the increasingly precarious condition of the Roman government is underlined by several short scenes of flight and fear: Macro's sending Caligula away, Agrippina's being restrained under guard, Nero's banishment, and Arruntius' complaint of the blindness of the gods.

Sejanus, wholly confident, swells with diabolic pride at the start of the fifth act and feels that nothing can interpose itself between him and success and that nothing will limit the extent of his fortune. He dismisses unfavorable portents, but no sooner have these been relegated than new prodigies spring forth. Some critics have wondered why at this point he denies the gods but also consults oracles and offers sacrifices. The contradictory actions, obviously, reflect his unstable temperament. Faced with unwanted facts, he prefers considering them superfluous, but bows in rites he has branded superstitions. Not quite aware of the significance of his own commission, Macro summons Sejanus to a meeting of the Senate. The report of that session, with the full panoply of the ceremony,[13] carries imposing legislative detail. The important members of the cast draw to the chamber, except, of course, the most powerful of all, Tiberius himself, a wonderfully appropriate touch to dramatize the whims which tyrants enjoy even *in absentia*. The proceedings indirectly denounce Sejanus by the letter, and his most avid followers desert him. The action is swift and, because at the moment of his fall he stands alone in a cloud of silence, terrifying.

> SEI. Haue we no friends here?
> ARR. Hush't. Where now are all the hailes, and acclamations?
>
> (V. 656–57)

Macro then rouses all senators, even the most obtuse, against Sejanus. He continues working with the crowd until hysteria unchains it, and it literally tears apart the former deputy dictator. The calamity of Sejanus' final isolation is direct and effective. His downfall leaves no doubt about the nothingness to which he is reduced:

> What cannot oft be done, is now ore-done.
> The whole, and all of what was great SEIANVS,
> And next to CAESAR did possesse the world,
> Now torne, and scatter'd, as he needs no graue,
> Each little dust couers a little part:
> So lyes he no where, and yet often buryed!   (V. 827–32)

No salvation emerges after this partial deliverance. Macro's manipulation of the mob already exceeds Sejanus' cruelty; the gods remain implacable, if not blind, and Fortune's wheel spins.

It seemed worth devoting an extended analysis to this play because it represents a kind of tragedy rare in English, and without many specimens in other literatures. *Sejanus* may not be an entirely satisfactory example, but, granted the outlook Jonson held at this period, it could scarcely realize better its intrinsic capacities. If slow and deliberate, the plot is well reasoned at each turn. The effect must be felt as a culmination of its pattern. To match this gravity, no notably brilliant single lines or epigrams adorn the poetry. The weight has a force which fathers respect by its own inevitability; the sure strokes permit objects and sentiments not ordinarily conceived as classic to achieve their places. The impact of the play overcomes one by a sustained vision, not through a series of partial insights. The ultimate tone eludes a single definition. The animus sustaining equally a contempt for rulers and people, while sympathizing with a protesting minority and past history, does not lend itself well to universal pity.[14] The whole combines intellectual toughness, a resilience against all sentiment, with a cold eye cast on all frailty; it reaches a particular sort of intensity, which, if something less than what currently passes for tragic vision, does, nevertheless, reflect upon what occurs when men lose all reason and become ambitious for any token of prominence.

The special brilliance of the achievement reflects from two different facets: knowledge of the specific story and an awareness of a mysterious necessity. With the uncertainties which last until the very end, the reality of dangers unassignable to a single exterior or interior motive forms a work different from those widely assumed in English tragedy where a villain or a hero grapples with unsympathetic forces. The emphasis here does not pit goodness against evil, but it introduces many

> shapes
> Of dangers, greater then they are (like late,
> Or early shadowes) and, sometimes, to faine
> Where there are none. . . .   (II. 384–87)

If no hero emerges, neither does society become the norm, as it has so far in the comedies. The group cannot correct; it cannot impose any standards; it must be weak and scarcely immune from the attacks of the men who help compose it. *Sejanus* does not appeal to one's immediate sympathies, but it magnifies the awareness of potential threats to the mass as well as to the members. It embodies as much pity as Jonson tolerated.

A production of *Sejanus* could be engrossing. It would require careful acting of a sort which no school now prominent in English practices. Much of its impact would derive from a unity of stage effects no director can handle any longer in stylized productions. Many of the speeches resemble self-conscious arias, which audiences no longer tolerate. Finally, in an era dominated by demagogues, the Cordus-like effort to draw parallels between the Roman fasces and modern counterparts would prove irresistible and distort the larger design: the charges of treason on trumped-up evidence, government by irresponsible deputies, the burning of books, and the despair of moral forces. The truth of *Sejanus* does not rely upon one kind of historical situation. Nevertheless, were such handicaps overcome, as a piece of theater it might prove effective. So much of the rhetoric is deliberately empty that the acting upon acting would make itself felt with a force refreshingly novel in a time of predominantly naturalistic productions which cut everything down to one life size. The verse, unafraid of itself, might prove that stage poetry need not sound just like conversational prose or like too rhapsodic poetizing. In distinction to mere sincerity, the callous condemnation of a whole social system might hold an honest, if unflattering, mirror up to modern practices at their roots, not specific malpractices on the body politic.

Such vain conjectures become too easily the idle sport of those who write about rather than direct plays. *Sejanus* was not well received when it first appeared. It seems unlikely to have much greater popularity in the twentieth century. Even a cursory reading will reveal devious twists on the emotions. The luxury, the vice, the ambitions, and the fears combine into a haughty commentary. The detached cruelty, which always seems to be admiring itself, hints at uncommon, unpleasant temperaments. The strength to outgaze unredeemable pride and anatomize it represents a unique realization in English dramatic tragedy. Upon getting to know it, one finds, in spite of the special outlook, a work which by its aspirations and achievements shows up the shoddy deceits of easier plays. It is a purer work than the English stage deserves.

CHAPTER VI

The Artificer

IF PRODUCTIONS are proof, the twentieth century has judged *Volpone* Jonson's most substantial achievement. Periodic revivals in English, the German adaptation by Zweig, Romains' French redaction of the German (and translations of one of these back again into English), numerous editions,[1] a French motion picture, and an operatic version:[2] all these attest its vitality. The tone pervading it matches the mood of desperate honesty which dominated continental European literature between World War I and World War II. It gladly pushes to extremes any of its assumptions. Gide, for example, noted in his *Journal* on 31 January 1929:

> Une certaine mélancolie devant le *Volpone* que Zweig et Romains viennent de mettre en scène. Il est peu de pièces que j'aurais autant souhaité traduire et que je sentais mieux sous ma main. J'en parlais à Copeau depuis longtemps, l'annonçais presque; et, sans doute, si le *Vieux Colombier* eût vécu... Mais je crois bien que, par respect du texte, je n'aurais pas osé *l'adapter*, ainsi qu'ont fait Zweig et Romains; fort heureusement, je crois. J'ai du moins cette consolation de savoir parfaitement mise en valeur cette pièce admirable.[3]

The adaptation, however felicitous, weakens the rationale by dismissing official justice and the complexity by omitting minor figures. Various added lines, situations, and characters, all closely allied to farce, provide comforting relief from the ferocity of Jonson's text. In the original the hard, logical progression works out implications with a ruthless thoroughness.[4]

On the other hand, Dullin's reproduction of *Volpone*, on which Gide reported, inspired sentiments which Jonson does not, as a rule, invite. Jean-Louis Barrault recalled his feelings as a young actor when he was poor and made the Atelier his home. One night he decided to sleep in Volpone's bed, foreshortened to uncomfortable dimensions:

> L'idée me vient d'aller ouvrir le grand rideau de scène. Je veux sentir la Présence de la Salle. La salle peuplée de fauteuils: tout un public virtuel. . . .
>
> Dire qu'au quatrième acte, à l'acte du Tribunal, je figure un sbire et que je suis incapable de me tenir de face devant le public, crainte de m'évanouir de peur et de me faire éclater le coeur: quel idiot de subir un tel trac! . . .
>
> .   .   .   .
>
> . . . et je me verrai toujours blotti dans le lit de Volpone, passant ma première et profonde nuit d'amour à la Source de mon art...[5]

Likewise, Yeats recalled a minor aspect of the play, quite out of context. "In Jonson's 'Volpone,' one of the greatest satiric comedies, Volpone goes to his doom but innocence is not rewarded, the young people who have gone through so much suffering together leave in the end for their fathers' houses with no hint of marriage, and this excites us because it makes us share in Jonson's cold implacability."[6] This explanation of how *Volpone* strikes one describes its effects but not how they are obtained.

In its own day and through the years following, *Volpone* has garnered high praise. Although opinions may vary, the persuasive arguments that it is Jonson's best play will be gainsaid only by sentimentalists or those committed to soft definitions of comedy. If such awards need to be determined, it is surely the most brilliantly executed comedy in English. Probably its excellences too uncompromisingly delimit its truths to permit this assertion general acclaim. Whatever ribbons one elects to bestow upon it, the unusual merit and skill have to be accorded some recognition. As with almost all Jonson's plays, this one draws on the attributes of the work just preceding it and modifies them significantly. If *Sejanus* at times, and for good reasons, bordered on the satiric, *Volpone* skirts around the regions of sardonic disillusion to impinge upon the tragic. Nevertheless, generous always in observing genre, Jonson keeps it by his standards an incredibly pure comedy. That he wrote it in five weeks argues a happy combination of skill and energy; that he dared dedicate it to Oxford and Cambridge, with an attack on inferior poetry, proves his awareness of its substance.

The firmly directed plot unrolls with the meticulous logic which guided *Sejanus*. No part yields to any temptations of turning aside from the facts as they unfold. In it are isolated, and perfected, for the first time the essential designs of the three ensuing great comedies. One person draws to himself a group of people caring little for each other and obsessively for the central attraction. Desire for control of that object leads them to extreme behavior. In this play that center is Volpone himself, a wealthy Venetian who pretends to be dying so that avaricious acquaintances, each expecting to be elected his sole heir, will bring him presents.[7] Because his imaginary illness demands that he lie immobile, he is assisted in his schemes by a parasitic servant, Mosca, a figure akin to Musco of *Every Man in His Humour* but more insidious and less ingratiating.

The first act presents the three clients as they visit Volpone: first Voltore, a lawyer, then Corbaccio, a doddering old man, and Corvino, a jealous husband. As in *Sejanus* the end of the first act begins the complication when Mosca praises Corvino's wife Celia. An auxiliary episode runs through *Volpone*, one which can more conveniently be dealt with later; it treats a foolish English tourist, Sir Politic Wouldbe, his equally silly wife, and another English traveler, Peregrine. At the start of the second act Volpone, disguised as a mountebank, enters the square under Celia's window, and, after a wonderfully managed spiel, lures her to look out. Corvino pulls her back at once, but the glimpse has aroused Volpone. Corvino decrees she may not leave the house, but Mosca brings a diagnosis from Volpone's imaginary doctors, who have decided that only by sleeping beside a young woman can the sinking man's life be prolonged. Mosca hints that to guarantee the inheritance, a suggestion Corvino cannot ignore, Celia should be offered. Corvino accedes to the scheme unenthusiastically, and Celia is kept ignorant.

At the start of the third act Mosca meets Bonario and cannot resist reporting, quite truthfully, to the youth that his father, Corbaccio, has disinherited him in favor of Volpone. While these couples draw to the house, Lady Politic Wouldbe assails Volpone, who finds himself helpless before her, the one character to defeat him in his sick room. Mosca finally lures her away with a report that her husband is keeping a rendezvous with a young woman. Bonario arrives at the same time Corvino does with a protesting Celia. The young man must wait while Corbaccio surrenders Celia to Volpone. Celia, not being a legacy hunter, cries for help to protect her from the onslaughts of a suddenly recovered Volpone, and Bonario blusters to her rescue. With Bonario and Celia thus informed of Volpone's duplicity, all seems lost, but Mosca arranges independently with the three men that they conspire under his guidance to substantiate Volpone in court, since Bonario has summoned the guards. The trial in the fourth act distorts evidence so that Celia and Bonario emerge the conspirators against the dying man, borne into the hearing on a litter. His exoneration encourages Volpone in Act V to pretend still further that he has died and named Mosca the sole heir. Mosca, faced with the possibility of seizing the wealth, betrays his master. In the confusions of his disappointment Corbaccio confesses his complicity before the attending officials. Volpone, disguised again, nearly saves the lie a second time, but rather than agree to Mosca's terms of sharing his money with the servant, he reveals everything. All are punished.

The subplot is tied to the main chiefly by Lady Politic Wouldbe who seeks out Volpone. Otherwise, it seems a series of episodes in which the tourist, Sir Pol, as he is called, tries to spy hidden secrets both in Venice and, from a considerable distance, in England. Finally, however, fear reduces him to hiding helpless under a tortoise shell he has constructed for an emergency while his elaborately worthless papers are confiscated and burned by a supposedly official searching party, which actually Peregrine and some friends lead. The two parts, however, in no sense constitute separate entities. Likewise, three entertainers for Volpone's idle hours, Nano, Castrone, and Androgyno, a dwarf, eunuch, and hermaphrodite respectively, have a function germane to the story.

This close obedience to the classical rules of time and place (and, as will be seen, action) transcends a ceremony of antique etiquette. The Venetian setting is indispensable. The city of Venice had long enjoyed a notoriety, well recognized throughout Europe, for corrupt luxury;[8] it is not just any distant Italian city in which an Elizabethan play happens. The play does not, however, document the more famous monuments and history. An enveloping aura of ease infuses Volpone's chamber. Sir Pol, the eagerly gullible Englishman, sustains this exotic atmosphere by contrast. Moreover, the reputation of Venetian justice for swift action was likewise established so that two trials on short notice within one day do not entirely exceed the probable.[9] The unity of time adds an intangible substance. Volpone worships gold. The opening finds him rising from the bed which he fills so often: "GOod morning to the day; and, next, my gold. . . ." (I.i.1) The treasure outshines the sun; as the action progresses references to time mark the hours with a chiming accentuation. The denouement accompanies dusk as the gold is confiscated and darkness descends. Nearly every detail of the text projects itself from the centers so that the design has an integrated totality.[10] The verse here modulates unusually pliant lines and extends the indolence both by its figures of vast softness and the slow rhythm of syllables. Beneath it all, however, runs an undeviating scorn of such surfeits. The rapid naming of delicacies overwhelms the senses and, simultaneously, cloys them.

> When you doe come to swim, in golden lard,
> Vp to the armes, in honny, that your chin
> Is borne vp stiffe, with fatnesse of the floud. . . .
>
> (I. iii. 70–72)

Volpone himself, purring on the bed as a lecherous, though supposedly dying, man, personifies the slough of unredeemable corruption. In this posture, and served by Mosca, he presents a figure not far removed from a prostitute. This effect corresponds to the teasing tactile sensation which Volpone desires to produce upon his clients:

> still bearing them in hand,
> Letting the cherry knock against their lips,
> And, draw it, by their mouths, and back againe. (I. i. 88–90)

The setting also lends the plot the sort of probability it must have to satisfy those whose imaginations are so literal that they accuse Jonson of lacking one. The method of acquiring wealth practiced by Volpone and the three Venetian bourgeois has not become widespread. Although scholars have, it is true, located historical antecedents, Jonson's scheme exposes primarily the general vices of greed. It condemns lust for mere money no more than it does gambling for a legacy. *Epicene* has been thought less "realistic" than *Volpone* because, presumably, in the value scale of modern life, with its mushrooming loudspeakers, critics still prefer gold to silence. Both comedies, however, portray in different ways the horrors which any immoderate desire, for gold, for silence, or for anything else, will engender. Venice, with its oriental trappings, happens to permit what elsewhere might seem an unlikely course of avarice; this minute localization suggests all the more strongly reasons for not supposing the vice to be just hunger for money. No one argues that *Poetaster* describes life and poetry in Rome under Augustus exclusively. The fortune hunters' peculiarities of conduct blend in as part of the tempo, but the climate includes more than Venice.

Along with this structure, Jonson evolved the ideal situation for embodying his meaning. Before this time the necessity of presenting his characters as moderately creditable beings, although they had also to be fools, hampered him and sometimes forced an underlining of the fact that his charade remained a contrivance for the theater. Such legerdemain, though intriguing, lay beyond the scope in which his abilities functioned best. By moving the calculating deceivers from the periphery to the center, by arranging for the leading figures to betray themselves, and by keeping justice marginal, Jonson made the illusions acceptable. Volpone and Mosca are the most consummate pretenders yet presented. Their attributes, of successful performers as opposed to the uninstructed poseurs of the humour comedies, allow a more nearly integrated play for this period when the stage was changing from a formal, stylized area toward the empty picture frame which reached its petrifying, if, one hopes, not ultimate, majority with the realistic plays of the late nineteenth century. Jonson, finally, utilized the full potentialities of the adult company for whom he wrote. Whereas it is unsuitable that any but boy actors play *Cynthia's Revels*, and even parts of *Poetaster*, *Volpone* demands adults. The whole work combines lazy sensuality with impotent desire, qualities which must be those of retarded men, not eager children. These, it seems, in terms of the theater itself, are the ranges of material which he had to work with. What emerged would have been quite unpredictable without *Volpone*.

One must, of course, have unlimited admiration for the care which C. H. Herford and Percy and Evelyn Simpson expended on the corpus of Jonson's works. As a model of textual editing, their volumes could hardly be more elegant and useful. But their notes sometimes tend to err on the side of stodginess. When they decide that there is "the suggestion of animal symbolism which runs through the play in the names of the characters,"[11] one wonders how far caution can go before it becomes misleading understatement; the answer probably is at the point opposite the one where overstatement becomes epic exaggeration, as when a play reviewer referred to "that terrible Noah's Ark of carnivora that Jonson, master-carpenter, beached on the English stage."[12] The imagery of *Volpone* is precise, and boundaries define its limits exactly. Like *Sejanus* it relies upon animals, but for a different effect. *Sejanus* implied a contrast: men, who should have better natures, unfortunately behaved like animals. Here, the men are animals. Their names, of course, merely use Italian words for beasts and birds: Volpone, fox; Mosca, fly; Voltore, Corvino, and Corbaccio, vulture, crow, and raven respectively. Sir Politic Wouldbe is Sir Pol, that is, a parrot, and Peregrine, the single sound person in the play, surely is the peregrine falcon, the pilgrim hawk. If this nomenclature were advanced by itself as an initial trick, it could be swiftly dismissed, but the connection extends more deeply. In both the quarto and the folio the running-title is *The Fox*, and the play was commonly referred to by this name throughout the century. Volpone himself mentions the association early in the action.

> Now, now, my clients
> Beginne their visitation! vulture, kite,
> Rauen, and gor-crow, all my birds of prey,
> That thinke me turning carcasse, now they come. . . .
>
> (I. ii. 87–90)

The complementary view follows at once:

> VOL. Good! and not a foxe
> Stretch'd on the earth, with fine delusiue sleights,
> Mocking a gaping crow? ha, MOSCA?   (I. ii. 94–96)

A statement so unequivocal at the outset allows a wide range of freedom for innuendo during the course of the struggle itself; not too insistent verbal parallels need be projected to define Volpone as a fox. Also, like an animal, he wears furs, and the dialogue tells that stage business between him and Mosca prolongs the process of dressing the fox in his skins to receive the birds of prey. When losing ground during the final trial scene, Volpone repeatedly refers to his totem animal, as though he sought a reassurance in the bare image. The three clients exhibit less than human traits: Corbaccio's glasses twist into "his foure eyes" (V. iii. 63), and his cane becomes a part of "that filthy couetous wretch, / With the three legges . . . ." (V. iii. 67–68) Moreover, other animals, as comparisons or in names used for expletives, keep their natures constantly before the audience through one rhetorical guise or another.

The profuse indications in the dialogue that none of the characters walks like a man make the intention sharper than inserted stage directions could. They prance, skip, creep, or slither, more closely resembling beasts or maimed men than any upright human beings. As Jonson noted in *Timber*, "Looke upon an effeminate person: his very gate confesseth him. If a man be fiery, his motion is so: if angry, 'tis troubled, and violent." (VIII, pp. 592–93) Actual animals spill over from the figurative descriptions. They leap forth as portents, but whereas in *Sejanus* supernatural appearances presaged fatal events, here the inept Sir Pol twists natural phenomena into dire warnings. A fantastic creature supposedly flies from Corvino during the trial, similar to the words which leave Crispinus in *Poetaster*, but here it is imaginary. Finally, poor Sir Pol becomes literally a reptile on stage when he takes refuge under his shell and Peregrine deliberately mistakes him for a turtle. The bouncing swing of this imagery has a grim elation, like a barbaric or medieval frieze in which the human and the bestial wantonly mingle. No implicit judgment blames men or animals, except that both are equally vicious. Their natures reinforce without hesitation the bases of the rationale. Animals denote not only a depth of cunning but also a height of luxury. Volpone during his frantic wooing of Celia plans an exquisite banquet on the brains of peacocks and ostriches, concluding with, if possible, the phoenix. Elsewhere, too, animals stand for the softest taste and sensuality, as well as the complementary side of these excesses, the crudest vulgarity and frenzy. The place is Venice; the people recognizable types; the time the late Renaissance; and the language serviceable English: yet, the whole offers startling vistas and nearly creates, transcending these, "a new element with creatures indigenous thereto, their costumes and cuisines,"[13] a feat supposedly beyond the reach of the imagination.

Throughout *Volpone* Jonson has mastered his poetry for swollen visions which are strikingly rich, if a trifle askew. With impeccable authority he names an object, then another, then another, and another without asserting their binding quality until through this progression the lines themselves clarify the complexity. This style ranges at random, and by its variations it unites everything from Volpone's vaunting declarations to Lady Pol's inane twaddle. The blank verse satisfies all occasions with two deliberate exceptions, the songs of the deformed trio and Volpone's mountebank salesmanship. These two provide revealing contrasts by their different idioms. Except for these excursions, it is Jonson's first comedy entirely in blank verse and in his mature style. Part of the effectiveness derives from another rhetorical device which might be termed the negative catalogue. This scheme lists attributes not possessed by the object or situation under discussion. Such items do not range across whatever happens to lie at hand but are carefully formed into a commentary on possibilities which might be, but are not. The contrast by negation presents no desirable values but evils which may be realized and happen, for the moment, to lack prominence. The temptation to quote long passages proves nearly irresistible, although any illustrations distort the tone. The verse always requires its context; the two reinforce each other, and both almost demand the stage for which Jonson designed them. The setting must give them life.

Some commentators have withheld approval from the long scene where Volpone goes out disguised as a mountebank to glimpse Celia because it contributes little to the play and because it may have been composed independently. Both charges look justified only after an imperfect reading. They undervalue the importance of the passage in relation to the structure. Volpone transcends being a simple hoarder, although, like Jaques, he buries his gold, granted that both the hiding places become profane shrines. For every penny he pinches, Volpone lavishes another upon an extravagance. The deceptions spun for his clients please him; while he performs for them, he watches them acting for him. For being happy and successful in his profitable business he is one of the most well-adjusted characters in literature. More than a mere cadaver, he does not ineffectually depend upon his accomplished parasite; far from inactive wits have already carried him high in the financial world. Thus, when he quits his room to act the mountebank, a convincing demonstration of his abilities dramatizes his prowess before a double audience: the one in the theater and the one on the stage. The resulting performance leaves no doubt about his talents for salesmanship. Among his admirers stands the rapt Sir Pol, who instructs an undeceived Peregrine; the scene further binds the two plots. The speech develops as a marvel of English prose, especially for this period. It moves with firm logic, wholly false, of course, and by the errors underscores misapplied knowledge and criticizes pseudo learning which perverts rhetoric to subservient ends by a crude ingenuity. Here the prose, which allows a greater semblance of this dishonesty within order, functions at each maneuver. As a set piece it has enough merit almost to justify its inclusion, even were it at the expense of the story. Perhaps this excellence in itself has contributed to its being misunderstood; it achieves its own ends so brilliantly that its essential ramifications have been neglected.

Throughout, the rhetorical devices which formerly expressed the humours now reach to different ends. Whereas the humours flowed on and on beyond the control of those afflicted, here the inventiveness, the elaboration of a single concept, provides Volpone and Mosca with the trappings of an ability as agile as it is mischievous and their dupes with the fixations of an immoderation which has but one goal in view. The comparison with the humours may introduce a misleading clue. The theory behind the humour comedies can scarcely be stretched to enclose a group as conniving as these men are.

For measuring the wide differences between *Volpone* and the earlier plays, a contrast of how they end will indicate the growth of Jonson's talents. A correction, of different degrees of severity, removed people from their humours, after which they were free to go their ways, no longer having much kinship with the beings they appeared during the affliction. If they had no afterlife to speak of beyond the final epilogue, this lack does not matter because their essence is that they must perish and that one does not care if they do. They might turn into almost anything. No cure exists for Volpone and his intriguing circle. Their punishment reveals them for what they are, and their follies, to the Venetian justices, are crimes. A momentary quirk will fall to the blandishments of common sense. A humour, by implication, sprang forth from idleness, where lack of restrictions allowed an accepted force to distend itself into futility. In *Volpone* the term describes an irrational deviation from the behavior which an individual exhibits generally; thus the primary meaning reverts back to its original status in the scornful comedies. The image of a stream subsides to an aside: "his sonnes ills / Growing to that strange floud . . . ." (IV. v. 57-58) Time and again Jonson tests his own assumptions of ridicule by ridicule, particularly when about to abandon them, at least deprive them of their force. Lady Wouldbe, still borne along on the old stream of humour, does not fit in with the rest and seems to bear a label "Not Wanted on Voyage," while she forges out over the play as a contrast with, not continuation of, the ruling passions of the other figures. Her primary trait consists of hopping from one correct observation to another without being able to hold any within a necessary connection. Superficiality is her chief attribute. She jumbles accurate and absurd literary judgments with so little notion of what she means that all may as well be wrong. Similarly, her opinions and observations about the humours and sickness are not so much wrong as wrongheaded. Her proffered diagnoses would nearly be a remedy in the earlier plays. Here, through Lady Pol, the prescriptions become a pompous mess, rendered more ludicrous when wished on Volpone who does not want to listen, who has long passed beyond a belief in sweetness and light, who is not ill anyhow, and who, should he wish the salvation almost any improvement would require, could not possibly achieve it.

If the reliance on a theory of humours falls into abeyance, sickness becomes more closely physical, although bound up in the psychological. Rhetorical figures keep up a running commentary. Volpone himself, pretending to be stricken, brings the embodied disease to the stage, and the clients' suggested cures, doubly ironic because they are gratuitous and because no one wants him to recover, swell the language. Further, to reinforce this point, gold and sickness are allied. The treasures the greedy offer represent an admission charged to watch a dying man, and Volpone obligingly stays ill as long as his box office puts out its S.R.O. sign. The contagion spreads as he infects the innocent Celia and Bonario when they come in contact with him. At the end his punishment fixes on him permanently the deformities he has been feigning. The objection that Zweig's adaptation is superior because it supplies a kind of release in squandering the evil money[14] instead of having it confiscated puts modern sociology and economics before Elizabethan dramaturgy. The gold must be condemned as a positive danger, not a neutral substance misapplied in the hands of its possessors as it appeared in *The Case Is Altered*. To have this plague showered down upon the unsuspecting poor is strangely gross sadism, if one understands the values in the play. Were the seized treasures tossed into the Grand Canal, that gesture might satisfy equally Jonson, *Volpone*, Elizabethan stagecraft, and modern critics, but not, surely, seventeenth-century Venice.

There can be no correction because no standard exists in the city. Any explicit disapproval of Venetian lasciviousness must be read into *Volpone* from the implicit condemnation in every line of the verse. After the enlightened despot Cynthia, the implacable Augustus, and the unredeemable duplicity of Tiberius, the justices and courts of Venice are refreshingly familiar: they know only what they are told, accept bribes, assume that a good reputation must hide an evil man, and can be molded by a lawyer's bombast. On the other hand, they do represent the forces of the law; when aroused they perceive the truth, rather later than anyone else, and mete out punishments. The state and its laws, consequently, cannot be guaranteed to deal fairly with their subjects, although there is as favorable a chance that they will as that they will not: scarcely a cynical view. Jonson preserved a fine balance between this newer mode and his older ones. The concluding punishment of Volpone is not too stern; he might have escaped entirely. The moral at this level does not preach the currently popular cliché that crime does not pay, but rather that crime does not pay indefinitely because it leads to success which can no longer contain itself within any limits and will, therefore, split apart. In terms of psychology and the law the fifth act fulfills all requirements: to carry any situation out to its bitter end, when not against the wishes of those indulging themselves, results in comedy. A corollary of this theory, that virtue does not pay indefinitely because it too reaches a limit so that eventually the good man becomes a victim results usually in tragedy. In both, the function of justice does not require it to investigate and uncover but to punish the uncontainable when enormities, from whatever violence, break laws.

Venetian justice, then, is not blind but purblind. A similar condition marks all the characters as well. *The Case Is Altered* championed the easy belief that the desire to see what the truth is will conjure its immediate emergence. The outlook has shifted gradually until here approximately a quarter-turn has been made. No one bears the qualifications to recognize what is true nor to appreciate it. The basis of disguise remains clothes, as Volpone, the master of deceits, concedes. Nevertheless, not alone by stagecraft—by the furs of the fox; by setting, the bed which commands the most prominent position; by make-up, the dissipation, which the squandering of money brings on and which in turn pays dividends; by direction, the placing of clients in Volpone's room; or by press agentry, Mosca's proddings—are the aspiring heirs taken in. Volpone is not a tyro like the humour characters who hopefully study one pose and trust this will suffice them until they become what they pretend. Rather, he throws himself into creating his role with the ardor of one of Stanislavsky's disciples.

> 'Tis well, my pillow now, and let him enter.
> Now, my fain'd cough, my phthisick, and my gout,
> My apoplexie, palsie, and catarrhes,
> Helpe, with your forced functions, this my posture,
> Wherein, this three yeere, I haue milk'd their hopes.
> He comes, I heare him (vh, vh, vh, vh) ô. (I. ii. 123–28)

The invalid, although his stellar part, does not exhaust his material; his mountebank disguise maintains a fine balance between convincing one that a mountebank speaks in this way and that Volpone as a mountebank would express himself in precisely this style. He later selects Proteus for an imaginary rival and recalls he acted in the form most dependent on metamorphosis, the masque. His declaration of lust to Celia mounts a finer repertoire for disguises than had beguiled the empty reveries of the static women in *Cynthia's Revels* while he recounts through how many masquerades he and Celia will amuse themselves in loving. The end finds him still pretending, this time as an official of the court about to unmask him.

This duplicity of appearance, as the action proceeds, twists all surfaces to whatever frenzy dictates; most ludicrous is Lady Pol's assumption that Peregrine is a woman in man's clothes, and, most shocking, the conspiracy of falsehood at the first trial. The innocent, but naïve, are accused of machinations falling beyond their abilities, interests, or understanding, though perfectly within the scope of their accusers. Celia is

> This lewd woman
> (That wants no artificiall lookes, or teares,
> To helpe the visor, she has now put on)
> Hath long beene knowne a close adulteresse,
> To that lasciuious youth there; not suspected,
> I say, but knowne; and taken, in the act;
> With him. . . . (IV. v. 34–40)

Before Voltore's rhetoric, Bonario's reputation melts away. Mosca, once again linking with Musco of *Every Man in His Humour*, has an identical function, that of keeping the action in motion. This time, however, not he himself but Volpone wears the disguises. In this society the parasite plies his trade without apology and achieves more rewards and amusement than his forebears did for all their multiple changes of costume. That he frankly recognizes himself and boasts about his position provides a likeness with Musco, but Mosca's temperament is treacherous and bent more on profit than on pleasure. He analyzes accurately the shortcomings of the clients and, incidentally, himself.

> Mos. True, they will not see't.
> Too much light blinds 'hem, I thinke. Each of 'hem
> Is so possest, and stuft with his owne hopes,
> That any thing, vnto the contrary,
> Neuer so true, or neuer so apparent,
> Neuer so palpable, they will resist it—
> Volp. Like a temptation of the diuell. (V. ii. 22–28)

Like Thorello's exposition of similar failings, this knowledge discloses the means of justifying further indulgences. At the end he is caught or, rather, catches himself. Everyone in *Volpone* shows the paranoiac's trait of rushing onward to the conclusion no matter how inevitable the defeat.

In *Sejanus* and *Catiline* night falls as the dimming of human insight before tragedy. Here the approach of dark becomes an accentuation in the comic pattern. It represents how an inevitable process catches up the deluded. Mistakes, close to unforgivable error, create a tragedy; in petty individuality and in choosing false standards lies the ridiculous. If one prefers hearing the still, sad music of humanity, the classical tempo in *Volpone* may sound repugnant, but this predilection merely tells one that audiences remain somewhat behind Jonson as connoisseurs of comedians. With disguise so convincingly pervasive, the eye cannot guide one, but this shift occurs because of the change in defining personality. Despite an undeniable cleverness, the clients are so obsessed that they see only what they wish, and, since it nearly amounts to the same thing, what Volpone wants them to. The voice continues to mislead when shaped by the rhetoric of Volpone and Voltore. There is, then, no accountable force to deliver moralizing speeches and to round off all corners nicely. Viewed in this way, the rationale of the play must be accepted as largely negative; judgments have to be brought from outside the dramatic frame by the audience roused through what the stage denies them.

Except as pure comedy, *Volpone* contains little of a positive nature. *Sejanus* substituted the broad effects of chaos for individual fates; here, the limited chaos within individuals permits a diminution of the enveloping social forces. *Sejanus* looks so long and uncompromisingly upon the cancer of evil that the tone must, because it is honest, occasionally be sardonic. *Volpone* keeps its attitudes focused on the protuberances of folly so steadily that its tone must, if it is equally honest, be wholly sardonic. The device of comedy generally composes a frame within which events are sometimes—and how infrequently depends upon the writer's skill—moved from what would appear a predestined end; a completed pattern emerges after a dexterous reliance upon what may be taken as logic not wholly predictable because of an ambiguously worded postulate. Obviously Dryden had some such formulation in mind for his famous examination of *Epicene*. In *Volpone* nothing is accidental and, at the same time, nothing forgivable. In this sense, that a clarity pervades every moment, it becomes one of the rare hermetic comedies in English and probably the only thoroughly successful one. The majority of them, even the best Wycherley and Congreve, demand that at a few, or many, points the audience take on faith the goodness of a few, or many, characters in a milieu which does not on the evidence of preponderant stress engender such virtues. By introducing this positive force for the inexplicable the comedy grows soft and untruthful; it no longer plays the game by its own rules. The humours, after all, no matter how fully bolstered, harbor this weakness. Their angry streams ravage a pretty landscape until, at the end, more like water from a closed faucet, they abate and send a munificent rainbow over everything, an effect as incongruous as this metaphor. *Volpone* remains resolutely true to its negatives; everyone is either a fool or a knave, neither condition necessarily better than the other. Such a rationale is not popular; if it suited the temperament between World War I and World War II, it lies now beyond the orbit of the prevalent hypocrisy and sentimentality in the commercial theater. To satisfy post-World War II tastes its *décor* would have to revert to the misty affection which Beardsley breathed into his illustrations for it. On the other hand, making sets and costumes as drab as those which Malcolm Pride designed for the Stratford-upon-Avon production in 1952 misses the chance for visual commentary by indirect display.

The strength of the play derives partially from its tensions which are fully comprehended not in isolation but as segments of the total structure. Nothing in the great comedies is idle; there are frills in neither detail nor design. Most comedy relies on improvisation, as, indeed, does some lesser tragedy. In the latter, however, drawing as it must upon hidden forces and motivation, the unforeseeable can be encompassed as nearly in the scheme of things, whether the fall of princes on an imagined Fortune's wheel or the keenest irony of a mind's self-discovery. At the core of tragedy lies a mystery of personality, inexplicable within the world of the particular play and at least partially vexing outside of it. For effective comedy this impenetrability must be eschewed. The great comedies of Jonson revel in the probable, if no longer the simply mechanical. The banana skin, the pratfall, the custard pie, and the double take are all irresistible after they have been planted. How to bring them into the plot poses the problem. Nothing limits their numbers and effects except the string of episodes itself. Jonson's design includes much more than skits and blackouts. *Volpone's* story begins where most others leave off, as the five main characters, already inured in their traits, clash against one another with misdirected cunning. When they devise ways for preying on one another, in the process they plant each effect until the climax. The trial which establishes Volpone's innocence in the fourth act, especially, points up how no momentary triumph can satisfy him or Mosca.

Perhaps an illustration will help pin down these generalizations, for example, the implications of the game Truth or Consequences. Basically, it is play, that is, it mimics lightly an activity and has no ostensible end except its own completion. If, however, the demanded consequences, upon the failure of truth, get out of hand, they may exceed the limits of amusement. Comedy is true because it is likewise inconsequential. Nothing follows from it; the final applause collapses the puppets, and the cast marches off or the curtain falls. Its very simplicity bestows its truth; one has enjoyed the illusion of having witnessed one world and its laws. Tragedy, in partial opposition, entails consequences. It cannot limit the qualities of its created world, and its ramifications point outside itself. In this sense no tragedy can embrace one truth, although it may hint at many. It depends upon a private spiritual mystery, the continuation in life of its theatrical game. The circus and vaudeville embody the nearly ideal comic forms because they correspond to nothing one knows except their own performances in a universe where legerdemain and prestidigitation rule. If the aerialist falls, one's sympathy extends beyond the act; the show itself is spoiled. The tightrope dancer is true to her art as long as she keeps her balance.

Some definitions by insisting that society sets the norm for comedy reduce the scope and exclude too much. Throughout every comic number there runs the sense that a standard is being upheld, the more fragile, the more interesting. In drama this code can most readily refer to social norms, as it does when exorcising the humours. Because the major part of comedy defies—without, however, breaking—laws (whether the law of gravity in trapeze acts, the law of cause and effect in magic, the laws of etiquette in farce, or the civil laws in *Volpone*) no rule can be taken seriously. In a word, true comedy must know that everything is relative and nothing fixed, but in the face of this awareness it pretends that absolutes exist. For the great Jonsonian pieces society cannot set punishments, and thus the Venetian justices are quite as corrupt as the people they try. The principle recurs in any memorable comedy: the Keystone cops chase ineffectually across the screen, and Chaplin must wander down a glowing road into another world at the end of his tales. In this light, the interpretation of justice in *Volpone* suits the *données* of the comic. Volpone ignores society and the laws, but until his uncasing no Venetian citizen criticizes him. Again, by keeping the comedy negative, its standards grow absolute; by defying the codified rules, it honors its own codes.

No one supposes that acrobats suspend the law of gravity while they cavort in the air. Their livelihood depends upon incisively grasping principles of weights and balances. With this special information they may in a measure of safety risk what for anyone else would be disaster. Beyond their moment of delight and astonishment, however, these performances cannot endure. They stay in a sense imperishable because one forgets them readily. Every circus act appears *sui generis*; one carries in active memory slight tokens for comparison. An awareness of this impermanence haunted Jonson; fortunately it prompted him to publish his writings so that they might "last beyond Marble" (IV, facing p. 348). Unfortunately, this drive toward the enduring beguiled him too often into tacking on voices of authority which draw their incongruously social moralizing from antisocial material. For *Volpone* he allowed the comedy to exist in its own right except for some inadequate didacticism at the end. One might consider the similar implications in the undervalued Auden-Kallman libretto for *The Rake's Progress*,[15] which shares with *Volpone* a grimly comic drive. The extravagances of Baba, bearded and endlessly talking, and of the turning stones into bread both have the requisite outrageous improbability for comedy. Tom Rakewell's pact with Nick Shadow must be strictly obeyed, and although Anne Trulove's devotion may save Tom's life, it cannot avert madness. The obvious moralizing at the close brings the final effect as close to *Volpone* as does any play in English. The opera has a meaning but nothing so pat as this curtain line supposes. Such reflections have strayed a distance from Jonson, but the three ensuing great comedies depend upon such points, and it seemed well to introduce the topics here. A few considerations about auxiliary action in *Volpone* remain and may, perhaps, expand these abstract speculations.

Volpone and his dupes observe the surfaces, and from these they try to deduce all. The mere sight of Volpone in his bed convinces everyone about his sickness; because all want to believe, and can believe, but one thing, no further investigation is required. The whole process of becoming his heirs, unlikely as it may sound at the outset, once taken for granted weighs upon their senses so heavily that it allows them to see only what they wish to, subject, of course, to a precautious correction by the wit which launches their scheming in the first place. These men pursue their singular desires as though all lay within easy reach; Mosca, as well, must finally play the comedy out to its end, aware though he may be of the stupidity of others. Their monstrous faith in the monster Volpone is not wholly misplaced. They are, after all, less deceived than Sir Pol, whose propensities lead him to see all as what it is not. He delves constantly beneath surfaces to emerge with the most unlikely set of conjectures, whereas the dupes require the prodding of Volpone's professional flashiness for their confusions. Sir Pol everywhere detects spies, portents, agents, and wonders. For him nothing is what it appears, but only what it might conceal. His wife, as has been observed, survives weakly from the humour comedies. She volunteers disconnected observations on nearly any subject, always in the manner of the humourists and always incorrectly. For her nothing exists but her own erratic universe. The sole character to regard the scene with detachment is Peregrine. His stability renders him powerless to turn aside the headlong plunge of stupidity. His standing to one side provides a weak counterbalance to the strong self-dramatizing centers. If he assumes the function of removing Sir Pol from his witch-hunting mania, this does not mean he could ensure any general improvement. Sir Pol is permitted, after his disgrace, to return home to England to try to reform. Like the second plot of *The Case Is Altered*, the auxiliary business here picks up, in reversed fashion, the concerns of the chief one.[16]

Yeats's opinion to the contrary notwithstanding, Celia and Bonario scarcely count in this welter of cheating. They neither know nor understand what they are doing, nor, indeed, much of what happens to them. Their virtue, such as it is, must be taken for granted, but it has affinities with nothing in *Volpone* itself. At Stratford-upon-Avon in 1952 the director saw fit to make them the intensely betrayed innocents with whom an audience might sympathize. This interpretation introduces a positive element into the action which may endear the performance to the tourists, but it reduces the comedy.

Every now and then a trio stumbles onto the scene to amuse Volpone, rather than to be entertained by him. This final aspect of the play consists of the dwarf, eunuch, and hermaphrodite. They may be Volpone's bastards; wherever they come from, they make external his inner defects. Their particular function, especially with their songs which Mosca writes and which inordinately amuse Volpone, suggests many overtones, most of which have already been well set forth elsewhere.[17] Their presence itself contributes a certain force. They keep before the audience the excesses of folly when carried to a second generation and help sustain the distortions which must at each point inform the drama. Their verses are jangling rhymes, quite at variance with the firmness of the blank verse itself. This crude expression comments adequately upon itself, for, as the main action of the drama demonstrates how desire can inflate itself by vanity, these three underline the level to which thought sinks by total surrender to deformity: Pythagoras is merely *"that iuggler diuine."* (I. ii. 7) Theirs is the negation of everything, a reduction to babbling imbecility. Volpone's final question to them, when Mosca has turned them out of the house, might, in addition to that of the fox and the crow, be designated the second emblem for the play: "How now! who let you loose? whither goe you, now? / What? to buy ginger-bread? or to drowne kitlings?" (V. xi. 8–9) To the deformed, both pastimes would be equally agreeable. In the play itself values reverse to the extent that pleasure may give pain, and pain pleasure, and both are weighed on the same scales. It is the destruction of values, but, because the characters themselves are held absolutely true to their deformity, the whole is wonderfully, if terrifyingly, comic. Jonson's control soars to such heights that it seems he adopted as his own goal the advice Volpone gives Mosca, "Play the artificer now. . . ." (V. ii. 111) In its manipulation of each nuance *Volpone*, in addition to all its other appeals, delights as a sheer marvel close to prestidigitation, the matrix of all comedy. In the respect that its qualities rest solidly on material luxuries and, somehow, tower into the heights of delicacy, *Volpone* resembles a description of Venice itself.

> A commercial people who lived solely for gain—how could they create a city of fantasy, lovely as a dream or a fairy-tale? . . . There is no contradiction, once you stop to think what images of beauty arise from fairy tales. They are images of money. Gold, caskets of gold, caskets of silver, the miller's daughter spinning gold all night long. . . .
> A wholly materialist city is nothing but a dream incarnate. Venice is the world's unconscious: a miser's glittering hoard, guarded by a Beast whose eyes are made of white agate, and by a saint who is really a prince who has just slain a dragon.[18]

After such an uncompromising demonstration of technique and subject, one should be satisfied by the competence itself. If anything more is demanded, it must be sought, and perhaps gratefully, not in the grandeurs of this Venice and its Volpone but back in the imprecisions of the merely living.

CHAPTER VII

Comoedy of Affliction

J ONSON'S great plays, in spite of the numerous cross references
so far invoked, exist sufficiently on their own merits. They
contain all one needs to know to appreciate them without distracting
glances before and after or behind the scenes at the working author.
At the same time, if only because of unusually imperceptive assumptions about them, the total sequence, how they inform and contrast
with one another, helps reassert the facts after centuries of misplaced
emphasis. *Epicene*, especially, must be regarded for both its internal
excellence and its position in the canon. It follows *Volpone* by four
years, but whereas that comedy declaims fiercely and directly in
poetry, this one speaks elaborately and obliquely in prose. Also, it was
written for and first acted by the Children. As in *Cynthia's Revels*, an
indirect piquancy attends the memory that these adults are not adults
and that the arch children's preciosity throughout all the scenes commented upon mincing attitudes of diffident men and women. *Volpone*
attains its severe intensity by heaping censure on the masters and ready
victims of folly. The punishments meted out here are less harsh; in-

deed, no legal body enters to name, least of all to sentence, the offend-ers. Seemingly this structure augurs a return to the concepts behind *Every Man in His Humour*, except that there a cure or a reprimand smoothed over the conclusion. Here the attitude accepts human aber-rations as a condition essentially comic but not wholly correctable. The play offers a last summary of many of the earlier themes shot through with predictions of debilitating compromises to ensue. Just as the earlier foreshadowings of what matured into merits often ap-peared a little ponderous by their too stern exercise, so, here, what later became vices resemble, rather, graces.

Notwithstanding its generally gentler views, *Epicene* embroiled Jonson in troubles when it was first staged. Perhaps Lady Arabella Stuart, a woman celebrated in court and literary circles,[1] took offense because the plot, based on a boy actor disguised as a woman, resembled her own escapades when she put on a man's clothes. (At least, one theory runs this way; why *Epicene*, of all plays which feature such turnabouts, should have been selected for the offending satire is less than self-evident. The incredible sensitivity which literary historians insist Elizabethans felt upon being caricatured makes the fairy-tale princess who noticed a pea beneath thirty mattresses seem compara-tively gross.) Possibly a rumored scandal resulted in its being sup-pressed, but a quarto probably was printed in 1612, although all copies have been lost.[2] It enters the folio, where both Beaumont's commenda-tory verse and Jonson's dedication to Sir Francis Stuart hint that when first produced it enjoyed a less than warm acclaim from someone pow-erful enough to transform his (or their) wounds into revenge.

According to scholars, several sources contributed the plot,[3] and still others provided the longer speeches. The plausible persuasions at-tending these arguments add up to the conclusion that it becomes one of those Jonsonian fusions which reveal unmistakable traceries from this or that work but which achieve an integrated stature. Many of the near recitations in the play, notably those rendered by Truewit, show lengthy borrowings from Ovid's *Ars Amatoria*. Truewit usually ridi-cules passionate attitudes toward love which in Ovid must surely be taken for sighing defenses. Moreover, some of Truewit's dialogue comes from Juvenal and other classical satirists whose scorns fit more coherently with the tone here adopted. All Truewit's discussions remain of a piece, so that, even to a sensibility well versed in classical poetry, the effects are not a montage of Roman sophistication superimposed upon a London scene. Part of the plot has evolved out of an oration by Libanius on behalf of a man who unwittingly married a garrulous harpy. Different studies, finally, connect *Epicene* with a play by Aretino[4] as well as with other works.[5] Yet it is misleading to force any single outside pattern upon the comedy, which in itself shows contradictions enough. Wherever derived from, since its composition it has trailed *Volpone* in popularity, if at a dim distance. Just as Zweig adapted that play into German, so he prepared the libretto for Richard Strauss's opera *Die schweigsame Frau, Epicene, The Silent Woman*.

The neatness of the structure also resembles *Volpone*. In the earlier play the pace of the conclusion was at times hard pressed to sustain the rapid beginning, and in this one the resolution has less verve than the complication. Also, the last act, while quite appropriate, does not in all respects convince one immediately of its own necessity. Though an acceptable outcome of the first four, it lacks the spurts of inventiveness which buoyed up most of Volpone's last trial. The bare action reduces itself to a fairly simple outline. Once again one man attracts a group of acquaintances to his house. Unlike Volpone, Morose does not seek the solicitations, nor does he promise any material gifts. On the contrary, he wants to see no one and to live in complete silence. The situation reverses *Volpone;* whereas Volpone and Mosca hypocritically salved their vestigial consciences by tormenting the clients, the visitors to Morose's house plague him. The action covers one day, the one which culminates a fit of rage Morose has been nursing against his nephew Dauphine. He has enlisted Cutbeard, a barber-detective, to locate a silent woman whom he may marry to gain an heir and thus be able to cut off Dauphine's inheritance. The play itself starts with a discussion of this resolution by Dauphine and his friends, Truewit and Clerimont. The second act shifts to Morose's dwelling where plans for the marriage are proceeding. Truewit, Dauphine's most active and irresponsible accomplice, interrupts these to point out the trials which matrimony entails, but Morose, bent upon his scheme, refuses to listen. The shouted warnings serve to strengthen Morose's determination. Dauphine and his collaborators decide to turn the quiet wedding into a noisy celebration by inviting a crew of silly acquaintances and festive equipage for the ceremony. These guests include the two gulls Daw and La Foole, a "college of women," Captain Otter with his overbearing wife, the barber, and, of course, Dauphine's allies. The third act depicts the revels which culminate in a sort of fox hunt through Morose's rooms. Amid the mounting noise Epicene, far from being demure and silent, becomes both demanding and vociferous. This discovery leads to the mock trial of the fifth act in which Cutbeard and Otter, disguised as a civil and an ecclesiastical lawyer, run through divorce investigations in shabby Latin without agreeing upon any proofs adequate to allow a separation. Finally, Dauphine rescues Morose by revealing that Epicene is not a woman but a boy actor whom he has hired in order to demonstrate for Morose the dangers to which a real marriage would expose him. Punishment for these follies is slight and rests with no official body.

A variety of minor characters and episodes round out the plot, which, until the fifth act, interlocks more tightly than in *Volpone*. In that play most incidents involve three or four characters because the clandestine nature of Volpone's traffic thrives on secrecy. Here the parade of outsiders tramples without impediment. Group scenes predominate in order to emphasize the two poles about which the action turns: Morose's desire for silence and the noisemakers who invariably defeat him. The changing pace accelerates steadily from the slow, thoughtful discourse of the opening to culminate in the hallooing chase of the climax in the third act. A different kind of comedy from *Volpone*, it flashes with an identical sort of intense luster; more than an improbable exercise for children, it catches up concepts which have great persistence, though it projects them with less bravado than those displayed in *Volpone*. Just what these are and how they become united must unfold with the progression of the analysis itself. One indication, which might be kept in mind, is Epicene herself (more properly, himself). No one, on the stage or in the auditorium, has any hint of how to see through his disguise. External perception no longer suffices.

Dryden's critical examination of this play sustains a high point of awareness for Restoration England. It praises especially the organization of the plot. Points for the construction by itself could have been gleaned from foreign sources. Dryden expostulates less fulsomely upon a more influential attribute which only English could furnish: the sheer technical dexterity of the dramatic prose itself.[6] Shadwell borrowed tricks for conversations from *Epicene*, and Congreve learned even more. Jonson here, and for his time uniquely, fused notable traits into a literary style which the Restoration elaborated and perfected. Although he took his point of departure from Lyly, *Epicene* catches more nuances. It is a mode of discourse tailor-made for bored, fashionable wits who enjoy a precarious detachment on the edges of poverty and their own insecurities. It discovers the prerequisites for a comedy of manners, and most later examples appear thin in comparison. Whereas from Sheridan to Noel Coward epigrams too often soar out of a flat exposition or explanation, in Jonson, as in Congreve, the flashing dialogue serves at every moment to define the speakers and their subjects. The balanced diction graces every member of the cast, but notably in Truewit's gently satiric speeches it reaches an easy sophistication which, even as it is spoken, points a demure finger at its own effortless virtuosity. The air of disengaged speculation resembles *Sejanus*, but prevailing standards make the comic tone more nearly acceptable. Truewit joins the insouciance of Mosca, without his treachery and final rashness, to the attitudes of Crites, without his heavy duties as the official spokesman for beauty, truth, and goodness. Just as the characterization, so the style represents no sudden development. It extends into a new sphere what have been abiding Jonsonian traits: a selection of general qualities rather than specific details and a rapidly shifting inventory of these to create a silver atmosphere. To enumerate the hallmarks each time they occur would clog discussion. One example should suffice:

> Many things, that seeme foule, i' the doing, doe please, done. A lady should, indeed, studie her face, when wee thinke shee sleepes: nor, when the dores are shut, should men bee inquiring, all is sacred within, then. Is it for vs to see their perrukes put on, their false teeth, their complexion, their eye-browes, their nailes? you see guilders will not worke, but inclos'd. They must not discouer, how

little serues, with the helpe of art, to adorne a great deale. How long
did the canuas hang afore *Ald-gate?* were the people suffer'd to see
the cities *Loue*, and *Charitie*, while they were rude stone, before
they were painted, and burnish'd? No. No more should seruants ap-
proch their mistresses, but when they are compleat, and finish'd.

(I. i. 114–26)

The tone satirizes what it pretends to praise, but merit and condemnation mix freely and neither emerges the victor. The counterbalances,
the holding in suspension conflicting attitudes, engage the suppleness
of the wit moving between the lines. One appreciates the artistry of
theories caught up, amplified, matched, and unresolved. The reflections can exist for their own sakes, apart from any program of the discourse. In this sense they more resemble set pieces, comparable with
Volpone's mountebank disquisition. Because everything else in the
play shares this tone, one accepts it as a consistent view of a society.
The opinions aim toward no end except themselves; the thought as it
forms and emerges is in itself enough, although, of course, it does project thematic lines for the dramatic tensions. Jonson said he composed
all his poems initially in prose, then versified them. This assertion does
not say that for him the two disciplines were identical; they obviously
were not. Each has its own limits and powers. Nevertheless, the practice presumably helps explain why the verse always retains a firm consistency, in Ezra Pound's dictum that poetry ought to be as precise as
prose,[7] and why the prose moves with a rhythmic balance to which
bare exposition could not pretend. Lyly's plays pointed the way, but
Jonson contributes a new resilience. Another beguiling contradiction
of this prose comedy is that attitudes more commonly assumed suitable
for poetry occupy the discourses: love, melancholy, speculation, and
reverie nearly dominate as topics. True, in contrast with these the
noise of the wedding festivities explodes concurrently, but this ex-
citement in itself arises from a background of idleness.

Jonson as usual turned to the classics for general concepts and
lines, but he localized such borrowings firmly in London, *Epicene*
being his first play with an English setting, and, traditional views to
the contrary notwithstanding, the first in which it is appropriate. For
example, one part of the speech quoted can be traced directly to Ovid.[8]

The contemporary city becomes a palpable part of the enveloping atmosphere, a force which the locale projected in none of the comedies of humour, including, of course, the revised *Every Man in His Humour*. Thus, however neatly managed by itself, the knowledgeable prose also fits into the major preoccupations of *Epicene;* it does not exist as an exercise undertaken for its own loveliness, although the characters may deliver it with that air. Its tensile qualities argue that behind the intelligences keen enough to shape these reflections lie minds as well. The strong rationale roots within the scene both the characters and the actions in which they participate. Affirming all this does not advance the contention that *Epicene* belongs with the contemporary "domestic comedy"; differences between it and Jonson's collaboration, *Eastward Ho*, will further set it off later. The pervasive influence is elusive and cannot be satisfactorily limited by an appeal to style, setting, or characters in isolation. Clues initially minor may supply the clearest hints.

Jonson's chief emphasis in the preceding plays has picked up a few points, turned them upside down or inside out to vary them with striking versatility. Except for *Sejanus* this packed construction has scorned minor effects; secondary ones, like the business with Sir Pol, propelled satire more directly along. In this one, and increasingly in those which follow, side matters, not incorporated into the texture, although tangential commentaries on it, begin claiming greater prominence. At first these are minute, and they might escape the notice of any but an overly fussy reading. Here they do, nevertheless, point up what the main routes of the drama are; later they so detract from it that they obscure the whole design, almost toppling it over. Three metaphors from a frozen or a thawing river suggest the theme. Aspects of these have been touched upon already on pages 10–11 above where the most striking was quoted. The other two do not call attention to themselves: "I, OTTERS wine has swell'd their humours aboue a spring-tide" (IV. iv. 168–69); and "Well, good master Doctor, will you breake the ice? master Parson will wade after." (V. iii. 64–65) Because this subject and relationship have not appeared in any earlier play, they suggest a new area; other figures of speech bear it out. A paragraph, *Iactura vitae*, of *Timber* condenses the language and climate of *Epicene*: "What a deale of cold busines doth a man mis-spend the better part of life in! in scattering *complements*, tendring *visits*, gathering and venting *newes*, following *Feasts* and *Playes*, making a little winter-love in a darke corner." (VIII, p. 565)

Up to this point all the comedies have justifiably lacked striking references to the outdoors. Here, in an urban setting, there are a number, and most of them refer to cold, bleakness, sterility, or winter. Taken together, they suggest a particular intention: "her autumnall face" [9] (I. i. 85); "That, which I haue plotted for, and beene maturing now these foure moneths, you haue blasted in a minute" (II. iv. 37–39);

Mor. Let his warming pan be euer cold.
Trv. (A perpetuall frost vnderneath it, sir);   (III. v. 79–80)

"but be like a barren field that yeelds little" (IV. i. 111–12); "Many births of a woman make her old, as many crops make the earth barren." (IV. iii. 60–61) Truewit, again, fashions the most extended discourse on the subject, as he ranges over the cold reigns of Ethelred and Edward the Confessor, before the refinement of manners, when one had a dull, frosty woman for a wife. In all of these runs an attenuated association of a country winter, old age, or impotency, with coldness. As negatives they link with the positive desire which leads Morose to search out a silent wife. The woman whom he marries obviously cannot be a bride at all, no matter what Epicene's sex beneath his veil may be. Silence renders "her" sexless or hermaphroditic.

In contrast with these images another, and far more obvious, group projects what Morose denies. In the two preceding plays animals in metaphors became the vehicles for figures of cruelty and cunning; generally they appeared in their native habitats. Here, in an indicative contrast, the procreative instincts, frequently of domesticated species, are stressed. Truewit mockingly cautions Morose that he not rush his bride away (Morose cherishing no such intention), "and not mount the marriage-bed, like a towne-bul, or a mountaine-goate; but stay the due season; and ascend it then with religion, and feare." (III. v. 46–48) The mountain goat does not conjure up a chamois but puns on and extends the meaning of the verb mount. If coldness becomes silence, impotency, and the country, which characterize Epicene, animals are noise, procreation, and the town, which Morose denies. Because the characters have a fashionable interest in sports, allusions to contests bring the topic into the dialogue, ties which Captain Otter's drinking glasses, christened bull, dog, and bear by him, strengthen. During the merriment the mock bearbaiting and a fox hunt with human contestants expand the subject. The culmination of the third act in a chase rebukes Morose not merely by its noise; its associations with the figurative language add complexity. Thus, the metaphors work themselves out: Morose's quest for a silent, unreal marriage invites the expected noises which mock it. Also, since this clamor swells from London life, it enlarges the conflict. Morose's nearly Proustian precautions against the swirling city which surrounds him make the intrusion one of, on the whole, the preferable citizens upon a moderately unpleasant individual. The surface judgment does not favor one side or the other; numerous qualifications hedge both in terms of theme, character, and language.

Zigzagging through these concepts, older preoccupations flash briefly and with less coherence. Although probably understandable in terms of the play itself, they emerge somewhat more clearly if one looks backward to their origins. The humours as a limiting concept of any sort, major, minor, marginal, or subterranean, have nearly disappeared. Although the word continues to be bandied about, its meaning varies, and it no longer exemplifies a single type of conduct. It becomes a cliché so ancient that no variation contributes new twists. The swollen stream, as has been seen, shrinks and freezes in the winter climate, except for a brief spring thaw. Daw and La Foole do exhibit the humour traits more elaborately than any characters since *Cynthia's Revels*, but it is extravagant to invoke the whole theory when their behavior can be taken for what it is by simpler explanations. Perhaps the attitude which Jonson finally chose toward the subject is best summed up in an opinion wrenched out of context: "humour is as tedious at last, as it was ridiculous at first." (IV. ii. 149–50) The psychology of flowing humours no longer adequately explains the aberrations; when storms occur in figurative passages, they describe noise: "O, the sea breakes in vpon me! another floud! an inundation! I shall be orewhelm'd with noise. It beates already at my shores. I feele an earthquake in my selfe, for't." (III. vi. 2–5) The initial vitality of unchecked individuality flowing outward has abated; a community now can channel its powers against one member.

Other devices to display the humours become casual digressions. An echo sounds notably in two passages. Once the pseudo lawyers, at a loss for words in their mock trial, repeat supposedly legal phrases while stalling for time. In the second, Daw and La Foole are urged to fight a duel, which both cowards want desperately to avoid. Daw claims his sword is being mended, an excuse La Foole immediately repeats. Both sections describe the speakers suitably, but their conduct is an isolated instance of what in *Cynthia's Revels* formed a heavy strand. The related rhetorical device, the insisting on a single word which chains the associations of the obsessed man, has matured steadily. Here, a number of especially brilliant examples define Morose, partly because prose accommodates this ranting more conveniently than blank verse, where the harping on a single term soon bongs like an inept metronome. Two of these, both too long to be quoted in full, move with decisiveness. The first is a tirade against Dauphine and his knighthood. In his scorn for this position, Morose moves down the London social scale and traces out an imaginary descent into poverty for the ruined spendthrift, a kind of rake's progress. The speed through the strata of failure increases, and at each station Morose reiterates scornfully, "knighthood." (II. v. 105–31) The second becomes a sort of malediction chanted between Truewit and Morose as an antiphon in which they vent curses against the barber, Cutbeard. Morose, carried away by anger, begins a splenetic outburst, and Truewit enthusiastically joins the game; each tries to outdo the other at inventing tortures which employ parts of the barber's equipment. Morose, finally, hears Truewit and himself shouting, and at once the noise pains him. He attempts, without immediate success, to silence Truewit, who, of course, quite consciously intends this effect. (III. v. 64–120) In both these episodes, however, the conduct refers more nearly to the humours as an explosion, the term in *The Case Is Altered*. These cataloguing tendencies show in Morose a break with the usual manner of behavior, not an accustomed method of discourse, and in Truewit a deliberate mockery. Closest to the old humours, the device scales to a similar pitch when La Foole outlines his family tree, the La Fooles, who inhabit every corner of the kingdom; La Foole still sees society in his own image.

These styles of expression, although cut loose from their accustomed moorings, are not mere survivals, banalities which the author could not rid himself of because they had become habitual. In *Epicene* any carelessness of speech seriously criticizes the group as a whole. Most of the cast are basically intelligent enough to command their elaborately wrought prose. They appear the most literate in any of the comedies, and their incoherence consequently shows up the more shoddy. Allusions to authors, made with a smattering of knowledge, draw out information, but literary criticism has become another fashionable pastime: "shee may censure *poets*, and authors, and stiles, and compare 'hem, DANIEL with SPENSER, IONSON with the tother youth, and so foorth. . . ." (II. ii. 116–19) Jonson, like other satiric dramatists, Aristophanes, Molière, Shaw, and Pirandello, is not averse to alluding to himself in his plays.[10] The references slip casually into the discourse: "As I hope to finish TACITVS, I intend no murder" (IV. v. 50–51); or "What's sixe kicks to a man, that reads SENECA?" (IV. v. 293–94) Such pretensions fall as no better than a senseless echo:

> CLE. They say he is a very good scholler.
> TRV. I, and hee sayes it first. A poxe on him, a fellow that pretends onely to learning, buyes titles, and nothing else of bookes in him.
>
> (I. ii. 74–77)

These familiar rhetorical tricks, tried as they have been before, fit into the play; the very assurance of repeating a theme with variations lends a virtuosity to the whole which culminates brilliantly both as language and portraiture. The relaxed severity of characterization and diction profits by the leisure which achieves its effects with a freedom from worry over scoring initial points.

More, however, underlies this play than an old master's reshuffling snippets into pleasing patterns. A new rationale begins, one which runs through the succeeding plays. In *Epicene*, for the very reason that it remains amorphous, since unfortunately Jonson never fully defined this style, it receives its most nearly satisfactory expression. As though it were the first fitting of a suit, a good deal of leeway for alterations permits the maker the benefit of reasonable doubts. Thus, somewhat unexpectedly, the familiar and the novel merge into a blend of tone and attitude which are striking. The old does not quiver as a feeble echo; the new does not clamor too assertively: the two are kept comfortably apart. The new attributes derive from noise and all that it stands for; those of the old are enclosed with silence or ineffectuality. The questions steering the complications center chiefly on four problems: what punishment can be dispensed and by whom; which prerogatives dare reason claim in a melee essentially unknowable; as an extension of this point, how strong are the powers of intuition in a tangled society, especially for those who feel that outside circumstances betray them; and, finally, do the ties of love, marriage, and family exert valid demands?

The standard which argued that a discernible unity binds interior and exterior fades. Some of the richness of language in *Epicene* derives from this ambivalence, which, strictly speaking, lies beyond the subject matter, but which indirectly permeates it. Truewit, especially, does not advance his opinions as necessarily true. His defending the use of cosmetics, before always a token of deceit, as perhaps attractive and justifiable reaches no conclusion; the balanced, suspended prose itself encourages exploratory reflections while it spins out its own musings without seeking to convince. Dauphine answers him by attacking rouge and mascara; because he reiterates the general attitudes of Jonson and the age, his convictions should sound forceful, vigorous, and final. When matched against a disputant, not an enemy, he must adopt an equally speculative attitude, and victory belongs to neither. Daw and La Foole, gulls of an older order, still believe that clothes make the man and that disguise is possible. They are unable to have their convictions gain attention, and the final reprimand, the dangers of gossiping, rebukes them on their own ground. Indeed, two other secondary characters, Otter and Cutbeard, succeed in their impersonation of the civil and the ecclesiastical lawyers. These two are endowed with gifts of altering the self formerly reserved for Musco. No notable trait sets them off to receive dispensation for their masquerade; on the contrary, they are, in the main, ineffectual men.

Moreover, before *Epicene,* any disguise had been censured, but Dauphine, the nominal hero, himself hires the actor to be the silent bride, and this deception redeems the whole situation. Whatever the general ethic which these practices entail, the pretense contributes directly to the instruction advanced. Epicene's hidden identity not only rescues Morose, but by giving the lie to Daw's and La Foole's boasted seductions he saves the reputations of the women. Tedious as the final passage of moralizing to Daw and La Foole may sound, it emphasizes the concept that defacing his reputation equals wounding the individual in this society where surfaces must count for so much. This tack, likewise, puts in proper perspective the sternness, bordering on a fussy Stoicism, of the strong men in the humour comedies whose belligerent detachment has about it an undercurrent boasting an indifference to the strength of words to harm. Here, the realities of slander and lies can injure dangerously that which is quite insubstantial and, nevertheless, quite real: the reputations on which some actual knowledge must necessarily be based.

Justice, the weighing of all evidence to sweep away false rumors, literally parodies itself. It is reduced to a mock disputation in bad Latin. Not only does the law receive an abstract rebuke, but Otter and Cutbeard in playing lawyers look like lawyers and, in this isolated house, are lawyers. Their bickerings deceive those on the stage, though the audience knows their secret. Like all good parody, their dialogue exaggerates to a point, but only to one which sounds as though it might not be parody. The interest lies in watching how closely the pretense parallels the real, how closely a noisy babbling becomes, while it comments on, a stern tribunal. Also, the individuals who earlier triumphed in trials were good, selected presumably for their virtue; the representatives of the law championed what was right. Here Dauphine, abetted by Truewit and Clerimont, a trio who are by no means depicted as endowed with only sterling qualities, though they lack Morose's gruffness, call the tune to which the rest finally dance. The line separating the true and the false runs less directly in dividing these crisscrosses. The final test is Epicene himself, about whose disguise no one on stage or in the audience has a clue. Before this no such figure has teased the comedies; Gasper and Rachel of *The Case Is Altered* hint to others their true identities and their noble parentage. Perhaps all the aspects of *Epicene* so far listed may be discounted as parts of a rapidly moving plot. This apology does not explain why the situation was chosen, why developed as it was, why written in prose, and why weighted as it is. Clearly Jonson was quarrying new materials and reforming old ones; neither of the processes quite fitted his former techniques, but both yielded enough so that only here and there does the furtive sentimentality protrude.

In *Sejanus* and *Volpone* the protagonist of the title dominated the scene and the dupes. Here, in stronger proportions, the entire design contributes to the interpretation of Morose, while he himself remains almost a neutral pawn. Volpone, as a deliberate fox, leads his pack; only an accidental lapse of his own wit, surely no sudden insight on the part of the abused, tumbles him down. Morose, at the center of the celebrations, has not invited his guests and cannot control their movements; the literal fox hunt in his home pains him. At most he represents one role; the orchestration becomes more complex, without solo passages. If in the humour plays the variety swallowed individuals and if in the later ones the threads of schemes centered in one man, here the segments affect Morose as much as, frequently more than, he does them. For the sake of sustaining emphasis, to consider first the pattern, then the man about whom it turns may preserve a balance.

The unifying theme of the play involves marriage. Love, it has been thought, did not engage Jonson as a subject suitable for his talents.[11] One need not quarrel with this assertion at its face value, but its scope stops short of total inclusiveness. Here, a satire on marriage, if not romantic love, in its muted manner engages the author almost as minutely as had the humours. While Jonson rids himself of subservience to a view or to a style by caricaturing it, he frequently introduces new ones by stealth. This double tendency served him admirably; although all his plays are experiments, none is unevenly experimental. In order to ensure quietness Morose pledges himself to a mute bride. The mania for silence exemplifies one avenue of immoderate desire, but marriage contains other facets which in themselves project different observations. A summary of points which have already emerged will suggest the direction: the action depends upon the wedding itself, which, perverted by silence, is not a marriage; the noise, associated with the accustomed hymeneal celebrations in town, fails because it seeks the wrong goal of tormenting Morose, the groom. If the party were a true one, the din would have its proper function. Such observations, however, do not imply that the issues are clear-cut, with Morose being blamable and the guests being right. The noise-makers personify depressing specimens of the failures of marriages and of love. Only Otter's rough, if not uncivil, tolerance saves his way of life from approaching pathos. Jonson here strikes the elusive tone of henpecked ridicule: "hee is his wifes Subiect, he calls her Princesse, and at such times as these, followes her vp and downe the house like a page, with his hat off, partly for heate, partly for reuerence." (II. vi. 54–57) Otter, dominated by his wife as he is, manages to preserve an open honesty toward his compromises. Whatever he and his wife lack as models, they do maintain a household of sorts, if all his interests lead him to his drinking cups and the animals they represent. For better or worse, they are the one couple who present a semblance of domesticity.

The college of women have resolved their unsuccessful marriages by a more striking project. This group have left their husbands and, maintaining a separate establishment, entertain young men of the town. Drawn to any lighted candle, they seek Morose's home, and all are attracted by Dauphine, whom they embarrass by their attentions. This mode of settling marital incompatibility depicts the failures of love, although not of sensuality; their affairs with their beaux are hardly Platonic. Their rampant sensualism permeates the play whether or not they are on the stage. The boy page in the first act describes how the *deshabillées* women to whom he delivers messages entertain him. "The gentlewomen play with me, and throw me o' the bed; and carry me in to my lady; and shee kisses me with her oil'd face; and puts a perruke o' my head; and askes me an' I will weare her gowne; and I say, no: and then she hits me a blow o' the eare, and calls me innocent, and lets me goe." (I. i. 13–18) The many reflections by Truewit upon women in general and the college in particular continue the theme. Feminine carnality, on the increase since Livia of *Sejanus*, here contrasts with masculine diffidence. Noise belongs predominantly with procreative instincts, and the wives, marshaled by Mrs. Otter, are shriller than their husbands. The page's experiences also hint at the effeminate traits which the men possess.

The male counterparts of the college of women are Daw and La Foole, two bachelors who express no intention of marrying. A fashionable interest in sex to which they pretend consists mostly of giggling gossip. Both boast of having been in bed with Epicene before the wedding. Their claim explodes with the revelation of the hoax, for they do not know of the deception. A reference to a poem of Daw's as "a *madrigall* of procreation" (II. iii. 138) marks him as an equally ineffectual littérateur. In all their activities these men are buffoons, incapable of decisive masculine conduct, a condition manifest in their every gesture and underlined by their fear of dueling. They suffer from a lack which in the collégiennes is an excess; indicatively La Foole's given name is Amorous.

Dauphine, Truewit, and Clerimont, whose names likewise describe their propensities, serve as a chorus of sorts and hasten the turns of the plot while they comment upon it. By deploring everyone around them and sustaining the sharpness of their wits, they range themselves as allies with the forces of sanity. Their own particular relationships with the patterns of marriage do not engage much attention. They perpetrate neither the puffed noises nor the aggressive silence but polish their measured prose to its most refined luster. Nevertheless, they do commit themselves as more than a distant chorus. Justifying their excuses entails unnecessary speculation; it is misleading to guess because no hints are given for tracing the sources of their larger responsibilities. Within the limits of *Epicene* their polite refusal carries its own acknowledgments. Vagueness about the three chief spokesmen stresses how tenuous, almost attenuated, the whole play is, but the exigencies of the plot cannot incorporate at any point actions to show them in other attitudes, and, from the evidence, it appears that Jonson at this time was incapable of executing such extensions. The ambivalence rests upon, chiefly, his indecisiveness about official spokesmen at this point of his career. The tricks of *Volpone* to avoid commitment could scarcely be duplicated. The most convenient dodge merely looks the other way when the subject elbows forward. By and large, conditioned by other comedies which frequently fall back on such sleights, one does not notice the omissions. One might draw a sort of analogy between this theme and the similar one detected in *The Canterbury Tales*.[12] The Chaucerian marriage group relates disparate segments dramatically through a device which, it seems, the author probably had somewhere in mind but for which not a shred of evidence remains. The function of Epicene himself, without such an explanation, becomes inexplicable, except as a prank of disguise and torment which reduce an otherwise sophisticated work to meager farce.

If the whole cast reverse the expected qualities of their sexes, the women unduly aggressive and living in a convent of lust and the men effete but pretending to a type of virility, then Epicene and Morose combine the two opposites to be archetypes. As a woman Epicene shows at first the demureness commendable in the play for her sex and, after the marriage, a deplorable tendency toward the prevailing garrulity. Since in neither role is he being himself, the conduct proves nothing because he is merely practicing skillfully his profession. In *Cynthia's Revels*, the queen stands in neither column listing the characters, but she occupies a place between the two at the top as mediator; by the same token, for all intents and purposes, Epicene deserves a similar elevation. Although he cannot judge, it is as neither man nor woman but as the final reversal of habits becoming the sexes, traits which he alone is free to put off, that the monstrousness of the rest is satirized.[13]

Finally, then, Morose himself remains, perhaps, in a similar midpoint at the end. If Epicene flaunts the satire blatantly to bring about a resolution, during the complication it is Morose's suppressions which mix the rationale with uncertainty. Both Epicene and Morose tend to be bisexual, the one by intentional design, the other by temperament. Had Epicene indeed been a silent woman, the ceremony would have become pathetic, motivated, as it is, not by love for a woman but by hatred of a nephew. The association of impotence and silence hides a special sting in one of Morose's confessions; he intends it as a lie to provide grounds for his divorce, but it rings appallingly true in its bluntness, "I am no man, ladies." (V. iv. 44) Furthermore, if Jonson actually did have Aretino's *Il Marescalco* in mind, the condition becomes less blatant than its source. "In this Italian play a Duke, knowing the hysterical misogyny of his gentleman-usher, a paederast, devises a rough practical joke, solely to make the fellow furnish the jaded court with an hour or two of farcical amusement."[14] Whatever the ramifications of Morose's eccentricity, its motivation lies imbedded in his psychic personality. The simpler humours made exploring such a depth unnecessary.

While undoubtedly adapted from Libanius, Morose's convincing portrait of himself suits the general pattern of development in these plays, much as it seems to clash with the intention of *Epicene*. "My father, in my education, was wont to aduise mee, that I should alwayes collect, and contayne my mind, not suffring it to flow loosely. . . ." (V. iii. 48–50) In spite of the fact that many of Morose's speeches extend at length and that others' conversations annoy him more than do his own, the explanation sounds plausible. Education has finally planted a humour in reverse, the humour which is not the absence of a positive. It becomes the stream of humour which refuses to flow at all. For Morose neither cure nor punishment exists. The play itself ends on the word silence, and the address to the audience requests their applause, a noise which may cure (a vain hope) or at least please Morose. Who before *in* a Jonsonian comedy has been pleased? This time the tone is not mocking. Until the very end, however, the brand of truth which this comedy depends upon has shifted from the kind which never hurt anybody to the sort which always hurts.

From start to finish *Epicene* is "an excellent *comoedy* of affliction" (II. vi. 36–37), the intention being comparable with the advice which Volpone tacks on to his injunction that Mosca play the artificer and "torture 'hem, rarely." (V. ii. 111) If the conclusion furnishes no punishments, the unfolding action itself sufficiently torments the foolish. The elements of the plot themselves do battle, but the contention has no clear-cut lines; indeed, the suave impartiality of the arbitration between the parts, when it does interpose judgments, sounds too aloof. The sentiments derive from Ovid's *Ars Amatoria*, whose intensities Truewit merrily waters down for his own ends. It presents a man who is no man who marries a woman who is no woman; but finally both the actor and the eccentric become figures who, in being honestly what they are, surpass the uninstructed mob which surrounds them. The rest, chasing worthless frivolities, finish as puppets doomed to go on incapable of pretense or honesty. The last authority rests with the three wits, who, claiming no particular ability, may with impunity appoint themselves judge and jury because they are clever and young.

All final verdicts must stay suspended, if the play succeeds; it perfectly balances its parts, none of which dominates.[15] One can, of course, condemn it as a grotesque failure in which perversions pull askew the comic lines, the ultimate one being the author's tormenting his own recessive nature.[16] Or, it may be dismissed as a meaningless froth about a man with an unlikely phobia and his not much more believable friends. Although not impervious to these attacks, it comes close by its own standards to being a wonder of complexities: style, character, attitudes, and meanings. These dissect quietly and daringly the uncommitted standards, match one extravagance against another, tie them together, and then unloosen everything—all this by a series of improbabilities which never break off into downright belief. An interpretation such as this seems not unduly generous but simply fair, if one will allow slight influences extending from other works into *Epicene*, which cannot quite account for them within its own limits. If it brings off all its intentional and unintentional indirections, it becomes one of the most coolly audacious comedies ever.

CHAPTER VIII

The Faustus

B ECAUSE *The Alchemist* has won lavish praise, any appropriate beginning must review its outstanding achievements; unqualified commendations have not rained down on Jonson's plays. Perhaps in the twentieth century *Volpone* has briefly enjoyed the first place, but through the centuries *The Alchemist* has been most highly regarded. For expertness the plot has ranked with *Oedipus Tyrannus* and *Tom Jones*,[1] a position not undeserved. The action flows with admirable swiftness and coherence; the period covered within *The Alchemist* builds brilliantly on the unity of time. Beginning, middle, and end follow duly, each situation implanting the seeds for the ones which inevitably ensue. Conflict breaks out near a climactic point and concludes with the finality of an exploding alembic. The language twists the jargon of alchemy into resilient verse; indeed, technical vocabularies from a half-dozen social groups blend smoothly within the wonderfully pliant lines. Characterization resolutely draws upon more than a single mania of the individuals. Subtle, the alchemist himself, juggles the multiple feats of inventiveness his name implies, but a minor figure, Abel Drugger, suggests quirks complicated enough to have allowed Garrick in his eighteenth-century production to assign him, eked out with lines pilfered from Surly, a nearly stellar spot.[2] It presents a view of almost unprecedented sweep for Jonson about the middle aspects of London society with the knight, Puritans, a clerk, a moneyed widow, etc. The secular vice it points out, gullible avarice, is chastised by corrections more agreeable to most standards than those dominant in *Volpone* and *Epicene*. In a word, the play is pleasant, all a comedy should be, and intelligent, besides.

One is not disposed to quarrel with the main contentions of these amiable views. The fact remains, however, that criticism of Jonson fails significantly to be judicious. With the other plays the faults are peevishly harped upon; here, as though to respect an unheeding urge for compensations, commentators pardon all weaknesses. A general rejoicing arises that for once in his career Jonson wrote a genial play. If the patter of alchemical terms resembles nonsense, this babbling reassures a proudly scientific age about the ridiculousness of quaint, old-fashioned views: no one could make sense out of that rigmarole, and Jonson was bright enough to expose it early. If the Puritans rant at wearisome lengths, the elephantine visions of Sir Epicure Mammon and his cohorts balance the ascetics. Above all, in production the action can accommodate a good deal of knockabout farce, which contemporary underlings demanded and got. Such uncritical excuses ought to stir one's suspicions about the intelligence behind the admiration. It is true that *The Alchemist* is a stunning comedy and that nothing else quite equals it in English.[3] It is true that it is very, very good; nevertheless, it has serious shortcomings. Not to see these overlooks the main points and misinterprets them. In broad terms *The Alchemist* may remain Jonson's greatest play; such gradations are somewhat beside the point. Possibly the virtues outweigh the lacks, and clever technique patches the flaws. An unqualified encomium dismisses the parts in wholesale acceptance; judiciousness demands that one try to separate the failures from the fulfillments.

The plot interlocks reasonably but unexpectedly; it deserves detailed attention. Written at a time of the plague, it concerns what occurs in a London house when its master, Lovewit, flees town to escape the contagion and puts his servant Face in charge. Face has invited Subtle, an alchemist, with an aide-de-camp, Dol Common, to move in. The action begins rapidly with a quarrel between Face and Subtle; Dol fails to calm them by warnings and finally resorts to threats. They gruffly agree just in time, for their clients begin arriving. First is Dapper, the clerk who seeks the money which the Queen of the Fairies, whose favorite he is convinced he has become, may bestow. Subtle, he believes, has the power to summon her; they send him off to prepare for this supernatural visitation. Drugger, a tobacconist who wants the most advantageous location, astrologically speaking, for his shop, comes on next. Act II brings the more ambitious. It opens with the appearance of Sir Epicure Mammon and Surly: Sir Epicure who desires the philosophers' stone in order to buy himself the more recherché luxuries; Surly, the detractor, who provides a counterbalance to his exuberances. To get Sir Epicure from the scene, Dol Common, now disguised as a bluestocking driven a little mad by her studies in the hermetic sciences, lures him away. Finally, the greediest of the lot is the Puritan Ananias, dispatched by his pastor, Tribulation Wholesome.[4] Drugger returns for his sign and promises to introduce Dame Pliant, a widow whom he loves, and her brother Kastril, an angry boy, a type of bucolic who lives riotously in town. By the end of the second act all have assumed their places.

Ananias conducts Tribulation onto the scene in the third act. They need the gold to convert the world to their own brand of holiness, just as Mammon would corrupt it by his idols. The ranting speeches, Christian or pagan, indicate Jonson's keen awareness of religious fanatics. The Puritans leave to consult the brethren whether counterfeiting may be practiced lawfully with their views. The pace increases as Dapper, Drugger, and Kastril arrive at once. Drugger and Kastril are shunted aside so that Dapper, blindfolded, may meet his supposed aunt, an interview consisting of pinches and squeals by the trio. Meanwhile, Sir Epicure, with Subtle's approval, attempts to seduce Dol. Kastril brings Dame Pliant, his sister, to the house, and when Surly returns, disguised as a Spanish captain, his intention being to expose the frauds, he is dispatched to her with the understanding that she is a prostitute. Mammon, forgetting that only those so pure that they scorn the wealth the stone brings can attain it, persists with Dol. An explosion supposedly destroys the long process of transmutation and blasts his hopes for Dol and wealth. Meanwhile, Surly, enraged that they expected Dame Pliant to submit to him, attacks Subtle, who, capitalizing on the fears of Kastril and the rest, incites them against the one undeceived man.

At this point, the opening of the fifth act, Lovewit, the master, returns to London and learns from neighbors the center of strange activities which his house has become. When Face is summoned outside, his excuses cannot stand against the presence of the enraged clients, who are returning, as well as the shouts of an agonized Dapper from within. Face, however, offers Dame Pliant as a bride and bribe to Lovewit, who considers consenting. Back in the house Face holds the controlling power over Subtle and Dol, whom he sends packing, and keeps such oddments as are left for himself. Lovewit drives those who were cheated away from the house. They have no recourse but to write off their losses.

The action, upon closer investigation, differs somewhat from that of the other plays. The typical figures in the comedies have been the somewhat schooled pretenders or the charlatans who disguise themselves to appear more (or less) than they are, as though the gesture were the achievement; this generalization applies comfortably even to Morose's marriage. Those of *The Alchemist* share this trait only incidentally. They happily brag of what they are in the expectation that through magic a wondrous transformation will be wrought. Subtle is a quack, but his quackery must refer to facts; his acting the part involves wide knowledge. Moreover, all his customers do not want one thing; their goals and temperaments differ, and they seek out Subtle not as an end in himself but as one through whose incantations they may obtain what they wish. Likewise, the deceivers, Dol, Subtle, and Face, are not taken in by their own masquerade, a possibility which always threatens Volpone and Mosca and which finally does overthrow them. At the same time, because these three are aware of their plans' never having a sustained success, theirs being at best a transitory arrangement, they can cavort as more extravagant and insouciant. After all, the eyes of the legacy hunters, deluded but guileful men, fastened hungrily on Volpone; one break could have tumbled down the whole structure. Here the crucial truth lies quite beyond the alchemist; his partial knowledge of arcana removes him from detection by his dupes. *The Alchemist*, concerned as it is with "projection," exploits the discrepancy between the actual and the impossible for most of its effects. The humourists diverted one because, within their ludicrously narrow compasses, they might convince themselves of their temporary success.

The characters exhibit a wider excavation of the social strata. These plays have before dealt with one segment of society; at least, most characters sought to impress the upper reaches. Here the range expands to depict the scope comparable with that encompassed by other precise, but less extravagant, British satirists, Chaucer and Jane Austen. Subtle, therefore, must exemplify more things to more different men; it is not a small accomplishment of Jonson's that he managed to vary Subtle subtly from encounter to encounter. The restricted scene, the comings and goings, the reciprocal motivations, the final resolution: all these deserve the praise they have received, but not because of their verisimilitude. The clients may reproduce specimens of townspeople currently on view, and alchemists undeniably practiced their craft in seventeenth-century England. The treatment of these subjects is no more realistic than is Bosch's painting of a conjurer. If the plot does not make this point undeniable, the language which the characters use does. No one group has before spoken with such a rich, hard vocabulary. The types seem to have been selected mainly because they all have special jargons.[5] Nouns pour forth with a rapid profusion which one scarcely expected to discover anywhere in literature, even in a Jonsonian comedy.

The rule of the catalogical imperative holds sway but in a new manner. The earlier subjects usually seized on the familiar, sometimes the too familiar, and small details, as in Morose's knighthood diatribe, could be borne up by the general subject. In *The Alchemist* such lists frequently abduct their terms from foreign places, either the advanced researches of alchemy or the more esoteric corners of London life. This vocabulary may have sounded slightly less exotic in the seventeenth century, but the plethora of technical items here, and their

omission from contemporary literary works, does not reinforce such
an impression. Almost like the sounding of a theme, in the violent
bickering which starts the play, Face, the servant, heaps scorn upon
the alchemist's equipment, and Subtle replies contemning Face's menial
household duties. As the dupes appear, each bears a cargo of specialized
words from his trade and unloads these immediately. The turns which
Dol, Subtle, and Face perform for their clients increase the possibilities. The two, however, who soar most aspiringly are the knight and
the Puritans: the former with his swirling dreams of luxuries, the
latter with their mean, magniloquent Biblical oratory. Not only do
these outpourings exist in isolation, but parts resemble flytings between
individuals. Surly parodies the alchemical vocabulary, "What a braue
language here is? next to canting?" (II. iii. 42), in lists which might
nearly pass for Subtle's own, but he then continues with his special
favorites, the wiles of Elizabethan cozeners, for a comparison. The
Puritans mistake part of Subtle's explanations of transforming metals
for *"heathen Greeke"* (II. v. 24), a suggestion which sends him and
Face off angrily with pauses now and then to reintroduce the offending phrase. It ends with a chant close to a blasphemy which mocks
both the phraseology of the creed which the Puritans rejected and the
trinity:

> FAC. 'Tis a *stone*, and not
> A *stone*; a *spirit*, a *soule*, and a *body:*
> Which, if you doe *dissolue*, it is *dissolu'd*,
> If you *coagulate*, it is *coagulated*,
> If you make it to *flye*, it *flyeth*. SVB. Inough.
> This's *heathen Greeke*, to you? (II. v. 40–45)

Such lists, which swell with a fancy no selection of quotations
can do justice to, mark the culmination of Jonson's style. Although
the primary concept of the humours has vanished, the stream flows on
in the verse, now bearing up the obsessed, now overturning them, but
always under control directed to a thoroughly unknowable end. Behind all of them continues the belief that a single passion rules the
individual, but the inventiveness and the ingenious illustrations have
never been surpassed. The terms do not particularly suggest one another, nor do aspects of one figure give rise to later imagery. The core

from which everything evolves is the ego itself. Granted that this patterning invites repetitions, the richness of the exhibitions forestalls any monotony.

Because of the intentional, and unintentional, obscurity of the alchemists and of the books they wrote, ascertaining what accuracy Jonson aimed for in Subtle's terminology and procedures has fostered conflicting opinions. Evidence has been advanced to prove that most formulae do not become nonsense in terms of alchemical lore itself.[6] The variety of the vocabulary, its orchestration and suitability, argues more than a casual familiarity with the field. This same thoroughness and precise usage undeniably guide the other speakers and multiply everything in the play. For example, when Subtle lures the Puritans to imagine the conversions which ownership of the stone will assure them, he ranges through many types, tying the bundle together with the catch phrase, "there you haue made a friend." (III. ii. 29–41) The fresh inventiveness lavished on *The Alchemist* can scarcely be overrated. Composing it transcended any idle act of the imagination: partial observation and partial reflection. It demanded the painstaking gathering of learned terms from obscure lore and then organizing them into a species of poetry for which English provided no model since Chaucer. The final test is that beneath this burden of slang and jargons the movement of the verse stays light and buoyant with not a hint of the extensive research which its composition entailed. Moreover, if the plethora of positive terms runs its course, the negatives of the catalogues can always be substituted. Almost any suggestion provides an excuse for grouping attributes; when Surly appears as the Spanish captain, the products of Spain at once are praised: horses, beards, perfumes, pikes, blades. Dol herself manipulates the style as she vents mangled quotations from the not quite lucid tomes of Broughton. The meek neighbors list the types who frequent the house, and Lovewit muses upon the kinds of attractions which might have lured the motley assemblage. When dividing the spoils, the three take time to name at some length who visited them and what each contributed. It is instructive to contrast a passage which describes the pleasures of London life by Face and those on the same subject by Truewit in *Epicene*.[7] While the variety of possible pastimes in both sounds equally ample, those in prose precisely balance against one another, but those of *The Alchemist* tumble forth in rapid succession, both styles adapted for the speakers and for their states of mind. The passages, then, while wonderfully accurate cannot be dismissed as mere journalistic reporting or realistic description. They become commentaries upon the milieu and the inhabitants.

Nevertheless, this mastery of the catalogue is achieved at an expense ruinous to the other effects of language in the play. The major types of images, although continuing almost unchanged from the preoccupations of the other comedies, are inserted less skillfully into the main body of discourse; indeed, they shrink to almost marginal places. In the opening quarrel the vituperations Face and Subtle throw at each other name dogs, qualities descriptive of the kind of snarling which flares forth frequently between the two men and later between them and their disgruntled customers. After this initial planting of the theme, unlike the effect in *Volpone*, figures rarely return to this metaphor. Other kinds of animal names recur in a sporadic fashion, as though Jonson had, at best, a passing interest in them, or he had grown weary of the old codifications. Little phrases, hardly worth noting, use birds for terms of rough endearment.

No author, of course, need be reproached because he chooses to vary his style; had the confining limits of the humour concept been observed beyond *Poetaster*, the major comedies would not have ventured far as experiments. Few authors have relied so persistently upon growth and change because few have found intellectual discovery so necessary to their temperaments. In employing the term Jonsonian, one does not mean that any single definition limits it; Jonsonian implies an adaptable process which within any work arranges every scrap of material in a definite way. Such a style risks rigidity, and so far all the plays have shown a salutary increasing of scope; up to *The Alchemist* this freedom has improved them. Now, however, the efforts to incorporate broader fields begin to stretch beyond manageable limits and to distend the form to its breaking point. This failure, and in terms of Jonson's ability a failure it must be counted, although temporarily it permits him his greatest triumphs, permeates several levels. For language, the reliance on set pieces as marvels of writing deprives sustaining passages of one of their double duties. They furnish exposition, but they fail to comment indirectly. A second weakness involves the abiding question of justice.

Problems about authority, what the good is and how to know and enforce it, haunted Jonson. In each play he invoked and tested different standards, only to reject them as unsatisfactory in the next. Here by his lights he drafts the strangest concept of all, a democracy, one unworkable and doomed by its constitution. Although Volpone saw himself the self-deputized agent to torment the would-be heirs, and Dauphine chartered a legal process to try Morose, their temporary usurpations got brief attention and no praise; the contexts made manifest their ephemeral prerogatives. Here the ideal principle becomes democratic; Subtle, Dol, and Face form an alliance part military, part commercial, and part civil, but the three pretenders are equal partners, whether as generals, shareholders, or a confederacy of sovereign states. Dol keeps insisting upon this point during the initial quarrel between the two men, and later the interpretations of their agreement furnish material for mild jokes. At the conclusion of the play Face, on questionable authority, dissolves the armistice, corporation, or alliance. Their contracts, of course, are parody. The three outlaws, pledged thus to their own charter, are interlopers in Lovewit's house during a season of plague. This isolation sets them off from the daily legal processes and grants them a modicum of immunity. Furthermore, this subterfuge does not have to stand under a direct force of outer stresses; at the end no constituted power can be summoned from London except, curiously enough, Lovewit's right of property. He allows Dol and Subtle, deprived of their loot, to go free and restores Face to his former position without any punishment because his is the greatest strength on the stage and happens, for accidental reasons, to favor the servant.

As the authority who resolves everything Lovewit shares affinities with Doctor Clement, but whereas the mad, merry magistrate fitted the right level for both plot and rationale in the original *Every Man in His Humour*, Lovewit's unexpected return to London creaks like a crane lowering a ponderous and desperate *deus ex machina*. He bears no warrant whatsoever except as owner of the house, and his judgments sound thoroughly whimsical. He appears a more prosperous version of the knaves, and his habits in discourse link him to them.

> I loue a teeming wit, as I loue my nourishment.
> 'Pray god he ha' not kept such open house,
> That he hath sold my hangings, and my bedding:
> I left him nothing else. If he haue eate 'hem,
> A plague o'the moath, say I. Sure he has got
> Some bawdy pictures, to call all this ging;
> The Frier, and the Nun; or the new *Motion*
> Of the Knights courser, couering the Parsons mare;
> The Boy of sixe yeere old, with the great thing:
> Or 't may be, he has the Fleas that runne at tilt,
> Vpon a table, or some Dog to daunce?   (V. i. 16–26)

This teeming wit dispenses punishments and rewards by passing upon all the deceivers and dupes. Lovewit's early return, when many citizens are absent and the usual affairs of city business are suspended, seems another effort to encase the action within a private niche. Face gets the uneasy last words, which confess that the resolution lacks the full range of edifying judiciousness it might have, although he insists that this break does not offend the rules of decorum. The plea does not convince logically; it merely insists mysteriously that the author has written and therefore is right.

This wobbly, nearly unresolved, presentation of authority does not exhaust the instances of weakness. Another contradiction threatens to overwhelm the flow of events before they attain a fifth act. Clothes and disguise loom as almost impenetrable. What lurks underneath surfaces changes momentarily. Except for his mountebank escapade and brief final impersonation, Volpone appeared an actor in one role, a great part and well executed but essentially limited in scope. Epicene, whose triumph as an actor may have demanded more histrionics, was necessarily restricted to a one-night stand. Dol, Subtle, and Face bow before no such limitations; the single change they are quite unable to effect is vaporizing base metals into gold. Otherwise, they improvise disguises and become whatever their clients yield to most susceptibly. Subtle plies each with his individual delusion: to Mammon he represents a devout holy man, to the Puritans a testy autocrat, always some variation on a wise father figure. Face, whose given name is Jeremy, sports a beard for the occasion and further serves as factotum and laboratory assistant, Lungs, for Mammon. Dol selects her parts as she chooses, and as the customer may demand, from prostitute to blue-stocking. Surly, the disgruntled but honest man, who once formed a chorus, now is reduced to a minor function and dons the costume of a Spanish captain; he belongs to an older order, the pretender with a single mask. These surface contortions glide more easily because the underlying personality assumes more complexity and because the people who witness them respond to varied stimuli.

Subtle's customers exhibit greater agility, within the style of presentation, than do those in any earlier comedy both for range of social types and as citizens bent on individual concerns. What links them together is their obsession with the treasures which magic will acquire for them. In consequence the dupes may imagine their own visions of grandeur all the while they consult Subtle. This freedom to be themselves induces an informality of behavior lacking in the first two great comedies. At the same time, though, this liberty joins them less coherently with the single pattern. The eighteenth-century theater, of course, played fast and loose with the scripts of Elizabethan drama. Because, as has been observed, Garrick did rearrange *The Alchemist* and puffed the minor character Drugger into one of his most celebrated performances, the flexibility indicates a difference. As a matter of fact, Garrick's script is not at all bad, quite acceptable within its own scope. Such a successful transference of emphasis is hardly thinkable for either *Volpone* or *Epicene*. Two figures, however, tower as incomparable inventions. On the surface their typical traits oppose them, but just beneath it they complement each other. In dramatic terms, moreover, they have the virtue of being solidly embedded within the rationale.

The others gamble on the philosophers' stone to win a private end or profit; both Mammon and the Puritans—Ananias and Tribulation Wholesome being in a sense one—aspire to nothing less than a conversion of the world. Mammon shamelessly admits that he seeks to ravage continents for his insatiable lusts. His daydreams swell into the most grandiose phantasies, appalling because every line criticizes the speaker: the greater the delicacy, the deeper the depravity.

Wee'll therefore goe with all, my girle, and liue
In a free state; where we will eate our mullets,
Sous'd in high-countrey wines, sup phesants egges,
And haue our cockles, boild in siluer shells,
Our shrimps to swim againe, as when they liu'd,
In a rare butter, made of dolphins milke,
Whose creame do's looke like opalls: and, with these
Delicate meats, set our selues high for pleasure,
And take vs downe againe, and then renew
Our youth, and strength, with drinking the *elixir*,
And so enioy a perpetuitie
Of life, and lust.   (IV. i. 155–66)

The Puritans, on the other hand, nastily anticipate subjecting civiliza-
tion to their views and drearily rejoice in the prospect of a mean
salvation. In spite of the gaudy religious rhetoric in which they vent
their disjointed Biblical images, they condone in themselves the worst
rationalizations, and by a false humility magnify their denials into
tyranny. If Mammon's honesty appalls one by its greediness, the
vengeful desires of the Puritans have the added taint of hypocrisy.
They command more cant than does Mammon, but the excited
temperament is identical:

                    ANA. Auoid *Sathan*,
Thou art not of the light. That ruffe of pride,
About thy neck, betrayes thee: 'and is the same
With that, which the vncleane birds, in *seuenty-seuen*,
Were seene to pranke it with, on diuers coasts.
Thou look'st like *Antichrist*, in that leud hat.
                                              (IV. vii. 50–55)

In Mammon's and Ananias' outpourings—and the shortest typical ones
have been quoted—the reflections dwell chiefly on surfaces and emphasize the physical, although their concern for the philosophers' stone
pretends to supraphysical transmutations. Mammon, honestly as he
confesses his immoderation, practices hypocrisy to the degree that he
imagines Subtle a holy man whose devotion will lead to unearthing
the stone, after which it will be surrendered to him. The Puritans deal
more openly with others because they recognize themselves as out--
laws, at least above or beyond the law of the land, and therefore they

willingly indulge in counterfeiting. Even with these, the most determined fanatics of all, Jonson preserves the trick of having them
fasten a last, idiosyncratic hold upon a reality in the midst of their
inordinate greed. While swollen with the prospect of treasure,
Ananias cannot forget his aversion to popish terms:

> Svb. And, then, the turning of this Lawyers pewter
> To plate, at *Christ-masse*— Ana. *Christ-tide*, I pray you.
>
> (III. ii. 42–43)

Mammon similarly keeps a firm grip over his own minimum gold
standard:

> Fac. Now preparing for proiection, sir.
> Your stuffe will b⟨e⟩'all chang'd shortly. Mam. Into gold?
> Fac. To gold, and siluer, sir. Mam. Siluer, I care not for.
>
> (IV. i. 2–4)

In these ways the usual rhetorical ingredients combine for new
characterizations. Mammon and the Puritans resemble neither the ineffectual little people of the humour comedies nor the readily victim-
ized clients, but those who by drives or positions have achieved an
amount of prestige in their areas of life. Although the quest for the
stone cannot succeed, their other schemes may. They loom as slightly
more sinister menaces than others encountered outside *Poetaster*. At
the end they share an identical debasement. Mammon, convinced his
own immoderation has lost him the stone, declares, "I will goe mount
a turnep-cart, and preach / The end o'the world, within these two
months." (V. v. 81–82) Shortly after these, his final words, he leaves
at the very moment when Tribulation and Ananias, not yet disabused,
rush on, expecting to rescue their base metals, which, they now
realize, will not be converted into gold. They shout, " 'Tis well, the
Saints shall not loose all yet. Goe, / And get some carts—" (V. v.
90–91) Nicely balanced as these two temperaments are, the fairly disjointed scramble of the action nearly buries them. Moreover, they
represent attitudes which challenge with genuine defiance the operative rationale of what has, up to this point, held the plays together.

When he worked the humours into a structure for comedy,
Jonson used his great ability for translating simplified psychological

quirks into their many physical manifestations. The old theory
equipped perfectly the new dramaturgy, but, as has been apparent, he
did not remain addicted to the concept, humours becoming self-love,
then false poetizing, then power, then immoderation, then sensuality.
However tangential the expression may have grown, beneath all of
them lay an understandable view of nature and of human nature. If it
advanced new expressions, it could always refer back to the basic
premise and thereby link with the original method. In *The Alchemist*
a different, and incompatible, standard shoulders aside the older ones.
The alchemical theory, while sharing a fondness for fours with the
humours, opposes them. A belief in the operation of the humours,
whatever other standards it entails, demands a recognition of the possible: an even mixture is good, an uneven one bad. Man possesses only
four; he cannot evolve for himself a quintessential humour. Alchemy,
creating water, fire, earth, and air into one, seeks a mystery beyond
human knowledge; its goals push toward what heretofore was counted
the impossible. The methodology of alchemy needs metamorphosis,
that of the humours growth. Humours arise within the individual; alchemy fixes upon an outside force, which, once controlled, transforms
any interior. No true alchemist can count nature immutable; all must
bow before a miraculous transformation. Mammon's explanation of the
properties of the stone defines the powers generally attributed it.

> MAM. 'Tis the secret
> Of nature, naturiz'd 'gainst all infections,
> Cures all diseases, comming of all causes,
> A month's griefe, in a day; a yeeres, in twelue:
> And, of what age soeuer, in a month.
> Past all the doses, of your drugging Doctors. (II. i. 63–68)

This claim, of course, is ridiculous, and Mammon is a fool. The ambition, however, links with the Faustian one of soaring beyond the possible, the magic of Daedalus, not the workmanship of Perdix. The late
medieval magician who prefigured twentieth-century man receives a
contemptuous rebuke:

> Or, he is the FAVSTVS,
> That casteth figures, and can coniure, cures
> Plague, piles, and poxe, by the *Ephemerides,*

And holds intelligence with all the bawdes,
And midwiues of three shires? (IV. vi. 46–50)

Nevertheless, once admitted, Faustus has a way of being unanswerable and ubiquitous.

If in all the earlier plays the pretenders and impostors have been satirized, the standards which checked them at each point have not demanded a laborious underscoring, thinly dramatized as some may have sounded. A universal reason operative within each man could not be gainsaid indefinitely; either one yielded to it or one perished. A fully constructed methodology was not required because a priori truths stood immutable, and short cuts around them never succeeded. The universe and man, macrocosm and microcosm, forbid a leap into the unexplorable. Here, however, Subtle occupies the scene as an arbitrator almost as strong as Cynthia. The courtiers, after all, envied her mastery, but her laws defied any breach longer than a momentary usurpation. One might argue that the more overreaching, the more puny and that Subtle in his lair, the most impossibly ambitious rogue of all, therefore needs no reprimand. This theory sounds pretty, and it should hold good, but the script scarcely bears it out.[8]

In the first place, Subtle wields an absolute dexterity in language permitted no other knave.[9] When Volpone acted the mountebank, his pleas sounded unlikely and, after all, they had as their immediate aim arousing one woman's curiosity. Subtle's spells spin more persuasive incantations. Also, no one effectively contradicts him. His chief critic, Surly, attacks principally by angry declamations which rant as furiously as do Subtle's and to less point. The spate of quotations reduces authorities to gibberish and misrepresents not only the alchemical tracts but Broughton, in Dol's parody, and the Bible, in the Puritans' zeal. This slandering of texts runs counter to respect for the word which these plays need, but no rebuttal topples it in dramatic terms. By these indirections reason itself falls under censure, and no one opposes himself to the anti-intellectual demonism. This objection may sound like naïve outrage, as though one insisted on evidence's being brought to bear against what rings patently false, but one has come to look for this very finality in Jonson to be handled with the greatest finesse. Its absence here might be dismissed from evaluations of the ultimate success or failure of *The Alchemist* itself, but any survey of his total development must note it. The lack of some criteria against which to measure the negatives does not stand alone as the single decline. In a more positive way a weakening has started.

Subject to however many abuses and ridicules, the eye remained the accepted medium of detecting deception. In a world as roundly sensible as Jonson's, it clearly had to be the sure instrument it was. Here, it no longer sees to its old tasks; the voice, rather, rises as an instrument of the oratory which later will dominate. The indistinct trustworthiness of Subtle's mumbo jumbo denies him respectability as a mere orator, but he escapes complete contempt. Everywhere, then, ambiguous forces move through the play, not to undercut and so cast its assumptions into a heightened relief but to undermine it and threaten both the story and the style. This indecisiveness may, nevertheless, help explain the marvels of the play; the vocabularies parade all their excesses because they can flow on their ways nearly divorced from the interacting personalities of the speakers; the effect of a newly perfect perpendicularity bolsters the plot. The characters, ultimately, need have no contact of any sort with each other; all their visions can be riveted on the same object, which, under Subtle's guidance, appears slippery as the stone itself, the embodiment of their own immediate desires. Lost in their phantasies, they require no eyes because they see nothing about them. The mean performances in the sequestered rooms soar upward toward an absolute principle which, if it exists anywhere, inhabits a Platonic firmament. Beguiled by their raptures, they can address each other without leaving their special spheres, for just as the projection itself is indefinable, so their own projections of it into their desires must be.

Perhaps one has been too much conditioned by the double pathos of Faustian man, from the simple fisherman who learns that "my wife, good Ilsabil, / Wills not as I'd have her will"[10] to the most refined delineation of aspiration:

> The greatest poverty is not to live
> In a physical world, to feel that one's desire
> Is too difficult to tell from despair.[11]

In grasping after mastery of the visible world, Faustus deals with an invisible one and so must lose both. Even when permitted a triumph, he institutes a strangely puny program of public works. One knows, of course, that the tenets of alchemy in this play and in experience have proved false. The very awareness, however, implies that the same sort of pseudo science still prevails and has swept all before it, that the crudest wishes of Drugger, Surly, or Dapper become mild in contrast with desires of their twentieth-century counterparts. Subtle's lies have affinities with the consequences which his modern heirs have unleashed. The comedy, thus, cannot be true because no adequate limits surround its assumptions either, a valid point, in its own period or, perhaps a sentimental complaint, for this age. It appears almost as though Jonson himself felt this inability to pull all implications of the play together because an unusual amount of camouflage, for him, disguises the loose parts and erects artificial bridges between them.

The setting itself in the deserted house makes graphic the isolation. Subtle, Dol, and Face partake of the atmosphere during a plague, insidious and hidden; when that clears they too will have to disperse. Yoking the cozeners and dupes in a town partially emptied by pestilence allies them with the abnormal, something which usual channels of business will not tolerate. The rough contract binding them furthers the impermanence of their partnership, footling from the outset. Lovewit's simple neighbors, too, express an awe before the decidedly exotic doings of which they have observed only the entrances and exits, descriptions which also divorce the alchemist from the everyday routines. Finally Subtle himself, to say nothing of Dol and Face, must remain an actor in a *décor* whose meanness mocks his pretenses to real accomplishments. If modern mountings of *Volpone* should beguile one with their luxury rooted in the poetry, *The Alchemist* profits from the incongruity between the ugly rooms and the promised riches. To this extent the enlargements upon time and place succeed, but, like the other aspects, beyond a certain point these defenses fall, and the shambles detract.

The trio unfortunately refuses to stay self-contained. The dupes must be dragged in from an outside, which impinges insistently. Illegal practices, such as Surly's recipes for cheating and the Puritans' decision that counterfeiting is legal, combine with Subtle's powers. Contemporary conjurers, charlatans who were apprehended and subsequently punished, are mentioned for comparisons. Of all superstitions ridiculed by Jonson, a belief in alchemy probably came closest to having a wide following among members of the audience. Nevertheless, while his subject became more concrete, his treatment of its ramifications became more amorphous. The follies castigated in *Volpone* and *Epicene*, if more remote, link with typical and enduring behavior. Because of these associations, although the activities do occur in a restricted area, one can view them as both self-contained and generally present. Should one wish to spin a moral that Subtle's and Dol's escape at the end compares with that of the Blatant Beast in the Sixth Book of *The Faerie Queene*, that pernicious lies will always flourish, the obvious reply says that nothing in the dialogue itself justifies this edifying interpretation. Perhaps comedy, perhaps great comedy, can be contrived from the merry pranks of that most fragile of all theatrical illusions, the likable rogue. If this sort of amusement can ever be pinned down to a general formulation, Jonson's tastes and predilections will render him the dramatist least qualified to succeed with it. Anyhow, for all his wiles and ingenuity, Subtle can hardly be called likable; indeed, no character in Jonson's plays is.

One other interpretation to defend the irresponsibility has been advanced: in *The Alchemist* Jonson struck his most mature note because he no longer forced an imposition of justice but merely depicted "realistically" the London citizens and their milieu.[12] Quite apart from the question of whether this glibness accompanies maturity, the fallacy of the rationalization soon appears. The one positive standard in the great comedies has been the negative pursuit to whatever end the consequences of an initiated scheme demanded. No compromise softened the material or the castigations which the subject made explicit. The full implications of any defined standard exploited the foibles ruthlessly. *Epicene* had to be carefully set off by Morose's padded house and the aloof language. In this play, as has been quite manifest, the control, while seemingly in operation, breaks down, however winningly, in its adherence to former views. The elusive failure is not just a deviation or a ruse but one which Jonson himself may have been only partially aware of, since he splashed about in this contradiction unconcernedly. The comic principle itself succumbs to the temptations which deluded alchemists. It resembles the fisherman's wife in the *Märchen* because, once an aggrandizement has started, it wills its power to equal god's until, like the description by Wallace Stevens, its enslaved imagination denies the physical world. Desire and despair accompany each other and lead precisely to the condition in which Dürer depicted melancholia. Comedy has abandoned the one world it can know to seek the one it dare not aspire to. At least, for twentieth-century man and his sciences this truism holds good, and Jonson stood, in this respect, at the very beginning of the modern era.

Finally, one must reckon with the principles and implications of alchemy as the progenitor of modern science, not a subject to approach lightly.[13] In spite of multiple abuses by false practitioners, its aspirations leap beyond the limits of Elizabethan comedy.[14] The other standards posited a ceiling; they grew from society and society could confine them. After the charlatans passed their zenith, a decline had to finish the trajectory. Even Sejanus could not escape Fortune's wheel. If the alchemist remains true to himself and his books, he braves all gods and taboos as a man armed with codified secrets of nature to batter down any mountain or unlock all doors. The other pretenders vainly assault a civil order; the alchemist-scientist challenges the cosmos itself, a bravura feat which comedy can scarcely contain. In contemplating the quaintness of the Elizabethan stage, one overlooks the canopy of the heavens above, which reminded contemporary audiences that immutable laws mocked ambitious heroes who seek too much. One of the few who might threaten the order was the alchemist. Being wise after the fact, later audiences assure themselves that the axioms and postulates which these men put forth held no seeds of fulfillment, but their heirs, the chemists and physicists, make tame the most unlikely medieval boasts. Only in the twentieth century is the time ripe for a comedy of pure science, perhaps the basis for the Intellectual Comedy Valéry wanted to surpass Dante and Balzac.[15] Were any to appear it would be so terrifying that no one incapable of appreciating Jonson could grasp its unnatural nature. In his age with his predispositions Jonson could not have composed one, but his shortcomings must still point the way: the subject must attack science, a method, not miracles, mystification.

In terms of his own work Jonson stood again at a crossroads; one development had achieved its maximum, and a break had to be risked. Once before he had occupied this position; once before he had chosen to do a tragedy from which he had emerged into a new understanding of comedy. It seems doubtful whether any intuition so uncomplicated motivated him, but it cannot be quite accidental that his two tragedies occupy almost identical spots in his career. After these remote speculations and before turning to *Catiline*, one should review what will remain a major, if not irreproachable, work.

The Alchemist, then, embodies these positive merits, virtues so genuine that few other comedies in English, or any language, can approach it. The structure observes all the laws of genre without having to apologize for any lapses. Moreover, this serving the rules hastens instead of impeding the general progression of episodes. The language moves with a firmness compounded largely from technical terms whose very association and arrangement suggest whole atmospheres and worlds, probable or improbable, which require no prodding by digressions. The characters, varied as they are, speak in one identical manner, but because of the peculiarity of their vision, this mode can, on one level, be taken as realistic while it soars quite beyond the limits of literal subservience. Subtle, for an alchemist, emerges as a figure of nearly impeccable proportions, one who puts his unbelieving faith in the wrong theory. His dupes follow him like the obedient sheep they are. In the main the deviation from the comic intent cuts into the rationale obliquely; at first glance the resolution merely rewards and punishes according to the most gentle reproaches. The whole is a triumph of stylizing behavior into a series of mechanical responses which have, except for alchemy, no consequences beyond themselves and thus are comic. If any ulterior assumptions prove at variance with this general scheme, that nature itself so far has balked at a thorough ordering—the tragedy of Faustian man from the Renaissance to the twentieth century—this discrepancy breaks open only after a probing which may push too far Jonson's reliable consistency. Without insistently pointing at the mended frame from which these surprises spring, one may enjoy the pyrotechnical wizardry of the language:

> Mam. I will haue all my beds, blowne vp; not stuft:
> Downe is too hard. And then, mine oual roome,
> Fill'd with such pictures, as Tiberivs tooke
> From Elephantis: and dull Aretine
> But coldly imitated. Then, my glasses,
> Cut in more subtill angles, to disperse,
> And multiply the figures, as I walke
> Naked betweene my *succubae*. My mists
> I'le haue of perfume, vapor'd 'bout the roome,
> To loose our selues in; and my baths, like pits
> To fall into. . . .   (II. ii. 41–51)

On and on the fabulous intoxication spreads. *The Alchemist* stands in achievement as worthy of a place almost beside *Volpone*, and that means a rank in pure comedy nearly without competition except from works by its own author.

CHAPTER IX

Prodigious Rhetoricke

Jonson may have learned slowly, but he retained everything. Initially incapable of gauging public reactions, he anticipated, after its theatrical failure, that *Catiline* might not please purchasers of the quarto. He defiantly appended two prefaces: one to the "Reader in ordinairie" and the other to the "Reader extraordinary." (V, p. 432) The former, in the majority, presumably will damn the play, but the latter minority will respond to its fine qualities. This dividing of readers into two camps may call to mind the other Johnson. His verdict, under different circumstances, voices the appropriate reaction to this hauteur: "I rejoice to concur with the common reader."[1] Years have not enhanced the reputation of *Catiline*, which T. S. Eliot has labeled with accustomed insight a "dreary Pyrrhic victory of tragedy."[2] After experiencing its juggernaut slowness, one feels that this estimation might err a trifle on the side of generosity. Pyrrhic as were the costs of battle, the Roman general, nevertheless, enjoyed a technical triumph.

For his tragic theme Jonson turned back again to a classical setting, the history of Catiline's conspiracy against Rome complemented by Cicero's defense of the city. His respect for sources betrayed him, although as usual he adapted and shaped these to comply with his immediate purposes. He may too uncritically have borrowed from Cicero's hysterically selfish and Sallust's malicious attack against Catiline. The effort to attain a classical unity breaks down, although more devices than in *Sejanus* bolster the gesturing at one. Sylla's ghost croaks the dire prologue as vindictively as does Envy before *Poetaster*. After every act a chorus tacks on reflections appropriately vapid for this vestigial appendage. The action, such as it is, starts with Catiline's declamatory resolution, an echo of Sylla, to beat down the Roman government from which he was rejected in the elections. After this soliloquy, like one by the outmoded Machiavellian villain, the conspirators seek their leader. They establish their individual temperaments and the attitudes they adopt toward the revolutionary movement. The general atmosphere emits a gloomy despair in contrast with the gusto which all parties of *Sejanus* brought to their illegal vocations. As *Sejanus* had the calculating Livia, so *Catiline* has Fulvia, and several other women, all siding with the rebels.

The second act starts with their discussion of politics and sex, and this time the women themselves are by far the more aggressive. One of Catiline's followers, Curius, loves Fulvia, but their affair consists mostly of quarrels. Fulvia cannot admire Curius while he remains a failure, which at the moment he is, and for peculiarly feminine hunches she cannot put any trust in the ultimate success of the uprising. So much ends the second act, with the inevitably perplexed chorus. The third introduces Cicero, somewhat less strikingly, surrounded by advisers. The members of the government pledge Cicero less lively loyalty than Catiline's outlaws promise him. Except for Cato, Cicero alone seems determined to save Rome, whose increasingly precarious position another scene with the conspirators, who continue making their elaborate plans, emphasizes. This third act, after the comparatively brief first and second, runs to unconscionable lengths. Fulvia and Curius from mixed motives desert to Cicero and reveal what they know of the insurrectionists' plans. On the other hand, Caesar of the government traffics with Catiline in a less co-operative, if more efficient, manner.³ The act closes on the implication that both sides have girded themselves and are waiting for the gong.

Because history supplied no break at this point, neither does the play.⁴ The chorus speaks; the Allobroges, partisans of whichever party will settle their grievances against Rome, shift from Catiline to Cicero. The scene moves to the Senate and Cicero asks in blank verse what in Latin is prose: "Whither at length wilt thou abuse our patience?" (IV. 175) The rhetorical question is prophetic. Nearly three hundred lines of a rambling monologue patched out from the orations *In Catilinam* test an audience's tolerance. This tirade forces Catiline's hand, and he leaves the city. At last, after more choruses and debates, the two groups draw together for some kind of conflict. With sporadic reports of battles, the play ends in more parleyings: Catiline is dead, Rome safe, the play finished, and Cicero still talking. The intention of the structure indicates an aspiration toward *Sejanus*, but in the first tragedy the several stalking factions confronted each other. Here two sides must, in general, be kept apart, and their common ambition, control of Rome, except for the ghostly Prologue, cannot be dramatized at all.

Jonson had decided exactly what a tragedy ought to be and what effects he intended to stress when he composed one. The brief fragment *Mortimer* (VII, pp. 58–62) obeys the same principles, although the first three acts, in the arguments, look more promising. Not only the sketchy outlines but also the language of *Catiline* have greater affinities with *Sejanus* than does either of these with any of the comedies. Nevertheless, because of the changing concepts which permeate the plays at this time the resemblance does slight credit to the second. Almost a stated theme of *Sejanus* took the recurring image of a giant or demigod supporting with his shoulders the world or comparable bulk. In Jonson this configuration appears nowhere else except here. At the opening Catiline invokes the god Atlas as a proper emblem for his own strength to bear the greatness and reputation of the Empire. Afterwards the image rises less pervasively, although allusions to giants mark every act and related passages invoke a sense of the oversized. A personified invocation of Slaughter as a Colossus materializes in:

CET. Slaughter bestrid the streets, and stretch'd
himselfe
To seeme more huge; whilst to his stayned thighes
The gore he drew flow'd vp: and carryed downe
Whole heaps of limmes, and bodies, through his arch.
No age was spar'd, no sexe. (I. 235-39)

The "flow'd vp: and carryed downe" repeats the related major theme of *Sejanus*, including the many changes wrought on that *locus classicus* for the figure, the Horatian "sublimi feriam sidera vertice."[5] On the whole, however, numerically or dramatically, reference to giants and rising is much slighter than in *Sejanus*, and appropriately so. The motivation describes ambitions, and the figures of speech cling to them, but the manifestations of immoderate desires differ.

The scheme to incorporate one major aspect of *Sejanus* into *Catiline* lost out; other transplantings flourish no more vigorously. Considering the older elements first will limit what otherwise might resemble an irresolute maze. Sejanus mounted higher to establish himself as the supreme power in the Roman hierarchy; he had to knock down obstacles. Cicero and Catiline, in contrast, command almost equal positions and spar to dominate the Roman Republic; in several senses *Catiline* is a more horizontal play than *Sejanus*. Tragedy, if the emphasis does not depict the achievements of greatness—the psychology of rising to which all is subordinated and which culminates in an inevitable fall—then usually traces one man's flight from the law or from gangsters. In this latter type, action frequently must be indirect, and *Catiline*, as has been seen, often becomes devious when it should be forthright. The match between the two contestants looks like feints of men fitfully unsure of themselves and surely uncertain of each other. This kind of mutual insecurity has produced some sardonic works, but Jonson does not point up this grimness. Were the man who flees not wholly good or bad and were the pursuing agents equivocal in their intentions, as in Kafka, the terror of chase could incorporate extensive enigmas. *Catiline* separates the criminals and the honest ruthlessly.

Sejanus and Tiberius to an undetermined extent shared one another's confidence. Members of the opposition did stand on the side to mutter unhappily, and at the end the Roman populace partook of its rulers' corruption. The struggle of the auxiliary forces never impaired the vision of the individual combatants. The nature of connections between a government and its people picked up the implications behind *Cynthia's Revels*, that the two areas interacted largely by sympathetic vibrations, the good or the bad sifting down from above. Here, however, all the tensions evolve out of two ideologies for which Cicero and Catiline serve as the designated leaders; their personal ambitions must share a place with considerations for the factions, good or bad, which they head. Perhaps drama, perhaps tragedy, can absorb this extraneous matter, but it seeks an essentially different treatment and, to remain engrossing in itself, propaganda less unilateral.

In *Sejanus* the progression of portents developed along definite lines. The series culminated in the fifth act when men outdid beasts. Here, reported signs burst forth early in the first act: the blazing torch which the conspirators observe over the capitol becomes their pillar of fire to symbolize their destructive bent. Indeed, before the start, Sylla's ghost sets the tone.

> What all the seuerall ills, that visite earth,
> (Brought forth by night, with a sinister birth)
> Plagues, famine, fire could not reach vnto,
> The sword, nor surfets; let thy furie doe. . . .   (I. 49–52)

This malediction establishes the direction of the contentious element both external and internal. Unhappily, after the bold announcement little follows; neither portents nor passions gather strength. They remain inert possibilities as do many other elements of *Catiline*.

Beginning with *Sejanus* and through the great comedies Jonson put animals through specific paces for different effects. Here, again, the purpose often falters or swings unhappily close to a parody of itself. Many of the animal images show domesticated species, those either spurred or yoked: the urging of activity on the lazy or the final subjugation of the already tamed. When animals run, fear drives them. Serpents or reptiles, the emblems of *Poetaster*, slither listlessly or crawl "with the same tortoyse speed." (I. 220) Strangely enough, only once does an animal rear with any bravery: a lion, which, as part of a detailed mosaic, adds a valuable courage. The anomaly is that this nobility describes the last doomed thrust of Catiline before he falls in battle. Nominally the villain of the piece, he alone exudes a kind of glory. Instead of becoming a mythical chimera, the last animal image turns into the one figure with exalted connotations. At least, the messenger who reports the episode speaks in neutral tones so that the incidental praise, such as "arm'd with a glorie, high as his despaire" (V. 671), hardly condemns his rebellion, however unlawful, as a thoroughly base deed. Presumably Catiline's defeat saves Rome from enslavement and plunder, but that deliverance in either language or action arouses no notable rejoicing.

The same lethargy dominates almost everywhere. Whatever the weary paces it has been put through, a soaring desire offers dramatically more promise than a cat and mouse game in which the mouse never emerges from its hole and the cat hisses without stalking. Lacking heights of eminence, then, the impact of the tragic consequences on the world must be geographical. Catiline and his gang have no boyish belief in power for its own golden sake. The Rome of *Catiline* is less hierarchical than empirical; with their positions the rebels want control of the gardens, villas, money, and provinces. Nor do they fall victim to the Marlovian drives which reheat their melancholia by reiterating names of distant places.[6] The most remote colony will bring in revenues. (The opening chorus chants a dirge on the theme of the dangers of the extended frontiers.) In *Sejanus* Tiberius got as far as Capri, whose vices the opponents did not begrudge him. The Empire played a slight part in the destiny of the Roman Senate and inhabitants. In *Catiline* the luxuriant Capri symbolizes precisely what world control bestows. With the appearance of the Allobroges from "beyond the *Alpes*" (IV. 6), a synthetic fusion joins the outposts with the dramatis personae. When Sejanus fell, Rome principally felt the shock, but the world must rock to the crash of Catiline. A warning implies that the threat to the safety of the mother city will disturb the zenith itself. Despite these exigencies of language and situation, the flat landscape does not enliven the flagging contest.

Another key to the differences between the two tragedies, and probably a deliberate deviation, lies in the subtitles. *Sejanus His Fall* carries metaphoric implications which all five acts thoroughly exploited; the full title of the second is *Catiline His Conspiracy*. Every-body delivers himself of long musings about what he will do, why he will do what he will do, his justification for what he will do, and the benefits of his deed, after it will have been done. These vaunted creeds amply convince one of the conspiracy, but the failures to obey them receive no explanation. The preoccupations with impersonal plotting rob the characters of credible motivation and throw psychological traits out in favor of the limply sterile debates about the body politic, which seldom looks engaging. Moreover, Cicero comes off little better than do the outlaws.

These five areas, which interlock with each other, indicate how seriously this play bogs down in the familiar, usually strong, configura-tions: its undefined conflict between two men, a loose incorporation of other elements in the story, the sloppy treatment of metaphoric lan-guage, the displacement in the rationale of the drive to power by a profit motive, and the irresolute declamations. These negatives cannot be dismissed as parts of the structure which simply get out of hand. They serve what must be taken for dramatic values: the recurrent theme that resolve is transformed into inactivity. In Chekhov frustrated suffering betokens effectively its own brand of pathos, but not in Jonson. The Prologue sounds the keynote to almost all the qualities, good or bad, planned or accidental, in *Catiline*. Sylla's ghost addresses an abstract Rome: "What sleepe is this doth seize thee, so like death, / And is not it?" (I. 9–10) This painful hibernation implies that the sleep which overtook the gods in *Sejanus* now grips the entire population. The actual historical sources provided scant material, Cicero notwith-standing, to make Rome a beehive of effective plotting; the burden of *In Catilinam* advances tangential evidence at best. Sleep and indiffer-ence become the most common charges which both Catiline and Cicero, as political men, hurl against their parties. Cethegus, likewise, berates the conspirators because of their proneness to slumber. In this vacuum which the indirections make inevitable, the ineffectual en-thusiasts resemble cheerleaders whipping themselves into a frenzy before a captive crowd which does not understand the strategy of the match it watches. If the energetic accuse their supporters of ennui, they themselves feel frequently melted away to a strengthless zero.

The condition grows from waiting for something to happen and, simultaneously, explains why little accomplishment distinguishes either side: failure, as usual, breeds failure. Catiline himself recognizes the onus which his nobility and inherited dignity impose; as one of the patricians he experiences a guilty pain at the discrepancy between his former status and his present occupation. "I then express'd my zeale / Vnto the glorie; now, the neede enflames me. . . ." (I. 340–41) He drives himself constantly against the anxiety that the accepted realities in which he places his trust will turn out to be nothing:

> CAT. How, friends!
> Thinke you, that I would bid you, graspe the winde?
> Or call you to th'embracing of a cloud?
> Put your knowne valures on so deare a businesse,
> And haue no other second then the danger,
> Nor other gyrlond then the losse? (I. 429–34)

Catiline's cry, modulated through a series of set responses by the literal and figurative contexts, is quite correct: "To what a shaddow, am I melted!" (III. 165) Sejanus, Macro, and Tiberius, however appalling their vices and treachery, at least behaved as though they believed in, frequently relished, their mischief. No one in *Catiline*, stymied as all are, speaks as though he believed very deeply in the efficacy of undertaking any enterprise. After a gory diatribe predicting Rome's destruction in a holocaust of frenzy and fire, the sensible observation dampens it, "But he, and we, and all are idle still." (I. 282) Part of this lassitude may be blamed on the total disappearance of the psychology of the humours with a concurrent lack of any substitutes to implant and explain the action.

As long as desires could, like raging elements, pour out of individuals, a persuasive intensity might lurk behind their most trivial gestures. No basic point of view operative for *Catiline* replaces them. Instead, the natural forces, which formerly were equated with humours, shrink to literal sources of external havoc, although sometimes, it is optimistically implied, they parallel powers released by the conspirators. The monsters of *Sejanus* predicted through abnormalities in nature the ruin of men; here man, almost like a pied piper, leads a tamed nature, when, indeed, he does not destroy it. Furthermore, before *The Alchemist* nature in every sense presided as an ultimate judge of all violence and as a standard of every ethic. No such position for it can be vouchsafed here; nature, in one sense, has shifted from a creative force to an inert backdrop; it lies flat to be exploited by any prowess. Where there exists no standard of external nature, nor of internal man, nor any consistent interplay between the two, a drama of the Renaissance can scarcely survive. This generalization does not imply that a playwright ought to forge a *Weltanschauung* for its own sake and then dramatize it. Such an approach fritters itself away in the dullest plays because disembodied ideas spout forth language pumped from behind a curtain and directed to no immediate audience. On the other hand, if the writer does not take over a moderately integrated order, the end result wastes away into disjointed fulminations unless, of course, the melodramatics gallop at a speed which beguiles one into mistaking horseplay for cosmic meaning. Jonson, almost congenitally, was incapable of sketchy razzle-dazzle, four-man armies, hobbyhorses, and sesquipedalian words. In *Catiline* the rickety props and supports might be overlooked, nevertheless, if the surface itself did not betray chinks. The curious indirections twist nearly every affirmation into a puzzle.

If the talk of the conspirators and Cicero comes from no assignable motivation, no immediate end directs it. When the climax occurs, it pops with a little fizzle which, true, kills off the protagonist and saves Rome. Because Cicero has named these two goals, an illusion of completeness accompanies the denouement. The two feats have no particular significance dramatically or, since they are not shown on the stage, as spectacle. The battle and deliverance could have happened at any point and been almost as appropriate. The first and second acts hold out a slight promise that something may emerge from all the fretting, but the third starts to bog down, and in the fourth all collapses. The dreariness of Cicero's orations on the stage staggers description. Whatever their merits may be in Latin, as vehicles of a human expression in English they huff and puff without yielding any insight into Cicero's hysteria, Catiline's inactivity, the theatrical context itself, or the civic situation. What Jonson was thinking of when he undertook this exercise perplexes one. Perhaps it is most charitable to write it off as part of a manneristic taste for bizarre bibelots which display old artifacts in new settings. Taking all these faults, granting the long translations and the choruses, one might respond more generously were there not an inherent division of loyalty, as though the mind of the dramatist in contriving the characters functioned almost wholly against its deeper sentiments. Not only the action but the playwright's mind, too, seems to have confronted a checkmate.

In the humour comedies and the great comedies, as well as *Sejanus,* almost everyone is appalling. Goodness, when introduced, flexes its righteous muscles gymnastically, and no one can doubt the intention of the virtue portrayed, although the persuasion may have to rest on a stated faith. Here the moral judgments fall in place less precisely. This attitude could signal an advance toward a novel presentation, granted that the actual circumstances imply little which this tendency might achieve. Catiline's traits, as already touched upon, show him a familiar character, the man of one idea who will push himself to any extreme in obedience to his passion. Accompanying this willing of one evil thing, or, at least, of trying to, goes a wistfulness, a tendency to stand off and regard himself with detachment. The habit engenders a surreptitious appeal especially because at such moments the justification for his bitterness directs attention to the cause (and thus the mixed consequences) of his becoming a criminal. This complication, introducing a human complexity, adds a sort of pathos which in terms of the structure must be out of place but which, nevertheless, cannot be quite ignored. A moderately appealing dedication to evil can blend into a tragedy of secondary status, but not one with pretensions of purity and one where the adversary is, or is meant to be, a man of unimpeachable virtue.

Cicero must be rejected as a complete enigma. The fall belongs to Catiline, who, granted his role, might make a proper foil of weakness against Cicero's strength. One assumes that the lawyer should appear the able, upright man. Anyone who favors the honor of public-spirited devotion must applaud the causes which Cicero champions. Moreover, in his preface Jonson praises the oration: *"Would I had deseru'd but halfe so well of it in translation, as that ought to deserue of you [readers] in iudgment, if you haue any."* (V, p. 432) Finally, looking still further from the immediate genesis of the work, one knows that Cicero's reputation dominated the rhetoricians of Renaissance Europe.[7] In light of this evidence, it becomes more surprising that Cicero emerges not just weakly, not just hesitantly, not just apologetically, but badly. Part of the indirection probably derives from Cicero's filling a responsible position which he was not born to occupy and which he won by oratory. Before his betters he sounds unsure of himself, and part of the deference must be deliberate. The constant protestations of unworthiness, which Cato laconically denies, might function to make him a less deified adversary for Catiline than is Tiberius for Sejanus. Unfortunately, when Cicero does exhibit resolution, it inclines one to believe the accuracy of the self-deprecations.

Because any decision of Cicero's rests on Catiline's striking first, his is the weaker position. He can only conjecture about Catiline or himself. Declamations by speakers' praising their own powers never carry much conviction in Jonson's plays. Laudatory passages not bound by irony always trail abstract fringes. The orator, master of the unreliable voice, has invariably been a charlatan, rogue, or self-deluded apostle. Moreover, the sniveling sort of self-love intruding into Cicero's rhetoric lacks the requisite modulation. Other characters find the loquaciousness wearying and criticize it sharply: "that talker, CICERO" (II. 108); or

> Why should he presume
> To be more learned, or more eloquent,
> Then the nobilitie? (II. 123–25)

again

> And, we must glorifie,
> A mushrome? one of yesterday? a fine speaker?
> 'Cause he has suck'd at *Athens?* and aduance him,
> To our owne losse? No, FVLVIA. There are they
> Can speak *greeke* too, if need were. (II. 135–39)

Sempronia, a woman priding herself upon her political and oratorical acumen, has all these lines. Her bitterness may sound merely like jealous aspersions cast upon Cicero by an outsider. Nevertheless, she possesses more knowledge than do the deluded women in the comedies, and her own prowess makes oratory an art which not only Cicero can master. Her contempt, moreover, hits the mark with the quips whose scorn was once reserved to dismiss the upstart courtiers. It is Cicero who, while listing his credentials, rambles onward in repetitious phrases, resembling nothing so much as a fool stumbling hither and yon about a point which everybody else has caught long before.

> I haue no vrnes; no dustie moniments;
> No broken images of ancestors,
> Wanting an eare, or nose; no forged tables
> Of long descents; to boast false honors from:
> Or be my vnder-takers to your trust.
> But a new man (as I am stil'd in *Rome*)
> Whom you haue dignified; and more, in whom
> Yo'haue cut a way, and left it ope for vertue
> Hereafter, to that place. . . .   (III. 14–22)

In the middle of his most impassioned declamations the detractors mutter against the emptiness of the speeches. The effect of the sarcasm does not ennoble Cicero's fight against traitors but highlights the weakness of his own arguments. In *Sejanus* the opponents of corruption had such lines.

What makes the problem of how to regard Cicero's addiction to language more disquieting is the lack of any effective force to counterbalance his enemies' ridicule. Cato, his principal backer, shoots out curt praises which resemble a reluctant fishwife's and barely escape being ludicrously rude. Cicero, however, come what will, never stops talking and, in contrast with Cato, draws more attention to himself. His affliction, of course, is the stream of humour without the label and without the saving triviality. The conspirators, Sempronia included, try at some point to be silent.

> AVR. You say,
> Women are greatest talkers. SEM. We ha' done;
> And are now fit for action.   (III. 679–81)

Catiline himself reinforces Sempronia's charges with more point just before and after the fourth act oration: "A boasting, insolent tongueman" (IV. 161), and

> CATI. If an oration, or high language, *Fathers*,
> Could make me guiltie, here is one, hath done it:
> H'has stroue to emulate this mornings thunder,
> With his prodigious rhetoricke. But I hope,
> This *Senate* is more graue, then to giue credit
> Rashly to all he vomits. . . .   (IV. 462–67)

As if this censure were not enough, Jonson, obedient to his sources, had to have Cicero rely on petty disguises, which, such as the armor worn under his clothes, make his hinting at shapeless dangers look more prissy.

Catiline is potentially a criminal traitor and Cicero a detective bent on forestalling violence. Almost inherently in the nature of the arrangement Cicero must resort to trickery, and Catiline, granted his conditioned nobility, has to resent impatiently any subterfuges. This configuration unhappily necessitates at least nodding toward disguise and chicanery with approval. The aspirations of the rebels fret against their enforced idleness. Catiline yearns for honest expressions as preferable to his dissemblings, no matter the price he might pay ultimately:

> CATI. I grow mad at my patience.
> It is a visor that hath poison'd me.
> Would it had burnt me vp, and I died inward:
> My heart first turn'd to ashes.   (III. 170–73)

Fulvia, as well, makes a declaration which, in light of the treatment accorded deceptive cosmetics, rings with unaccustomed crispness:

> I loue valour
> Better, then any lady loues her face,
> Or dressing: then my selfe do's.   (II. 338–40)

At the climax when a liberated Catiline breaks forth he fuses appearance and beliefs: "His count'nance was a ciuill warre it selfe." (V. 644) In contrast with the rebels, Cicero pretends. He must procrastinate and win by his own inflated rhetoric, which frequently gets out of hand. For example, his interview with Fulvia, when she informs on Catiline, puzzles one. What effects does it produce? The feigned shock cannot be pardoned as a clumsy effort to stir up an audience's horror indirectly. When a group has just drunk a pledge in blood on the stage, little more nausea will be produced by mere outraged expressions. Moreover, Cicero all along has been cognizant of plotting, so his quivering anger does not carry conviction as sudden surprise unless he is more naïve than other passages indicate. To quote a snippet of his amazement would serve no purpose because it gains chiefly through its inordinate length, which for sheer calculation resembles the enticements of Mosca or Subtle before their most willing clients. Perhaps one must assume that, like an educated cousin of Juniper's, he enjoys hearing his own words. The trouble with any of these assumptions is that his listener is Fulvia, an intensely practical Roman who shares none of his illusions. She puts no faith in a dedicated or disinterested patriotism from which she cannot profit. When the vertigo of speech turns to praise her in the very terms which have before been reserved for the good man in plays, patrons in dedications, royalty in masques, and, indeed, the unstained immortality of Virgil's epic, one cries out for the conscious undercutting of satire. None seems intentional in the ponderous encomium, although Cicero later expresses a contempt for her.

> Here is a lady, that hath got the start,
> In pietie, of vs all; and, for whose vertue,
> I could almost turne louer, againe: but that
> TERENTIA would be iealous. What an honor
> Hath shee atchieued to her selfe! What voices,
> Titles, and loud applauses will pursue her,
> Through euery street! What windores will be fill'd,
> To shoot eyes at her! What enuy, and griefe in matrons,
> They are not shee! when this her act shall seeme
> Worthier a chariot, then if POMPEY came,
> With *Asia* chain'd! All this is, while shee liues.
> But dead, her very name will be a statue!
> Not wrought for time, but rooted in the minds
> Of all posteritie: when brasse, and marble,
> I, and the *Capitol* it selfe is dust!   (III. 341–55)

Suppose, however, Cicero does act this grandiloquence for its private ironies, the passage, merely a culmination of one long part which leads into another, would be a nightmare for any actress portraying Fulvia, unless she were Hermione Gingold, who might point up the parody it deserves. Were Fulvia, who obviously does not believe one rumble of all this thunder, to decide merely to stand and listen without comprehending, this ruse would not solve the next problem, which should be set as the final examination for all actresses' ability. At the end Fulvia, the hard-bitten, must say something, and the line has a macabre fascination: "Your honor thinks too highly of me." (III. 356) One would be hard pressed to cite a more gauche understatement in a drama.

On the other hand, Fulvia alone in her sinister dialogue with Curius during the second act achieves the mocking directness which distinguishes almost all *Sejanus*. The two are quarreling (and this is the same woman who soon stands meekly before Cicero).

> Cvr. Nay, then I must stop your fury, I see; and pluck
> The tragick visor off. Come, lady Cypris,
> Know your owne vertues, quickly. Ile not be
> Put to the wooing of you thus, a-fresh,
> At euery turne, for all the Venvs in you.
> Yeeld, and be pliant; or by Pollvx— How now?
> Will Lais turne a Lvcrece? Fvl. No, but by Castor,
> Hold off your rauishers hands, I pierce your heart, else.
> Ile not be put to kill my selfe, as shee did,
> For you, sweet Tarqvine.   (II. 277–86)

Since *Epicene* the women have gained in force and here sound wonderfully convincing with their discourses upon sex, politics, intrigue, and cosmetics. Their portraits, however, are Jonson's and not directly drawn from sources, except for a few hints. This precision makes impossible a more charitable reading of the other, infinitely longer, adaptations.

Jonson, then, chose the interpretation, apparently standard for the age, that in his orations Cicero gave a true account of both his own activities and Catiline's. That he intended any inconsistencies in his presentation may be doubted, but fidelity to unworthy historians in part betrayed him. Even more damaging, his inability to quite believe in Cicero, in spite of protestations, must make the result vexingly contradictory. The effect of the play relies wholly on the triumph of rhetoric, but rhetoric, by its very definition here, cannot yield such an overwhelming victory. The weapons of Cicero are ineffectual; the thrusts of his detractors strike home. Were Cicero allowed to show himself as a man essentially right but pledged to an ambiguous cause, then a play of conflicting tension based upon its inherent weaknesses, such as *Epicene*, might result. This pulling together of opposites lay beyond Jonson's abilities when the split had become fundamental. Furthermore, Cicero's whole character apparently puzzled Jonson, whose respect for royalty and authority may have driven him to demand better authority and so, in the process, express a censure of careless royalty, but until that point a noble pedigree consistently argued a supposedly elevated personality. The self-made Cicero, although nominally the hero, engages one less favorably than do aspects of Catiline. The new man matches his rhetoric, a poor ally at best, against Catiline's ancestry. Which of the two men is actually the better need not be questioned; what matters is that between a hero without credentials and a villain with them, the roughnesses of both portrayals tear the fabric.

If during this discussion it has been necessary to draw upon more conjectures about Jonson's personal predilections than one ordinarily wishes to borrow from biographical guesses, the failure of the play must be blamed. Whereas up to the present the adequacy of the scripts themselves in isolation or set side by side allowed their author to remain somewhat anonymous, here, where nothing in the text can illuminate or justify the shortcomings, one must turn to the next immediate cause of possible failure. The sources themselves have helped to explain part of the difficulties, although not inconceivably a satisfactory tragedy of some sort might be composed about Catiline, if Cicero proves nearly hopeless as a dramatic figure. The trouble, though, lies farther back; it is the author himself. This is not to say that Jonson had suppressed sympathies with Catiline. No other playwright of the Renaissance thought less restrictedly in terms of character even at a time when that concept had considerably less importance than it usurped in theatrical and critical vocabularies during the nineteenth and twentieth centuries. Where he did fall short was in assigning a harmonious group of motives to individuals who had to give the illusion of showing an integrated progression of growth or disintegration, especially when this sentimental development infringed upon standards previously sacrosanct for satire.

Keeping *Catiline* in a fair perspective makes heavy demands upon any reader, and it seems unlikely that many audiences will see it staged. One may, of course, project a modern political implication back into it.[8] This expedient instills a certain unhistorical, and unhistrionic, immediacy into it. To make the intent a plea for democracy—the triumph of Cicero, a common man undistinguished by birth—ignores the undercurrents which detract from this easy moral. To be judicious in the evaluations imposes a burden because the few well-realized sections contrast with the imperfect ones. Finally, it predicts the dotages, and looking forward to a decline never opens charming vistas. Fortunately, *Bartholomew Fair* rather gloriously intervenes.

CHAPTER X

Adam, Flesh, and Blood

Bartholomew Fair could not be better. Elements formerly restrained by a nervous insecurity follow an easy course, and standards once squeamishly championed tolerantly yield to being parodied.[1] In its own terms it lies beyond criticism, one of those works which, granted the goals, realize perfectly their inherent implications. It has attributes of an *Alterswerk*, although Jonson wrote it in 1614 when comparatively young. An atmosphere of mellow discovery prevails; an accomplished master suddenly occupies himself with a form and subject which have not before interested him. The novelties, graced by the sure touches, combine into a product eccentric, unclassifiable, private, and, nevertheless, wonderful, although for literary history it becomes a side eddy, a dead end, a culmination, or a last fling. While never pretty or smooth, its own vitality, a necessary part of the very aesthetic impulse which gave it life, overwhelms academic objections as timid or impertinent. *Bartholomew Fair* stands alone in English literature, perhaps in world literature, and is purely Jonsonian. One can, nevertheless, discern how it combines, in reversed form, three of the more striking aspects of the preceding comedies. Instead of being decoyed by a cadaverous Volpone on his bed, the Bartholomew birds seek the roast pig sold at Ursula's stall; not the idle London wits' carefully phrased prose but the tradesmen's extravagant exclamations swell the dialogue; replacing the learnedly exotic vocabulary of alchemy, the equally occult, but uneducated, terminology of shills exploits the Fair. Only Jonson was energetic enough to undertake a comedy like this; it is moderately surprising that even he carried it off. His power to raise realistic subjects to a literary level and to sustain them here pushes to its ultimate peak.[2]

Humours, as a concept, no longer influence the portraits. What supplants them, approximately, although with neither their precision nor emphasis, connotations of the term "vapours" indicate. One editor has counted its use sixty-nine times in *Bartholomew Fair*,[3] but no consistent denotations can be assigned it. Its charm derives from this vagueness. Basically, it seems to be a game, and a marginal note explains: "*Here they continue their game of* vapours, *which is* non sense. *Euery man to oppose the last man that spoke: whethe⟨r⟩ it concern'd him, or no.*" (IV. iv. 27–38) Similar to other games in which the comic characters indulge, Vapours serves the dramatic function of ridiculing the players. It does not extend to being one more aspect of a mania dominating individuals, such as the courtiers' parlor games in *Cynthia's Revels*, which exposed the participants' vanities and boredom. Vapours does not voice an inherent criticism that these characters have anything better to do, or, for that matter, that they might do anything better. It wastes their worthless time, inanely and harmlessly.

If stylistic affinities link *Bartholomew Fair* with the great comedies and with the earlier plays, several important advances open into novel forays. For the first time since *Every Man in His Humour*, considering their family relationships helps motivate the characters. After that play any ties of blood heightened antagonisms: the ridiculous given names in *Every Man out of His Humour*, Augustus' tyranny over Julia, Volpone's stunted progeny, or Morose's harsh guardianship. As usual for a major feature of the plot, the theme crisscrosses on various levels. One group comes to the Fair because of a pregnant woman's feigned craving for roast pig; a man from the country tries to restrain the enthusiastic sightseeing of a betrothed youth in his charge; rival suitors clash; and a mad justice searches out a foster son: "If I can, with this daies trauell, and all my policy, but rescue this youth, here, out of the hands of the lewd man, and the strange woman. . . ." (II. iv. 64–66) Ursula, the strange woman, keeps a booth where she sells the roast pig. In a sense she becomes a kind of universal mother, indiscriminately, for all the Fair's businessmen and visitors. From the multiple family ties and human affection, gruffer than life as they are, a flourishing source for action flows, which, with its outdoor locale, nearly doltish characters, relaxed construction, and multiple episodes, resembles in its sprawling vitality the animated masses composing a Breughel kermess.

The structure is slight, and episodes digress at many points, a treatment similar to that of *Every Man out of His Humour*. It begins with John Littlewit, who wants his wife to go to the Fair so that she can watch a puppet show he has composed. To get the consent of her mother, Dame Purecraft, a convert to Puritanism, and of her mother's mentor, Zeal-of-the-Land Busy, both of whom must disapprove the worldly Fair, she pretends that pregnancy has afflicted her with a desire to eat the roast pig for which Smithfield is famous. Also drawn to Ursula's tent are Waspe and his charge, Cokes; Justice Overdo, with his wife and her ward, who is engaged to Cokes; the men who want to marry Dame Purecraft; and Edgeworth, a young wit. These round out the chief characters who live in London and visit Smithfield. Mixing everywhere with them, the usual habitués of the Fair engage in their professions and crimes, the two often being identical. The troubles which beset the visitors need not be recounted. Although cause and effect help determine the arrangement of episodes, the construction does not seek tightness; everything depends upon the prevailing atmosphere.

In *Catiline* emphasis awkwardly fell on space, the continuum of the Empire, which tremblingly bore the weight put upon it. This expansiveness likewise dominates in *Bartholomew Fair*, but it partakes of the strong, disorganized, amorphous, and amoral arena which the Fair itself is. The inhabitants stretch lightly across the Atlantic Ocean from London to Virginia, where refugees from Smithfield have begun peopling the New World. The word which Overdo applies to the Fair with repeated scorn puns neatly on its two traits: enormity. Technically enormity is a crime, but the overtones of largeness relate the description to the teeming sideshows themselves. His shibboleth comments on his own exaggerated contempt for, and fascination with, the Fair. In his special taste for what he believes degenerate he rambles onward with a vocabulary more varied but just as insistent as that stamping others who have already spoken this sort of discourse. One of his diatribes pulls out practically all the associations the term acquires. (In contrast with *Catiline* and *Sejanus* this play stresses Hercules as a traveler rather than giant.)

> Ivs. Master *Winwife?* I hope you haue won no wife of her, Sir. If you haue, I will examine the possibility of it, at fit leasure. Now, to my enormities: looke vpon mee, O *London!* and see mee, O *Smithfield;* The *example of Iustice,* and *Mirror of Magistrates:* the true top of formality, and scourge of enormity. Harken vnto my *labours,* and but obserue my *discoueries;* and compare *Hercules* with me, if thou dar'st, of old; or *Columbus; Magellan;* or our countrey man *Drake* of later times: stand forth, you weedes of enormity, and spread. (V. vi. 31–40)

As an instance of ranting under rhetorical control, even Jonson had not achieved anything quite like this gradual yielding to self-intoxication. Zeal-of-the-Land Busy likewise launches sermons against the popularity of the Fair, with individual variation in cant derived from the Puritans' ejaculations of faith. He continues the patterns of Ananias and Tribulation Wholesome, but the general tendency harks back to Captain Tucca. Although all the characters do not share propensities of discourse to the same degree that those of *Epicene* did, a surprising number command a home-grown variety of jargon which they muster with alacrity. Appropriately, Ursula herself, at the center of the Fair, feels no inhibitions; her ample vocabulary fits her figure. She weighs a prodigious amount, and her flesh overflows into a kind of quagmire. "Yes, hee that would venture for't, I assure him, might sinke into her, and be drown'd a weeke, ere any friend hee had, could find where he were." (II. v. 95–97) All the elephantine passages draw upon stylistic habits which prevailed in the great comedies, but in those the exaggerations were primarily intellectual or imaginary. Here, they refer to the enormities of sights on or just off the stage: when Waspe lists the freaks in the Fair, the catalogue tells what he has seen, not possibilities, as in Lovewit's conjectures about the monstrosities which have attracted the mob to his home.

The very expansive, substantial scene and the weighted language are complemented by the ordinary people and commonplace sights. Volpone's and Sir Epicure Mammon's sensual visions of exquisite delights stay within the confines of the comic because their essence is that no one will achieve them. As empty reveries, the precise details comment upon their wasteful creators. Here, the descriptions, more fleshly than erotic, spring from and return back to the Fair. If not exactly vigorous and muscular, they neither appall nor surfeit. The rage against hollow men, those who boast achievements without any accomplishment, continues on a vulgar level. "A poxe o' these pretenders to wit! your *Three Cranes*, *Miter*, and *Mermaid* men! Not a corne of true salt, nor a graine of right mustard amongst them all." (I. i. 33–36) This censure comes early in the first act and the following four repeat it. The bulky Ursula personifies the flesh; no camouflage makes her attractive or disguises the appetites to which her booth caters. With its practical nature her traffic, whether in food or prostitutes, becomes the Fair itself: "This is the very *wombe*, and *bedde* of enormitie! grosse, as her selfe! this must all downe for enormity, all, euery whit on't." (II. ii. 106–8) That Justice Overdo offers this evaluation does not rob it of correctness, although it sounds unnecessarily biased. The business enterprises she controls dramatize her unrestrained and unadorned appetites. Her most energetic opponent is Busy, the hypocritical Puritan, who pretends to asceticism. He had, however, been a baker before his conversion to the cause and is initially introduced eating. Whatever may be Ursula's and the Fair's faults, dishonesty about themselves and meddling in others' private affairs do not occupy them. Busy can analyze his enemies both realistically and symbolically. "But the fleshly woman, (which you call *Vrsla*) is aboue all to be auoyded, hauing the marks vpon her, of the three enemies of Man, the World, as being in the *Faire*; the Deuill, as being in the fire; and the Flesh, as being her selfe." (III. vi. 33–37) No one would attempt to deny that on one plane the charges of Overdo and Busy have certain justifications, but those bringing the complaints and the way in which they phrase them give Ursula the benefit of any doubt about the unqualified truth of the men's opinions. Moreover, Ursula, while always a comic figure, scores a victory in appearing openly what she is.

Busy, in contrast, as soon as he begins searching out her tent must reduce himself to an animal. So that contact with the Fair will not corrupt him, he closes his eyes and sniffs his way along, his nose alone guiding him by the scent of the roast pig. Overdo wears a futile disguise from the time he enters Smithfield so that he may better detect the criminals. By the last act almost all the townspeople have, likewise, masked themselves voluntarily or been reduced to subterfuge. This cliché of farce goes beyond its origins. Ever since *The Case Is Altered* appearance and pretense have dramatized the main themes. For *Bartholomew Fair* the matter of dress spreads to become nearly a subject in itself. The Fair, by bringing out an inherent insecurity in the visitors, when frightened into denying who they are, boasts a valid function in comedy. Significantly, Ursula and her associates accept the whole scene with the warmth of those who love a humble home. Through them the audience can view the Fair without worrying about sentimentality and extraneous moral issues. Smithfield exists in its own right without any softening of its sordidness. By the completeness of all details, by the sort of critics it inspires, by the casual progress of action, and by the winningly relaxed prose, it neither attracts nor repels. As a literary work *Bartholomew Fair* is consummately realized.

In those passages which invoke animals figuratively, the same easy mingling of scene with language, of the human with the animal, contributes to the mellow tone. Characters bearing animal names, such as Waspe and Nightingale, form no discernible pattern as did those in *Volpone*. The Fair itself manages to pull them together so that they ultimately fit into or contrast with the setting. Moreover, heterogeneous species of animals comprise a caricatured carnival when their shapes invade the stage: the hobbyhorses of the morris dancers or the outline figures of the gingerbread cakes which Joan Trash sells. Many quasi-figurative terms associated with horses and asses grow from the vocabulary of the horse courser, Jordan Knockhum, whose preoccupations rarely wander outside the stables. This unforced interplay of all its elements bestows a tolerant quality to the genial script. In the great comedies animals represented a warning level to which, or beneath which, an individual might sink; in the tragedies they sometimes reproached man's greater cunning. Here, the two exist peacefully in one landscape which can accommodate both.

All the matters so far touched relate to a further development which for Jonson constituted a problem whose solution he saw in many guises. This statement does not imply that the late ones look better or more probable; they are simply different. Whatever motivated his ceaseless redistribution of stresses, an aesthetic sense guided him in welding his beliefs to his effects more economically. This dilemma may as well be put in its broadest, and overly familiar, terms: appearance and reality. The configurations have ranged from the assumption that the two are naturally related to a questioning of any ultimate reality under chaotic appearances. Efforts to disentangle the true from the deceptive necessitated various compromises until here the appearance is the reality, and appearances have the last word. No denouement explains or corrects the Fair; the surface dominates in substances as undefeatable as Ursula. As a principle this rationale sounds purely Jonsonian, and special qualifications couch it. Nevertheless, it defines an affirmative grasp of experience with such vitality that almost no one can face it. Although in 1950 the Old Vic staged a notable revival in Edinburgh and London, it proved too much for critics, who could only dismiss it as "the most crashing old bore. It is realistic comedy."[4] Of course, if one mistakes its keen techniques for realism, one probably has such weakened energies that any imaginative discipline bores one. *Bartholomew Fair* offers more than a series of sketches taken from Smithfield.

Three visitors seek to alter the Fair because they, like the critics, mistake its reality. In the great comedies the majority, almost the whole dramatis personae, had to undergo correction because they were in the wrong. Those winning, like the three wits in *Epicene* or, elsewhere, the official spokesmen, always stood off to one side to avoid the risks of soiling themselves in the stupidity of the main action. Here the central attraction, Ursula as opposed to Volpone, Morose, and Subtle, triumphs; the fools, the deluded as opposed to the naïve, stalk the edges of the Fair and exhibit their idiosyncratic, disproportionate responses to it. What relates Busy, Overdo, and Cokes (with Waspe as an aspect of his lack of caution) is that none of them can visit Smithfield and accept the Fair for what it is. Their misunderstandings take highly individual paths, but they claim a single source: the three either misinterpret the appearances or spy to uncover its reality, both pursuits based on the wrong assumption that any qualities divide the essences from the elements composing the object. The three differ as much from each other as do Subtle's customers, but here the delusions refer to an object which can be dramatized. The Fair is as obvious as the philosophers' stone was elusive.

Cokes, perhaps because of his country origins, behaves like the gulls in the humour comedies. In part because his first name is Bartholomew, he invests the Fair with a specious glamour and tries to extend its falsely conceived enticements into his own provincial life. Before his visit he has whiled away his rural hours by singing its ballads and catches. The projected excitements he has aroused blind him to what the locale itself is. In his naïveté he opens himself as a victim for all the cheaters in Smithfield, but so enchanted are his responses that being repeatedly robbed does not dampen his spirits. Nothing he could suffer in the Fair would cure him. In an uncritical way his pleasures approach being a species of love, satisfied by seeing what he admires. His enthusiasms bubble happily, almost triumphantly, to the end. Waspe, his guardian, picks up a theme not encountered for some time: the older man who gruffly disapproves all that his charge does. His annoyance against the Fair describes nothing inherent in it but the trouble it causes him by inciting Cokes to folly. His petulance has none of Augustus' hauteur. In a marvel of spinning a silken passage from the least likely material Jonson leniently combines Waspe's attitudes to Cokes and the scene.

> WAS. Would the *Fayre* and all the Drums, and Rattles in't, were
> i' your belly for mee: they are already i' your braine: he that had
> the meanes to trauell your head, now, should meet finer sights then
> any are i' the *Fayre;* and make a finer voyage on't; to see it all hung

with cockle-shels, pebbles, fine wheat-strawes, and here and there a chicken's feather, and a cob-web. (I. v. 91–97)

Although deluded, Cokes escapes lightly from his folly except for being duped at every corner. On the whole, his small wants deserve the holiday they get.

It is Busy whose anger drives him to denounce and try to destroy the Fair. His superficial soul harbors the mightiest tempests. Seeing the worldly Fair well enough, he takes refuge from wanting it in hating it. In his thoughts Biblical sins and the London scene mingle to design a more sinister institution than Smithfield could harbor. The misinterpretations of Ursula's tent contort a simple situation with an ingenuity which Sir Pol might envy. By translating the invisible into a vocabulary made up from symbols of his own manias and by exaggerating these private discolorings until they glaze all corners of life, Busy deceives himself. Unlike Cokes, he prevails upon others to follow along with his fantastic aggressions which he thinly disguises as religious dogma. Jonson, perhaps because he shared some of the sounder Puritan principles, pricked their inflated bombast with malicious accuracy.

Justice Overdo, rightly the most deluded of the three, searches for too much meaning beneath surfaces and, furthermore, disguises himself in the process. His opposition to the Fair rests on better ground than does Busy's, but the egotistical Puritan, at least, never stoops to the lawyer's conniving. Although many criminals infest the Fair, Overdo, pathetically costumed, can never approach one crime soon enough to snare the culprit. In employing too much finesse, he fails to weed out enormities because they are unabashedly on the surface. Busy and Overdo, in their specific traits, represent comparatively new developments; they look outward. Although personal rewards motivate them in part, they approximate more closely the habits of the public-spirited nuisance begun with Sir Pol. This increasing use of a civic standard as a meddler's justification indicates both how little this criterion counted for earlier and the difficulties which beset Jonson when he tried to embody it. Here, whatever the labors, the broader scope blends well with the tendency in *Bartholomew Fair* to allow surfaces a greater importance and not to worry much about underlying secrets. In keeping with the preference for the popular, the inhabitants of the

Fair understand what they are and what surrounds them; they harbor no illusions of dwelling in marble halls. Those who fail to come to grips with the scene, or who put on a particular garb for it, make themselves ridiculous.

What shelters the unprepossessing and defeats the reformers is the Fair itself. Ursula's being a woman and a personification of Smithfield assumes a meaning beyond the confines of one comedy. Remembering that Ferneze's wife died before the action in *The Case Is Altered* started, one sees in that detail a significance which extends beyond the costuming of the Milanese courtiers and servants in black. It also sounded a knell for nearly all mothers or references to them in the comedies. The fathers, Lorenzo Senior, Ovid Senior, and Sordido, must be widowers. Cynthia behaves more like a nurse than a mother for her courtiers; at best she retains an abstract authority which suits a virgin queen. Ursula bulks as an incredible but recognizable mother figure with a rude force in caricature. Jonson again parades a novelty by overstatement, although later it will shrink as satire and almost dominate the action. Ursula pushes her path through Smithfield with shameless violence and asserts herself everywhere. Her unequivocal triumph presents no claims to power beyond her own invincible strength. If her will becomes almost an independent creation, Jonson does not permit it to range wholly at random across his scene. For example, her victory cannot deliver the last word. For the climax of the plot and of her sway, the meaning must find an alliance at the greatest comic distance from her mountainous flesh.

The puppets, who at the inception draw Littlewit, the author of their piece, to the Fair, complement Ursula and speak the vocal condemnation which she cannot deliver. Throughout all the acts references remind the audience of them, and finally for the conclusion most of the cast, itself by now parodying the usual conduct, has been lured to attend their *reductio ad absurdum* of the favorite Elizabethan erotic subject drawn from the classics, Hero and Leander. Changes from Marlowe's retelling have modified the exotic original: "that is too learned, and poeticall for our audience; what doe they know what *Hellespont* is? Guilty of true loues blood? or what *Abidos* is? or the other *Sestos* hight?" (V. iii. 110–13) The revised story shows London watermen in a clamorous plot. Although Pepys recorded his distaste for the puppet show,[5] and critics do not take kindly to it, the performance has a logical, almost inevitable, place in the progression of *Bartholomew Fair*. Without it the end seems sentimental. The dialogue of the puppets bounces along in the same jingling verse which the freakish trio chants to while away Volpone's idle hours. There it contrasted with the steady blank verse and commented on the main characters deprived of their trappings; in a sense the jesters portrayed Volpone's soul. Here the crude versifying clashes less with the seemingly relaxed prose of the rest.[6] It does not condemn the members of the audience within the audience who have rejected pretenses; in a phrase of Valéry's, which is happily appropriate, they have killed the puppet of the ego,[7] or probably they never developed one. After one tires of the game Vapours, one may as well look at puppets; either activity carries slight blame.

The puppet show rounds out the play in exhibiting what the Smithfield men and women are not. By the same token, it becomes the critic of the men who misunderstand the Fair. Potentially the dolls embody the inert stupidity of Cokes, whom they enchant, the uselessness of Overdo, who would make them criminals, and the blindness of Busy, who wants them destroyed. At the same time, obedient to the puppeteer, they remain harmless pipings, incapable of any force on their own, if at times they appear nearly independent entities. Their refutation of Busy, who attacks them with the pledged enmity which the Puritan must bear against all players, meets him on his own, otherwise unanswerable, level of inanity. The dialogue effectively pits the wooden heads, chattering like gnats, against an overly stern man.

> Bvs. Yes, and my maine argument against you, is, that you are an *abomination*: for the Male, among you, putteth on the apparell of the *Female*, and the *Female* of the *Male*.
> Pvp. *You lye, you lye, you lye abominably.*
> Cok. Good, by my troth, he has giuen him the lye thrice.
> Pvp. *It is your old stale argument against the Players, but it will not hold against the Puppets; for we haue neyther Male nor Female amongst vs. And that thou may'st see, if thou wilt, like a malicious purblinde zeale as thou art!* (V. v. 98–106)

This last reference to Busy's blindness ridicules the weakness which his sniffing out Ursula's booth started.

All mechanical aspects of behavior have been poured from the characters of the Fair into the puppets who must obey accidental impulses. The humour figures, as has been seen, resembled marionettes, jerked this way or that by their irrational phantasies. These characters of *Bartholomew Fair* can, in a general manner, make decisions for themselves based to an extent upon a valid comprehension of situations in which they find themselves. They can sustain a balance between internal and external with an acceptance of the obvious. Lady Wouldbe and Ursula have no traits in common. The puppet show must revel in all its vulgarity: debased plot, crude versification, slapstick, and ludicrous characters. Nevertheless, unlike the disembodied echoes of *Cynthia's Revels*, the inanimate voices fulfill their single functions, as their master explains: "they are as well gouern'd a company, though I say it— And heere is young *Leander*, is as proper an *Actor* of his inches; and shakes his head like an hostler." (V. iii. 103–5) Not only do the squeakings of the puppets exist without pretense, but they mock inflated rhetoric as *Catiline* should have, except that Cicero's precarious eminence made such attitudes untenable.

In a place which the eye must regard with candor, Busy drones out his sermons: "he breaks his buttons, and cracks seames at euery saying he sobs out." (I. ii. 72–73) He rants onward into grandiose visions about an apocalypse in some of the most tortured imagery ever wrenched from a scriptural context: "I haue gaped as the oyster for the tide, after thy destruction. . . ." (V. v. 23–24) More extensively it can be:

> . . . that heathenish *Idoll*, that remaines (as I may say) a beame, a very beame, not a beame of the *Sunne*, nor a beame of the *Moone*, nor a beame of a ballance, neither a house-beame, nor a Weauers beame, but a beame in the eye, in the eye of the brethren; a very great beame, an exceeding great beame. . . .   (V. v. 4–10)

Obvious affinities link it with earlier styles, and Busy must surely be Ananias' and Tribulation Wholesome's brother in religion and blood. The prose permits a more relaxed intensity and betrays fewer compulsions to exploit all the neatest variants. Except for Busy, however, the voice too tends toward a harmless babbling. In comparison with Hedon's forced vocabulary of *Cynthia's Revels* and even Subtle's nimbly inventive one, Littlewit's puerile, if winning, conceits irk no one. Ursula's flow of ready invective too shrivels, at last: "I finde by her *similes*, shee wanes a pace." (II. v. 140–41) Poetry, associated frequently with the voice and vain affectations, returns again as an issue for both discussion and motivation. This topic, generally staple as a garden vegetable, puts forth strange blooms when nurtured in the climate at the Fair. Littlewit writes poetry as a hobby; his talents run to puns, which fall below the tolerant Elizabethan standards, and to the verses, which become the puppets. The same prejudices which fathers once lodged against poets because their sons practiced versifying now belong to the deluded Justice Overdo. The parody increases because a mere ballad seller has aroused his anger and because Edgeworth, whom he suspects of poetic inclinations, has livelier activities in mind.

> I haue followed him [Edgeworth] all the *Fayre* ouer, and still I finde him with this songster: And I begin shrewdly to suspect their familiarity; and the young man of a terrible taint, *Poetry!* with which idle disease, if he be infected, there's no hope of him, in a state-course. *Actum est*, of him for a common-wealths-man: if hee goe to't in *Rime*, once. (III. v. 3–9)

The choices of debasing or praising poetry fall beside the mark. Overdo's inverse criticism does not, of course, vindicate the balladmonger any more than his wild-goose chase pardons the Fair. The censure and the circumstances giving rise to it are false and may, therefore, be dismissed as pointless. The question of defending poetry does not need to be answered in the play because no necessary debate on justification arises.

In part this wholesale acceptance of the physical may have been dictated by the main target of attack: the Puritans. Busy, as his name implies, seeks converts; his zeal spreads through the land to influence others. Dame Purecraft confesses the cheating in which she has indulged for the sanctified cause. In contrast with the noisy affirmations of the Fair, the zealot's destructive negatives, because they emptily deny everything except their own hypocritical asceticism, find positive ridicule at every turn. Many of Jonson's habitual traits have a moralizing, nearly Calvinistic, aspect. Because at his best he cannot permit the innocent and guilty to share contiguous qualities for which only the guilty receive chastisement, here he eschews any temptation of trafficking with a more palatable brand of Puritanism. Smithfield represents all the world the stage contains, and it surpasses the Puritans' narrow preaching. The Catholic concepts of original sin and invincible ignorance neatly juxtapose as the distinguishing marks of Busy's brand of stupidity;

> by his profession, hee will euer be i' the state of Innocence, though; and child-hood; derides all *Antiquity;* defies any other *Learning,* then *Inspiration;* and what discretion soeuer, yeeres should afford him, it is all preuented in his *Originall ignorance;* ha' not to doe with him: for hee is a fellow of a most arrogant, and inuincible dulnesse, I assure you. . . .   (I. iii. 142–48)

Busy's ranting does not indicate merely failure of expression. The Puritans' vices of speech, like those of Crispinus in *Poetaster*, describe their underlying psychic confusions. By allowing other characters freedom from Busy's besetting faults, Jonson points up the preacher's foibles as the more stale and ridiculous. The device of making Busy an ineffectual critic of a holiday scene he cannot enjoy comments adequately on him. The Fair, set within its special context, emerges less reprehensible than he.

The Fair transcends being a flat quicksand in which to snare fools or to provide criminals a refuge. Comparable with *Epicene*, here marriage preoccupies many of the characters: Cokes' betrothal to Overdo's ward and the rival suitors, Busy, Winwife, and Quarlous, for Dame Purecraft. The accommodating noises and cries of the Fair triumph unequivocally, and so does marriage. The vendors fill the stage with their hawking, and the concluding events point up the marriage theme directly, more richly voiced than it could have been in *Epicene*. This development pushes as far as it will go Jonson's assumption about characters' chances of escape from their limitations. The behavior of the afflicted in the great comedies and even more in the humour comedies cuts them off from an aspect of life usually considered essential. The satirized figures had to stay partial; their incompleteness being necessary, the eccentric behavior took them to out-landishness lying beyond redemption. The end had to see them killed off as monsters. This inhumanly harsh code started to fray at the edges in *Epicene;* with *The Alchemist* a tentative compromise rent almost embarrassing seams. *Bartholomew Fair* celebrates its tatters and ragged characters who not only win forgiveness but, slightly modified, live happily ever after in what will be, presumably, their family circles. As a fully comprehended work, *Bartholomew Fair* must rank close to *Volpone,* but its merits differ. In fact, for sheer inventiveness it prob-ably surpasses the Venetian comedy, although marks must be scored against it: the argot at times goes slack; a good deal of horseplay for its own sake inevitably steals scenes; the episodes stretch somewhat out of hand; and diversity cannot always be introduced into the isolated Fair.

The genial Prologue indicates that Jonson had something special in mind. It takes the form of a legal contract between the author and the audience about the rights of both. Unlike *Catiline* no division separates the public into two groups. All are welcome. Not only with the course of action inside *Bartholomew Fair* does Jonson acquiesce to his subject, but within the larger frame of the theater he announced a different intention. The affirmation in such terms cannot, however, win all points without some sacrifices. If the guiding control rarely falters, it lacks a specific direction in which to go. In the close con-fines of Venice, Morose's house, or Lovewit's cellar, a single theme replaced a larger diversity. Those comedies triumphed through their negations. By concentrating on the positive aspects of the Fair, and by being always honest about them, Jonson handicapped himself. Ursula, after all, cannot quit the Fair; outside of it she would be quite unbear-able. This limitation of characters to their milieu suited the three pre-ceding comedies, but, when the end points outward, the boundaries seem curious. The Fair must remain one spot, no matter how great the enormity and how wide the geographical imagery which expand it. Momentarily, perhaps, it may humble, chastise, correct, and enlighten, but it stays, nevertheless, an underworld. Perhaps one consents to leaving Ursula, Joan Trash, and the other inhabitants there, but the

Londoners should emerge into a different sphere. This very transition occurs, largely, on faith.

For *Bartholomew Fair* this kind of rebirth may not be requisite. All that the citizens need do is to come to terms with the Fair under its own rules. When Quarlous, the short-tempered voice of reason, resolves all the dilemmas with dispatch, he suggests that the judge pause "and remember you are but *Adam*, Flesh, and blood! you haue your frailty, forget your other name of *Ouerdoo*, and inuite vs all to supper. There you and I will compare our *discoueries;* and drowne the memory of all enormity in your bigg'st bowle at home." (V. vi. 96–100) Overdo, who, like Sir Pol, has a middling ability which might yield to reform, rises to the suggestion, and he accepts it with a touch of learning neither wholly false nor misplaced: "I inuite you home, with mee to my house, to supper: I will haue none feare to go along, for my intents are *Ad correctionem, non ad destructionem; Ad aedificandum, non ad diruendum:* so lead on." (V. vi. 110–13) For the first time since *Every Man in His Humour* the suggestion appears that after the characters march off, they will go on and develop into something else. If once the satiric purpose implied that after seeing the plays the audiences, having hated monsters, would like men, it now comes dangerously close to hoping that they may not condemn the characters themselves after a metamorphosis. The play accepts all conditions as they are and nearly hopes that from such unlikely materials may emerge a slight improvement. With such centrality comedy appears most joyful because desire has, largely, been banished or tamed. The euphoria may end as mere philistine smugness which deifies the *status quo*.

Justice does not reside with rulers, with courts, with officials, nor with sentimentally deputized agents. To dramatize any concept of justice proves almost impossible in this setting, where the Pie Powder courts farcically intrude. Not only Overdo's follies but also Troubleall, who has gone quite mad serving under his stern principles, satirizes it without contributing any positive standards. Less than Lovewit can Quarlous rise above the milieu which he sometimes controls. The concept of judging must itself undergo a drastic revision in the light of the Fair, whose characters could not, even should they wish to, alter themselves completely. Parts of their propensities have been inherited and defy immediate correction. Thus, their surnames describe their ludicrous but innate qualities: Littlewit, Cokes, Waspe, Overdo, Wellborn, and Trash. Their given names sound unexceptional: John, Bartholomew, Humphrey, Adam, Grace, and Joan. Although Bartholomew and Adam may heed the admonitions which other Bartholomews and Adams receive, as Cokes and Overdo they share only the human frailty which makes them liable to stay their faulty selves. The conclusion grants the futility of demanding a complete reform and accepts Bartholomew Cokes and Adam Overdo as capable of some improvement but essentially unchangeable. It affirms this condition in the face of the Fair; the honesty and humility are thoroughly disarming. Indicatively, too, these names suggest how "realistic" the comedy is. It depicts more nearly recognizable types than do Jonson's other plays, but its style and patterning transcend any slice of life, just as Ursula's roast pig does not equal a tinned Smithfield ham.[8]

Unquestionably Jonson had begun exploring the materials for a domestic comedy, a topic to which he restricted himself in his last four plays. These do not, however, wholly repeat the sentimental errors of other middle-class dramas of the period, a flaw which clings inherently perhaps to the subject matter itself. Because he collaborated with Marston and Chapman on *Eastward Ho* and because this composition almost ideally illustrates its type, a few notes about it will further point up just what he does in *Bartholomew Fair* and later ones. Efforts to break down who contributed which passages have proved, by and large, inconclusive,[9] but Jonson must claim the smallest portion. The assumptions demanded by domestic comedy from *The Shoemakers' Holiday* onward mean, in a Jonsonian sense, no comedy at all. It appeals to the bourgeois conviction that a restricted social scope holds a little misbehavior and quite enough goodness not only to cancel all evil but to convert it. In his dealings the sincere businessman already owns the philosophers' stone; he cannot sublimate base substances into gold, but his gold transmutes all baseness into purity. A lip service to an original charity may explain such miracles with greater piety, but a popular playwright clearly has no need of this hypothesis.

Several satiric passages in *Eastward Ho* duplicate in subject and style Jonson's abiding themes, but far outnumbering these are stretches where values which he scorned rise triumphant. The plot itself could claim kinship only with *The Case Is Altered*, although lacking the appeal to an aristocracy and its inherited virtues which bolster that play. Touchstone, a goldsmith of humble origins, has two contrasting daughters, Gertrude, with ambitions to marry Sir Petronel Flash, and Mildred, happy as a citizen's daughter and wife. The names of his two apprentices, Quicksilver and Golding, sufficiently underline their diametric temperaments, the mercurial and plodding respectively. These characters themselves undergo more disillusions and reforms than Jonson's views of psychology and dramaturgy would tolerate. The size of the cast equals the one of *Every Man out of His Humour*, but this play wastes its minor roles on momentary effects. The action threatens to reach Virginia, although accidents interpose and it ends in jail. Here neither magistrate nor judge imposes the punishments. Instead, Touchstone with his successful son-in-law Golding redeems the wastrels, who have already undergone a hasty conversion to the gold standard. The setting in prison and Quicksilver's song may suggest the trifles which round off *Die Fledermaus* sweetly, but that concoction belongs to another age, another country, another genre, and another class.

Ten years earlier than *Bartholomew Fair*, *Eastward Ho* could not have been composed by Jonson at any time. Quicksilver points the moral (as does almost everyone else at some point) in his song, "*Seeke not to goe beyonde your Tether, / But cut your Thongs vnto your Lether*" (V. v. 119–20), a sentiment rejoicing more patly in human limitations than any in *Bartholomew Fair*. This play contends that *laborare est orare*, a view not distant from Jonson's as a craftsman. Nevertheless, two differences cut him off from the definitions in *Eastward Ho*. For him the master by employing his skill fully transforms the materials at hand. Value resides in creating a whole greater than the sum of its parts, an accomplishment not commonly vouchsafed the worker in leather or even gold. Furthermore, he took the artist's position that the achievement carries its own reward and that profits must be relegated to a secondary concern. He dissuaded Drummond of Hawthornden from poetry "for that she had beggered him, when he might have been a rich lawer, Physitian or Marchant." (I, p. 149) To regard *Eastward Ho* as a sermon preached exclusively to the middle class assigns Jonson a brand of snobbishness he was not guilty of. When justifying his morality, he could not appeal to an elastic civic standard which popular practices had enshrined.

In consequence of this sternness he failed to write what still passes in the common view for comedy, a play depicting a social and a world order which triumphs and looks unanswerable to the degree that its examples teach expediency. The tone must be genial toward the erring and little short of worshipful toward that monument of misplaced concreteness, the commercial hierarchy. Such comedy lacks the savage indignation of satire and the honest conviction behind parody. In the scornful comedies the correct code represented not the standard of their day, about which Jonson betrayed few illusions, but an elevated greatness which probably has never existed outside the heads of a few writers and philosophers. The ensuing problems have been analyzed sufficiently. *Bartholomew Fair*, no matter how closely it scrutinizes an annual outing, neither becomes *The Shoemakers' Holiday* nor quits Smithfield with its puppet watermen's shouts of "Eastward Ho." The roots of Jonson's supposed groping after realism had to penetrate more deeply than the shallow soil of Jacobean society.

This growing awareness, more likely despair, on his part of the stronger influences which a commercial Puritanism exerted over England has been ably traced by L. C. Knights in *Drama and Society in the Age of Jonson*.[10] Although his observations cannot avoid all the snags inherent in sociology, his study does help explain an aspect of the direction taken in the late comedies and why, even in decline, they remain nearly unique. A more obvious solution to these problems might appear a retreat to a foreign setting, but such a stratagem would have defeated itself. The very belief in enduring virtues, as well as follies, bestows validity for London on action in Florence, Gargaphie, Rome, or Venice. When the challenges to correctness took on uniquely English guises, then geographical parallels no longer sufficed. At the same time, desperate problems need specific remedies which, less than ever, dare plead eternal codes. Thus the setting could no longer be taken for granted nor could the cast parade to reformation or forgiveness. The favored characters, in themselves a novel concept for Jonson, must escape from an emotional dead end since nothing in the scene can bestow life on them. This striving, which eventually defeated Jonson, is the theme of human growth.

No longer does the primary conflict push monstrous behavior to its inevitable and ridiculous conclusion. No one in *Volpone* could live happily ever after because he had no life of any sort. As entities all were fully revealed and end-stopped from their first entrance. In *Bartholomew Fair* the process of character development begins to pre-empt all other matters. It is a vexing concept to work with, especially in drama. It insists that an altered personality gradually emerges through three hours by a series of trials and errors. If the standard of the great comedies has been that every experience resembles the person who has it, the new one implies that every event changes the individual involved. How much more congenial the first is to comedy than the second need not be elaborated. In fact, the action of the late plays often sounds like a prologue to a reformed life after the comedy ends. The dramatic consequences seek a meaning outside the frame which starts them. However desirable this declaration may look in the abstract, it does not make the most effective Jonsonian theater.

Such conjectures, however, invoke standards not required for an appreciation of *Bartholomew Fair*. This play, more successfully than *Epicene*, balances its conflicting themes. It remains sure enough so that it need give neither view the last word and honest enough so that it does not have to suppress its differences into tedious equivocations. The language flows with such grace that one accepts its forthrightness. This aspect shows it one of the few poetic but unsentimental folk plays in English, and, understandably, Synge could learn from it.[11] It nearly beguiles one into a genial tolerance of Bartholomew Fair, Smithfield, and society; thin as the ground which the Fair spreads for such tender sensations is, their brief flourishing provides more than one usually receives from literature.

CHAPTER XI

Shutting Up of His Circle

P ERHAPS yet another statistician ought to instigate yet another survey, this one to determine whether some generations respond less to individual works than to the author's age at the time of their composition. The nineteenth century seems to have preferred a romantic youth's excited raptures. Ardor and fire won prizes; if the poet as adventurer perished in his assault upon Parnassus, the more pathetic and the better. The twentieth century surveys the total output. If an author's stature does not advance, and worse still if a decline sets in, one squirms with the same annoyance as at a novel each of whose chapters becomes less sure. "Of all fine sights in the world to me, the best is that of an artist growing great, adding to his art with his years, as his life and his art are inseparable."[1] European sages, such as Gide, Yeats, Mann, and Claudel, improve with years. Critics sigh that in the United States native authors write themselves out, after the rounds of New York and fitful expatriation, by their forties. The fact that they were patent flashes in the pan and that everyone, the authors included, allowed himself to be deceived does not mitigate the disappointments. Writers do, in as general a sense as any metaphor can have, grow, but as with all expansions a limit at some point defines them. Its being encountered early or later does not reflect on the worth of any essentially realized piece. The lacks tell one something but not enough to justify total condemnation. If one appreciates Jonson sufficiently, one may forgive his dotages. On the whole, recognizing them for what they are damns them less than comparing them with such oddities of old foolishness as *Parsifal* and *Prince Hohenstiel-Schwangau*.[2] Jonson titled four of the late plays *The Devil Is an Ass*, *The Staple of News*, *The New Inn*, and *The Magnetic Lady*, indicative, perhaps, that comparably with *Bartholomew Fair* the concentration on a central character subsides in favor of exploiting a scene. This broadening forces attention outside the general drift of the great comedies. In a sense, taking them together produces an erroneous impression. The intention in all differs markedly, the demand on a rationale and the impetus to explore being as powerful as ever. With a failure, however, one concentrates more on what is not present than on what is, if merely to explain the peculiarities one encounters. Although their positive effects vary, what they lack refers to one subject, which grows increasingly strong.

The most promising in conception, and the most disappointingly executed, leads off this group. Performed in 1616, two years after *Bartholomew Fair* and in the same year as the appearance of the folio, it has, however, few affinities with that resounding affirmation and heralds the irresolutions. *The Devil Is an Ass* falters with doubts where Jonson before proceeded without hesitation. He fails to define effectively the number of levels on which it operates and their relative values. Before this play the dichotomies halved themselves along moderately assured lines, a quality which this commentary may have insisted on excessively. Here, a heterogeneous group of characters and actions cross lines, but, bafflingly, no checks restrain the scramble. In barest outline the plot of *The Devil Is an Ass* points toward great rewards of comic possibilities. An apprentice knave and an eager gull join forces and exploit each other. Oddly, neither one maintains his traits consistently, and their bungling ineptitude for mischief weakens the satiric drive. Fitzdottrell, yielding to Subtle's Faustian ambition, longs to control the devil who will endow him with wealth; Pug, a minor functionary of hell, begs his chief for a holiday to experiment in human depravity. Pug gets his wish and inhabits for one day the body of a criminal who has just been executed. Almost at once after taking up residence, he confronts Fitzdottrell, who does not recognize the answer to his prayers: "I look'd o' your feet, afore, you cannot coozen mee, / Your shoo's not clouen, Sir, you are whole hoof'd." (I. iii. 28–29) The rest of the action proves how the flesh outdoes the spirit, even an evil one, in malice. Pug, however, lacks the inventiveness to launch many machinations, and he serves at last merely to explain away the human complications: "You talke of a *Vniuersity!* why, *Hell* is / A Grammar-schoole to this!" (IV. iv. 170–71) In spite of lending himself to the title, the asinine devil sinks to a minor role, like a sluggish Mosca who instead of steering affairs bungles them to his own chagrin. Fitzdottrell attracts vices but more like a victim than master. As taken with clothes as any courtier and with money as Volpone and Subtle, his brand of stupidity turns to business and patented gadgets.

Fitzdottrell is a capitalist looking for new inventions and schemes upon which to make inordinate profits. Meercraft, a man as full of wiles as Subtle, readily obliges him with such doodads, which he carries about in a pouch. The ideas range from worthless pipe dreams to the nearly practical. Whether innately they sound feasible or hopeless matters little, and Fitzdottrell's inability to judge between the two kinds marks the satiric point. Also, just as the alchemist's customers would have wasted the philosophers' stone, had there been one and had they owned it, so Fitzdottrell must fail no matter how well a project might succeed theoretically. Because of its insight into business methods, which had to wait several centuries to overtake Jonson's parody, one almost forgives the failures of *The Devil Is an Ass*. An outline of an advertising campaign catches the manufacturers' reverence on which twentieth-century merchandising thrives. It is worth quoting at length both for itself and as proof of Jonson's powers.

> MER. For seruing the whole state with Tooth-picks;
> (Somewhat an intricate *Businesse* to discourse) but—
> I shew, how much the Subiect is abus'd,

First, in that one commodity? then what diseases,
And putrefactions in the gummes are bred,
By those are made'of'adultrate, and false wood?
My plot, for reformation of these, followes.
To haue all Tooth-picks, brought vnto an *office*,
There seal'd; and such as counterfait 'hem, mulcted.
And last, for venting 'hem to haue a booke
Printed, to teach their vse, which euery childe
Shall haue throughout the kingdome, that can read,
And learne to picke his teeth by. Which beginning
Earely to practice, with some other rules,
Of neuer sleeping with the mouth open, chawing
Some graines of *masticke*, will preserue the breath
Pure, and so free from taynt—ha, what is't? sai'st thou?

(IV. ii. 39-55)

Being a professed opportunist, Meercraft will sponsor any harebrained scheme for others to invest their money in. Although Jonson's temperament has nothing of the seer about it, his training in tracking down the ultimate pursuits of folly led him in these late plays to satirize institutions which he could observe only in embryo. The bourgeois fixation upon practical gewgaws and uncreative piddling has not since been more effectively ridiculed in English; for anything comparable one must look to French literature, and there not until Flaubert and the nineteenth century. Meercraft, then, represents the common desire for worldly power, of which Pug, whose evil is otherworldly, must be innocent.

Fitzdottrell's weakness for clothes introduces the third aspect of the plot. He allows Wittipol to talk to his wife for a few minutes in order to get a cloak from him. Wittipol loves Mrs. Fitzdottrell in spite of the moralizing sermons his friend Manly expounds to warn him away from the temptations of adultery. Although Fitzdottrell mistrusts his wife almost as grossly as does Corvino in *Volpone*, here virtue resoundingly triumphs. Wittipol gives up his love, and the wife remains true to her doltish husband, who promises to reform. This victory may stand for the transcendental good which finally crushes evils. Jonson fails to sustain these levels with much ingenuity, let alone work them out in the desired alignments. Moreover, how shall the ideal virtue be embodied on the stage? Such a quality never before figured so elusively in any of the plays. The closest approximation occurred in *Poetaster*, and the embarrassing circumlocutions that play invoked have already been listed.

Jonson's solution gambles on an extreme novelty, although its approach may be traced from afar. The voice takes over as the primary instrument of truth, and long debates ramble onward in moderately heated succession. Such a series supposedly leads one to an insubstantial piety. Until this point the rhetoric, even in the magniloquent *Catiline*, has referred to character and situation; one could profitably cite few passages divorced from context. Here the composition sounds petrified, a studied system of declamations which depart from the strict ordering of the action and which say nothing in themselves. One cause of this divergence harks back to the irresolution; the value to which these speeches refer holds a quality of goodness above the devil and the flesh, but being transcendent, it has no chance of surviving on the stage of *The Devil Is an Ass*. The logic surrounding the action boils down to this: an evil which is not evil when embodied in the flesh conflicts with a good which is good only when it exceeds the flesh. The resultant shadowboxing leaves the flesh amorphous; it outdoes evil in spite of propensities for virtue and often wanders about lugubriously without any sense of direction between what to shun and what to seek.

Many plays exhibit beliefs more confused and manage to squeak by, indeed, to be acclaimed. This kind, however, subdues objections by treating less and being glib. In *The Devil Is an Ass* the episodes ramble inconclusively. The main drift shows Fitzdottrell's being tricked into signing away his fortune, but the surprise announcement that, without his knowledge, he had earlier put his property into his wife's name saves it and him. The fifth act, again, contains a trial, but it lacks the justification for this contrivance which the earlier plays provided. Indeed, all problems have been largely resolved by the time it occurs, and it does little except perfunctorily mark time. Not in this act alone but throughout the play a series of digressions distract one's attention, a diversion pardonable were the interruptions agile enough. Such inventiveness does not distinguish the description of a "Dick Robinson," a boy actor who crashed a party of women in his female disguise nor, an extension of this report, the role of a "Spanish Lady," who is really Wittipol. Both fumble their effects which, one feels, under the most favorable circumstances could scarcely be put to much account.

In language the changes exhibit a decline toward specious sentimentality, a tendency which magnifies the structural cracks and whose own weaknesses are no less thoroughgoing. In passages of invective the terms hammer on the disagreeable and the ugly without forming an adequate criticism of the speakers. On the other hand, when Wittipol pleads his case with Mrs. Fitzdottrell, the declaration of love has a clubfooted rapture of purity not attempted since *Poetaster*. It hits the mark no more effectively than did Ovid Junior's suit. Manly, the confidant of Wittipol, prates of "the braue occasion, vertue offers you, / To keepe you innocent" (IV. vi. 29–30), the sort of moral stupefaction which would not have dared show itself in the great comedies. The trouble is that its chances of success are not much better here. The most unaccountable detour of language and situation, however, involves two minor figures, a father, Guilthead, and his son, Plutarchus. They aid Meercraft in his cheating of Fitzdottrell but hint at more complexity than the knaves who have filled secondary roles with gratuitous malice. Guilthead's nearly wistful ambition for his son's cultural growth breathes a pathos formerly foreign to the comedies, and the son's moody indifference to these improvements expresses a tension between the two close to the pitiful. Contrasting with the sardonically christened children of Sordido, Plutarchus' name carries a hope.

> Gvi. That yeere Sr,
> That I begot him, I bought *Plutarch's* liues,
> And fell s⟨o⟩' in loue with the booke, as I call'd my sonne
> By' his name; In hope he should be like him:
> And write the liues of our great men! (III. ii. 21–25)

One is tempted to say that in addition to predicting the methods of the businessman Jonson also foresaw his domestic disappointments.

In many ways *The Devil Is an Ass* fails more seriously than do the three ensuing plays.[3] It holds more potentialities and realizes fewer: the satiric targets show clearly, and the misses, consequently, appear to fall further afield; the beginning moves briskly, and the conclusion dribbles away; segments, especially Meercraft's schemes, speak with Jonson's vigor, but the sentimental ones intrude awkwardly. Jonson, who fed his critical sensibilities no less fiercely on his own texts than on those of his adversaries, perhaps discerned his decline. At least, nine years passed before he turned again to the popular stage. If this quiescence did not strengthen his powers, neither did it diminish them.

The Staple of News mixes the standard ingredients of the late period: a greater ridicule of contemporary business practices, increasing reliance on family relationships, a tendency to portray allegorical virtues instead of specific vices, and a stated desire to please *some* public. Although nowhere can *The Staple of News* touch the better sections of *The Devil Is an Ass,* it does present less violent contrasts of parts; the whole impression seems more nearly uniform and slightly less meandering. The satire is directed against a "News Office" where, however, current events are not printed but sold directly to the clients. This scene gives an excuse for a chorus, a group of women who presumably would patronize a news office and the public theater. Addicted to whimsical opinions, they comment unintelligently but not unpleasantly upon what they watch. This much adheres closely to the standard effects of the great satires. The main plot, however, traces the fortunes of Peniboy Junior. (The nomenclature imposed on this play makes any discussion of it cumbersome.) His father has just died, and, since one Peniboy Canter, a beggar, brings him news of his inheritance, the younger man adopts the older in place of a father whom he scarcely misses. Peniboy Junior loves Lady Pecunia, a partially allegorical figure whose servants, Mortgage, Statute, Band, and Wax, further link her with acquisitive instincts. She is the ward of Peniboy Senior, a miser more vicious than the others who have sporadically appeared since *The Case Is Altered.* The action concerns Peniboy Junior's investing in the News Office, the plans to cheat him of his inheritance, his turning the tables, and the final revelation that Peniboy Canter is actually the missing father. (Peniboy Senior is Peniboy Junior's uncle, not father.) Obviously no one could surmount these situations and characters, but, granted the improbabilities, quite a few superior episodes come through. In the general intention the play proceeds with greater resolution than did *The Devil Is an Ass*, although in the levels of their satire the two have similarities. In *The Staple of News* the episodes take nearly mechanical people and, after five acts, drop some as potential human beings. The scheme parallels *Peer Gynt* or *Pinocchio*. This sort of moral fable does not strike one as ideally suited for Jonson's talents, but, if he felt compelled to steer them in this direction, his discernment proves some awareness of the difficulties.

The opening reverses *The Case Is Altered*, where Juniper went into mourning; here Peniboy Junior boasts of having reached his majority and independence. His pride has some of the stilted wonder which the humour characters experience.

> P. Iv. Look to me, wit, and look to my wit, Land,
> That is, looke on me, and with all thine eyes,
> Male, Female, yea, *Hermaphroditicke* eyes,
> And those bring all your helpes, and perspicills,
> To see me at best aduantage, and augment
> My forme as I come forth, for I doe feele
> I will be one, worth looking after, shortly.   (I. i. 3–9)

Elsewhere the verse also snaps with some of its previous verve. Where Peniboy Canter reduces the vocabulary of trades and professions to "canting," one hears again a collective contempt for mystification by obscure terminology. The ridiculous "news" reports of simple-minded phenomena, "of Ghosts, Apparitions, Monstrous Births, Showers of Wheat, Judgments of God, and other Prodigious and Fearful Happenings,"[4] which formed the stock in trade of ballad dealers, here stretch out to seemingly impossible lengths. The absurdities did not span far enough to outdistance contemporary credulity, and in part the initial failure of the play may be blamed on the acceptance of the caricatured reports as actual.[5] Too often, however, the language loses the vital touch of objects elbowing each other and comes to resemble the ugly arrangement of utilitarian pieces on pipe racks in a shop window: a series of metaphoric descriptions of drab insects, an insistence upon the infirmities of old age, the harping on heavy foods, and a general inelasticity of associations in many figurative passages.

Conceding such weaknesses does not deprive the plot of its better moments. The invective against business and greed strikes with bitter accuracy when showing the News Office, Peniboy Junior's purchase of it, and the final legal complications. In a more general sense Lady Pecunia, who has antecedents in contemporary and Aristophanic satire,[6] embodies the same drives abstractly. The tirades against money gain a melancholy which nothing shown on the stage quite suggests, for example, Peniboy Canter's dirge, "How hath all iust, true reputation fall'n, / Since money, this base money 'gan to haue any!" (III. ii. 247–48) In spite of this admitting a decline and fall, the play as a whole says less than the author indicates in parts he hopes it will.

The minor characters go through their turns with the expected alacrity; Madrigal, Cymbal, Picklock, Shunfield, Almanac, and Lickfinger are, respectively, poetaster, businessman, lawyer, sea captain, doctor, and cook. Their routines frequently depart from the action which involves the three Peniboys. In this element *The Staple of News* imitates a humour comedy, where, however, the discontinuity itself formed part of the satire. Here, when the chief theme appears the growth of Lady Pecunia and Peniboy Junior, such auxiliary episodes more nearly resemble distractions. Each exploits a technical vocabulary; their penchants ridicule their special jargons. On the other hand, the practice descends into one more game called, this time, "Jeering." Throughout the plays a recurrent tendency has stopped the plot while the actors perform such exercises. In theory this device may sound workable because it does liberate the characters from any obedience to outside forces and present them an ideal freedom. The trouble arises from this very disaffection. When, as in *Cynthia's Revels*, Substantives and Adjectives complements the main themes, or, as in *Bartholomew Fair*, Vapours nearly persuades one by its own simplicity, such idling has a point, and it does not annoy unduly. These excuses will not serve Jeering, which envelops the whole stage to seize anyone in an epidemic of invective worthy of *vetus comoedia*.

> MAD. We ieere all kind of persons
> We meete withall, of any rancke or quality,
> And if we cannot ieere them, we ieere our selues. (IV. i. 7–9)

Most notable, if not most successful for this play, is what happens to the practice of justice. Almost without exception the fifth acts have culminated with some trial or official speaker to resolve the confusions. Agents of the law have become increasingly less trustworthy, except in *Catiline*, part of whose confusions hinge on this uncertainty. In *The Staple of News*, whose subtitle might be the one bestowed on *The Devil Is an Ass*, "The Cheater Cheated" (VI, p. 161), nobody attempts to reconcile the dispensing agent with a legal force. Peniboy Junior takes the law in his own hands and saves himself with his father's blessing: "To cheat the *Cheater*, was no *cheat*, but iustice. / Put off your ragges, and be your selfe againe...." (V. iii. 21–22) For the first time in any of the comedies the righteous individual triumphs over the institution, although the victory does not convince one, and it is scarcely comic. Moreover, this cheater of cheats becomes himself by wearing his own clothes. The authority for authority develops from no corner of the play itself. It descends as a crude *deus ex machina*. Lovewit's opportune return to London, at least, was based on property related to the scene; the advance of Peniboy Junior and Lady Pecunia into human status must be taken on faith. This rejection of the codified laws, whether of society or psychology, touches the design at many points. Peniboy Senior goes mad and tries his two dogs, a parody of the legal process gloomier than any Jonson displayed before.

These two plays illustrate an aspect of a change in outlook which has already been sketched. With the rise of the Puritans, the shopkeepers, the "practical" men, Jonson realized the impossibility of his own standards in poetry and justice:[7] However haughtily he may have railed, however proudly he may have blasted the pit, he had, after all, his rights not from heaven but Olympus. His classical mind codified principles which developed through his literary disciplines. At first all sins for him violated the senses or the intellect. Later, such assurance went against the social powers gaining control on every side. The middlemen, who recognized only means, had won places of might; their laws had, *ipso facto*, to be corrupt since they were designed not for the sake of the good but for the profits they distributed. Standards had shifted so that, whereas salvation before lay in obeying what the best social behavior demanded, now the individual had to hope to summon the strength to proceed beyond the group into unknown territory. One cannot deplore Jonson's honesty; one can hardly blame him for failing to discover what three centuries have not formulated. The final lines of many Elizabethan plays sound maudlin, at best. Having observed what significance Jonson attached to the circle, one hears in the routine conclusion of *The Staple of News* an indirect irony. Lady Pecunia and Peniboy Junior will marry so they "ioyne their hands. / P. CA. If the Spectators will ioyne theirs, wee thanke 'hem." (V. vi. 57–58) The audience and cast unite in an act of faith based on no belief.

The New Inn followed with greater difficulties. For reasons which so far have defied explanation, the audience demonstrated against the name of a character, Cis. At the next performance she was hastily rechristened Pru, but the makeshift camouflage does not alter the conditions of *The New Inn*, which seems beyond redemption. Tendencies of the other two plays here reach forth and wrench the whole design into a form hardly Jonsonian. The scene moves from the corrupt city to the country, a place called, of course, The New Inn. Staffing it are a host, his son, an old Irish nurse, and servants. These servants with soldiers indulge in slapstick, but it does not interlock directly with the main action, which demands most of the space. To the Inn comes Lovel, who suffers from lovers' melancholy with more sighs than one would have believed possible for Jonson. Soon to arrive is Lady Frampul, who has lost her father, mother, and sister; her servant Pru (nee Cis) accompanies her. These two women, so that they will not be companionless, borrow the host's son and disguise him in girl's clothes. To while away the hours they set up a mock court in which Pru presides over Lovel's pleading the cases of love and valor. If all this fretting were an allegory on the soul, it might be simpleminded but understandable. The action needs a nearly literal interpretation. The preposterous denouement throws any last shred of caution outside the Inn. It transpires that the host, removing a false beard he has worn for years, is Lady Frampul's father; the Irish servant, lifting her unnecessary eye patch, becomes the wife and mother, and —one shrinks from contemplating what these strokes cost Jonson— the host's son is not a boy after all but the missing daughter and sister.

Astonishment reunites the family. By dragging in other characters the final procession leads neither to court nor to dinner but "Let's all goe sleepe, / Each with his Turtle." (V. v. 123–24) One assumes the ending not deliberately scandalous, but several of the "turtles" have not yet been married.[8]

Indeed, Jonson seems to have nodded during the labor of composition. Sleep permeates the play in language and through the characters; the Irish nurse, when not speaking her brand of native dialect, slumbers. The topic blends well with the dominant rhythm, which flows almost indolently, although the rural atmosphere bestows on the heaviness more validity than lethargic Rome does on *Catiline*. A certain purpose directs the situations. Lady Frampul and Lovel must seek their way through a maze analogous to the one which Lady Pecunia and Peniboy Junior traverse. Because their discoveries rely upon oratory instead of commercial undertakings, the progress commands less conviction. If the low comic elements have too little to do with the rationale, the same charge may be lodged against the higher. Lovel's rapturous improvisation goes to excessive lengths of abstraction, and it must be written off as philosophizing, in the worst sense of the word, for its own sake. Thus, although *The New Inn* tolerates moderate digressions from the story it tells, that story itself ambles at a sluggish pace with so many detours that dramatically nothing in it reaches a climax. At no point does any passage have the tautness which distinguishes parts of *The Staple of News*. What serves as secondary relief must have embarrassed Jonson himself, who dropped the servants and soldiers rashly before the final scenes.

Another aspect of the story could be omitted, but this one does, in its quaint manner, suit the main plot. A tailor coincidentally arrives at the Inn with his wife, who wears a dress which he has made for Pru. It turns out that he regularly dresses his wife in customers' clothes and takes her to an inn where they pretend they are an unmarried couple having an affair. At their most deluded the courtiers and humourists did not push their perversions this far. In part the difference depends simultaneously upon the greater importance allotted the physical and the higher value allowed the transcendent. Whereas the earlier characters respected substances too little, here the ideal becomes one of grasping after the most elusive emotion, which must then be embodied in the seeker's conduct. The masquerading tailor and his wife offend both because of their gross natures and crude pretenses. Lady Frampul and Lovel, on a different level, work out a more complicated formula to attain success; like Lady Pecunia and Peniboy Junior they must lose their stilted responses to others: Lady Frampul to feel a true love, and Lovel to find someone whom he can love. The voice serves as match-maker. By orations Lovel wins Lady Frampul in the slow passion of defining love and valor. They do not "see" each other; both fall in love with the concept of love itself. The scheme is thoroughly Platonic by the Renaissance interpretation and does not, on the whole, sound in prospect more improbable than the humours as a basis for drama. For whatever reasons—perhaps because Jonson had grown older, per-haps because idealized beauty lends itself less readily to the stage than particularized affectation does, or perhaps because a mystic growing cannot mature in a few hours—the static qualities triumph.

The action, nevertheless, does not depict wholly disembodied pleasures. For a while Lady Frampul's raptures convince those who know her that she merely pretends to Lovel's insights and that beneath lies a mockery of him. Phoenixella in *The Case Is Altered* likewise confused Aurelia about her intuitions. Here, however, after the insight comes matrimony; while more transcendent in its ideals, the play like-wise insists more cogently upon the physical. If Lovel's voice wins a lady, it must be the Lady Frampul. Indicatively, the missing mother, the Irish nurse, wears a patch over her eye while she remains separated from her family. The voice, when gaining ascendancy over vision, does not throw the eye into eclipse. The two should combine: sight dealing with the corporeal, speech with the conceptual. Because one can devise neater schematizations for the early and the late plays than for the great comedies, it may seem that the first and last should, like-wise, turn out more effectively, the theory most flattering to criticism. With some writers this correlation holds good. Jonson, when he diagrammed his meaning to the last curve, lost the flowing strokes which permitted him to impart vitality to his arabesques.

Being also a personal document, *The New Inn* through its auto-biographical parts gains a more poignant force than anything it offers on the stage. After the ridicule heaped on the performance, Jonson brought it out as a book but in octavo instead of quarto. The designs of the publications keep up a running commentary on the plays. In this late work he summoned back the intimidating devices which launched *Every Man out of His Humour*, but in the reduced format they seem a feeble gesture toward the first success. The title page carries its Latin motto and the insult, "As it was neuer acted, but most negligently play'd, by some, the Kings Seruants. And more squeamishly beheld, and censured by others, the Kings Subiects." (VI, p. 395) Then, however, the reader, ordinary or extraordinary, becomes the judge and the jury on both this title page and in the dedication. After that follows "The Argument," to explain the construction, which sounds somewhat more coherent in outline. The old character sketches return, less lively than before, with a few comments on the ability of the actors at the opening performance. Finally, the Prologue gets action under way. It concludes with an antepenultimate Epilogue, a penultimate Epilogue, and, finally, the strongly moving "Ode to Himself," one of the most resounding assertions Jonson ever formed. Nevertheless, brute determination cannot sustain the whole, and the first Epilogue concedes:

> for he sent things fit,
> In all the numbers, both of sense, and wit,
> If they ha' not miscarried! if they haue,
> All that his faint, and faltring tongue doth craue,
> Is, that you not impute it to his braine.
> That's yet vnhurt, although set round with paine,
> It cannot long hold out. All strength must yeeld.
> Yet iudgement would the last be, i' the field,
> With a true Poet.   (VI, p. 490)

Perhaps other poets have been equally dedicated but none, surely, in spite of colder appreciation and more stingy rewards.

Faced with this resilient assurance, one hesitates to side with those who decide that Jonson did not know what he was doing. Perhaps one may silently ignore *The New Inn*, but *The Magnetic Lady* puts forth claims which must be refuted.[9] The idea of the circle, of completeness, operates everywhere in this play and nowhere to the advantage of the action. The Induction, in itself a pleasant conversation, shows a boy's superiority to two men representing the audience who question him about what they will see. He informs them:

> The *Author*, beginning his studies of this kind, with *every man in his Humour;* and after, *every man out of his Humour:* and since, continuing in all his *Playes*, especially those of the *Comick* thred, whereof the *New-Inne* was the last, some recent humours still, or manners of men, that went along with the times, finding himselfe now neare the close, or shutting up of his Circle, hath phant'sied to himselfe, in *Idaea*, this *Magnetick Mistris.* . . . hee makes that his Center attractive, to draw thither a diversity of Guests, all persons of different humours to make up his *Perimeter*. And this hee hath call'd *Humors reconcil'd.* (Induction, 99–111)

In the most generous interpretation this explanation describes neither the progression of Jonson's career nor *The Magnetic Lady*.[10] For example, in the comedies of humour no central attraction drew the cast together, and in the great comedies the types presented considerably more diversity. Other objections seem self-evident.

In execution the plan goes awry. The characters' names indicate the confusions. The Magnetic Lady is called Loadstone, and the nominal hero Captain Ironside, a couple clearly destined for each other. To fit in Compass, who steers rather than points, already stretches credulity. On the perimeter flit Sir Diaphanous Silkworm, Sir Moath Interest, Doctor Rut, Parson Palate, Tim Item, etc., all types whom one has observed before. Between the prancing characters and false reports, the proceedings suggest a troupe who decided to play Menander like a French farce. At points the plot defies paraphrase, and one inevitably finds one's attention drifting off to happier memories of the true comedies.

The humours, as they are called, become mere exaggerations of conduct, a prediction of what later years would make out of them. In other words, Jonson has at last descended to the kind of comedy that he supposedly wrote throughout his career and that almost anyone else could contrive. To appreciate the characterization one must invoke the contemporary standards of conduct and see how the portraits match or distort the models. To sympathize with the outcome one must forget the approved standards of justice and applaud the private triumphs of those who ignore the law in favor of their own feelings. To respond to the ending one must take the alliances as gratuitous, for nothing in the course of the play points toward them. To approve the sentiments one must banish critical standards and beam with a benevolence which believes that an educational reform may be wrought within the scope of three hours. All these conditions apply to the usual comedy which reassures audiences about the simplicity of all choices. The subtitle "Humours reconciled" defines the difference; until *Bartholomew Fair* no reconciliation could have freed the deluded. The play, thus, predicts Dickensian humor; it lacks Jonsonian humours.

One notable difference, as apart from careless ineptitudes, does distinguish it. The central attraction is the Magnetic Lady herself, almost Ursula metamorphosed. The heroines have become increasingly important since *Bartholomew Fair*. Mrs. Fitzdottrell saves her husband financially and promises to assist his reform. Lady Pecunia shares Peniboy Junior's achievement of maturity, but she already has a degree of independence which none of the other women has attained. Lady Frampul sets her own standards and appears Lovel's superior. Loadstone completes the reversal; she brings the situation around to herself and to her own advantage. She makes the final dispositions. If one could trust Meredith's formulation that comedy arises only from a society and a drama which permit women stellar roles, again toward the end of his life Jonson would have stumbled on to what he imagined he was doing all along. The conditions apply to one kind of comedy, and, in the light of the Jonsonian formulation, an inferior sort, at that.

If it continues telling the unvarnished truth, comedy can do little with romantic love. The drives of sex, translated into ritual, lie at the source of much comedy at any time, and Jonson often employed this impulse, particularly in his four great plays. Otherwise, confusions between sex and romantic love have so permeated western culture that even seventeenth-century audiences must have automatically identified one with the other. Starting with the troubadours, through the Platonism of the Renaissance, the two values have claimed disputed spheres in literature. The finest analysis of how sex and romantic love end in their mutual destruction, *Madame Bovary*, hardly resembles a comedy at all, although its complex levels depart from a French province close to satire. Romantic love, in spite of an addiction to self-examination, shuns a conscious awareness and worships a transcendent truth, one understandable only through legends. When love links with the death-wish upon the frustrations of its longings, the result may become tragic. Comedy insists on vitality and human freedom, both antithetical to romantic moods. For example, the three young men in *Epicene* do not have any affairs which would have to depart from the world of the play and exploit another, foreign one. The late plays, thanks to Jonson's unfailing taste, try less for romance than the kind of forgive-ness associated with Christian charity, granted that such emotions can scarcely be dramatized.

Although these four plays differ widely, they share in broad out-line more with each other than do any two of the rest. Three thema-tic treatments set them off: the stage tableau veils many mysteries about the actual situation; characters likewise shift their natures unex-pectedly; the end has citizens triumph over society. The audience is deceived increasingly by people who turn out to be actors rather than women or by strangers who unmask to become long-lost relatives. In the last plays the eye, closely allied with the senses, sinks, and the voice, communicating emotions beyond words, soars upward. On the other hand, for this very cause, words harm deeply, and, being related to no inherent pattern, surfaces likewise gain significance. In turn, this confusion leads to a stress upon disguise for its own sake, particularly with the elaborate private trial scenes of *The New Inn* and the misun-derstandings about who has given birth to a child in *The Magnetic Lady*. The author, as well as the audience and the work, enjoys extrav-agances under this dispensation. The indecisiveness frankly encourages capricious indulgences. Instead of obeying any inevitable laws, it con-structs a maze which temporarily flaunts the rules it finally obeys. The lambent shadow play may yield eventually a scepticism of the sort which romantic ironists of the nineteenth century and Christopher Fry in this one have exploited. The mock seriousness may in time ex-pand the comic or convert it into something else. An extended specu-lation has no bearing at this point. It runs the risk, however, of accepting the paradox that the comic is more tragic than tragedy, a merging of emotions which Jonson could not have brought himself to recognize.

This ingenuity depends upon glancing effects, a few touches here and there of the sort which fit with the structure of *Every Man out of His Humour*. For Jonson in that play the strength which held all together lay in the inevitability of the humours which could not change. In the four last plays metamorphosis no longer resembles Musco's disguises but something which lies deeper or which stays nowhere permanently and crops up sporadically. The main design does not sketch a façade but a shifting phantasmagoria of altered costumes and personalities. It involves, to reverse the concept behind *Volpone*, consequences without truth, that is: the comic game becomes a gamble in which the loss may represent a beguiling mischance rather than justice and, in the long run, seem a gain for the specific individual. Seated before this spectacle, an audience ought to experience an involvement with certain characters and want one of two, or more, possibilities to transpire. The intricacies of empathy eluded Jonson; he failed to come close to encompassing it.

The law vanishes as a principle except where it works against the innocent individual who seeks to go beyond its unjust restrictions. Superficially a general social order may prevail, but the community does not exert a vital force to correct or set standards. A terrifying anarchy rules the world, and it is this chaos which the heroes and heroines strive to avoid. In *Volpone* the most nearly satisfactory practice won; justice in Venice forms a contradiction in terms, but nothing else avails against monsters. Eventually it does, or may, see the truth. The comic possibilities of this disinterest hold considerably more promise than the tracing of individual fates. Within this welter of late uncertainties, the language collapses. Just as the structures appear more desolate because the ruins suggest a grandeur and here and there a nearly intact episode shows through, so a few speeches do not lack inventiveness. Various set pieces, some of which have been mentioned or quoted, progress with irreproachable correctness. Often in the main action and usually in secondary plots jests grind along without satiric impulses; the clowns sound as labored as only bad Elizabethan jokes can. The lovers' outpourings, especially Wittipol's and Lovel's, resemble grammar-school exercises which mouth the approved sentiments instead of creating observations from any valid experienced or imagined encounters. The piety which the endings demand, while everyone compliments himself on how splendidly it has all turned out, sounds sanctimonious. Nevertheless, at times a surpassing ineptitude bubbles forth and almost wins one over to the simple-minded confusions, as when Miles Metaphor, a character whose vocabulary makes John Littlewit's inventions seem almost decorous, cautions:

> *Met.* Let not the mouse of my good meaning, Lady,
> Be snap'd up in the trap of your suspition,
> To loose the taile there, either of her truth,
> Or swallow'd by the Cat of misconstruction. (IV. iv. 25–28)

These lines occur in *A Tale of a Tub*, a play unquestionably by Jonson but so far relegated to a note here. Its place in the canon provokes disagreements because it may antedate *The Case Is Altered*, be one of his last compositions, or represent a mixture, an early one later patched with new episodes. Its disjointedness has been blamed on a novice's inexperience and an indifferent old man. The parts ridiculing Inigo Jones as a maker of gauche masques must belong to a time not long before the play's performance. Otherwise, authorities, summoning their favorite criteria, have come to different conclusions. To embark on the intricacies of conjectures would distend a work which, in the perspectives of Jonson's development, deserves no such notice by itself.[11] If he composed the play in the 1630's, the choice of subject throws light on his career. Nevertheless, even if he dug out an old manuscript, the gesture itself and the reasons for his choice say something about a temperament as deliberate as his. The point is that, new or old, this play, rather than *The Magnetic Lady*, rounds out Jonson's career and in a sense nearly links with *The Case Is Altered*.

The parts involving a rustic masque and satire on Inigo Jones, the names In-and-In Medlay and Vitruvius Hoop, in themselves devastating, matter less than the two central themes on which the episodes depend. One depicts a hue and cry designed, however, not to torment a man who wants a silent bride but to unite two lovers. The second is a mother's search for her missing son, a point beyond which

The Case Is Altered began. The English setting seemingly puts *A Tale of a Tub* with the part of Jonson's career long after he discarded the *fabula palliata* for the *fabula togata*. More deliberately than the comedies, this play seizes on what look like native English types without counterpart in other theaters. Nevertheless, the action approaches a pastoral lyricism unlike any work yet considered. It flows across the Middlesex landscape on St. Valentine's day. The country, winter, and love develop patterns already associated in *Epicene;* more appropriately than in the confines of London, the hymeneal masque takes place to the satisfaction of all concerned at the conclusion of the play. In the majority of Jonson's plays the time of year does not have much bearing on the action. When it does impinge, it usually concerns heat as in *Volpone* and *Bartholomew Fair*. Nevertheless, having at the end turned decidedly to winter, Jonson did not leave matters there. Surprisingly enough, in his last work, which remains incomplete, he attempted to evoke spring with its traditional associations.

The Sad Shepherd surprises critics who have inflexible notions about Jonson. On the surface it looks almost unique and unexpected. Its versification reaches a purity and elegance rare even for the delicacy which English pastoral poetry sought.

> *Aeg.* A Spring, now she is dead: of what, of thornes?
> Briars, and Brambles? Thistles? Burs, and Docks?
> Cold Hemlock? Yewgh? the Mandrake, or the Boxe?
> These may grow still; but what can spring beside?
> Did not the whole Earth sicken, when she died?
> As if there since did fall one drop of dew,
> But what was wept for her! or any stalke
> Did beare a Flower! or any branch a bloome;
> After her wreath was made. . . .   (I. v. 33–41)

As an exercise in the pastoral genre, it owes little to any model. The characters do not join the thinly veiled classical figures who migrated from *The Shepheardes Calender* into English poetry; they comprise Robin Hood's band. The villains take the supernatural guise of witches who can assume varied shapes, but they belong to British mythology. The plot concerns life among this group with emphasis on their outdoor sports. As the quoted passage indicates, although the season is spring, a bereaved Aeglamour mourns his missing beloved. All this sounds like a drastic change from what have seemed Jonson's chief preoccupations. In one sense it is. In another way, however, it proves once again that his method bestowed such thorough mastery that he could direct his talents as he wished. Any method must impose limits, and so did his; it operated with amazing finesse within its boundaries which expanded slowly.

The musicality of the verse finds antecedents in songs and the masques where, however, he could resort to the more accommodating stanzas of lyric poetry. Here, in the passage quoted, the impulse behind the blank verse of the great comedies shapes the lament. The list of weeds chooses the appropriate objects. The pathetic fallacy of a mourning nature belongs to the accepted conventions in Renaissance elegies where the landscape joins human sorrow. The adventures of Robin Hood and Maid Marian set this grief in context and keep it from dominating. Here, again, Jonson took familiar matter from books and used it as he chose. Although he read up on the methods of hunting and dressing deer,[12] he versified his description skillfully. So, too, Robin Hood and Maid Marian cause many puzzles in legends. Through their banter they become a sensible pair (a unique achievement for Jonson), able to be deceived by a witch but less given to despair than Aeglamour. Likewise, the witch has the right amount of power for a native spirit, a command of magic but easier to oppose than absolute deities. Of course, his research into these matters, such as with *The Masque of Gipsies*,[13] stood Jonson in good stead for the topic. Far from being a decision to try something else, *The Sad Shepherd* becomes an adaptation of abiding practices, particularly in view of the masques.

The tone of the work has no direct precedents. The stage directions list a variety of settings which derive more from the masques than the plays. Caroline drama may have tended in this direction, but *The Sad Shepherd*, like the humour comedies and the great comedies, does not exploit the latest fad for mere novelty. It corresponds with nothing else in the English theater. Its unfinished condition, although like *Hero and Leander* others' pens have given it an ending, means that a satisfactory performance is impossible, and visualizing it proves moderately inconclusive. The characters have strong allegorical tendencies which depict virtues rather than the vices of the comedies. The witch Maudlin and her daughter Douce sound, on the other hand, too expectedly like human beings; the contrasts might, however, disappear or add depth in a performance. The whole has a pleasant unity which the Prologue announces. The pastoral should not be solemn, and the English subject can *"match, or those of* Sicily, *or* Greece." (Prologue, 14) Set apart from the country mirth, the title figure develops another aspect of the plot. In many ways it represents Jonson's most diversified achievement.

It asks, perhaps, a more detailed examination than the one accorded it here. Its incompleteness, however, requires rather rash conjectures for any generalization. It undeniably fits into a career whose totality reflects back upon it, and the last chapter may better explain it as part of an outlook. *The Sad Shepherd* helps prove how right one of Jonson's faculties—and one for which he is given least credit— always is. It might be termed an intuition of decorum. Thus, when he chose to write a play dealing with the outdoors, he picked with surprising appropriateness the one English rural deity of any significance. Whatever one makes of Lord Raglan's assertions in *The Hero*[14] on the origins of Robin Hood, there can be no doubt that the folk hero exceeds mere historical proportions. Each of Jonson's plays is an individual exercise, valid in its own right. Taken together, thanks to his intuitive powers, they form almost a lexicon in the art of comedy. The definitions at no point in his works receive a full statement, but his methodical traits make one inevitable. In his books he inscribed the motto " 'Tanquam Explorator' . . . . from Seneca's *Epistles* (ii. 5), 'Soleo enim et in aliena castra transire, non tanquam transfuga, sed tanquam explorator'."[15] What he returned with he arranged with a new coherence, not merely for phrases and lines but also for concepts and ideas. Some of these remain in *Timber*, whose disorganized state does not reveal them at their best.[16] The full title of *Timber* is "DISCOVERIES; MADE VPON MEN AND MATTER: AS THEY have flow'd out of his daily Readings; or had their refluxe to his peculiar Notion of the Times." (VIII, p. 561) As much can be claimed for the concept of the comic truth itself.

CHAPTER XII

Virbius

To claim that Jonson's plays encompass the major modes of comedy without yet having mentioned the most common pragmatic test must seem a crippling oversight. Laughter, however forcibly expressing itself, springs from mixed sources at unpredictable times. Physiologically and psychologically it proves so baffling that reliance upon it for any proofs turns into a whimsically subjective measure. Jonson, along with other theorists, took diametric views. In the semiprivacy of *Timber* he confided, "Nor, is the moving of laughter alwaies the end of *Comedy*, that is rather a fowling for the peoples delight, or their fooling. For, as *Aristotle* saies rightly, the moving of laughter is a fault in Comedie, a kind of turpitude, that depraves some part of a mans nature without a disease. . . . In short, as Vinegar is not accounted good, untill the wine be corrupted: so jests that are true and naturall, seldome raise laughter, with the beast, the multitude." (VIII, pp. 643–44) Publicly, echoing Horace, he promised in the Prologue to *Volpone*, "He'll rub your cheeks, til (red with laughter) / They shall looke fresh, a weeke after." (Prologue, 35–36) The trouble with laughter as a standard rests in its mercurial appearance from one night to the next and the shifting tastes between country and country or century and century. British audiences find stock Elizabethan clowns less of a trial than those in the United States do. The Channel makes an insurmountable barrier which has defeated everyone, Gide included, who transported Elizabethan tragedy into French. (A Parisian performance of *The Changeling*, a translation dispensing with the second plot, amused the spectators, who treated it as Grand Guignol; de Flores' announcement of severing Alonzo's finger brought down the house.)

Elusive as external sources of laughter may be, what inner sensations it expresses or distorts remain likewise hidden. "When you see with what hypochondriac profundity an earlier generation of Englishmen discovered the ambiguity which lies at the root of laughter, it is enough to cause a feeling of anxiety. Dr. Hartley, for example, makes the following remark: 'When laughter first manifests itself in the infant, it is an incipient cry, excited by pain, or by a feeling of pain suddenly inhibited, and recurring at brief intervals.' What if everything in the world were a misunderstanding, what if laughter were really tears?"[1] Kierkegaard's perverse epigram delivers a less shocking paradox now than it must have to a complacent age and land. Twentieth-century existentialists have insisted upon the inseparability of the two emotions. "On ne découvre pas l'absurde sans être tenté d'écrire quelque manuel du bonheur. 'Eh! quoi, par des voies si étroites...?' Mais il n'y a qu'un monde. Le bonheur et l'absurde sont deux fils de la même terre. Ils sont inséparables. . . . Il faut imaginer Sisyphe heureux."[2] Lacking facts and confronting these opinions, one has no choice but to relegate laughter itself to a marginal position. For the time being it may serve as a welcome addition to comedy without becoming crucial. Were anyone thoroughly trained in the techniques of psychology, drama, acting, and folkways to undertake a survey, he might emerge with statistics on why and when his chosen group laughs, but his report would not penetrate the structure of comedy itself. No ready-made criterion defines the genre more adequately for Jonson's achievements. If one had Aristotle's full speculations, how to begin might pose a less confusing riddle. As things are, other rule-of-thumb measurements stand up no better than laughter.

For example, at a considerable distance from pragmatic investigations, literary theory fails to say what comedy achieves and where to place it. Until recently, few have deigned to regard it seriously in fear, perhaps, of sounding incongruously solemn on a frivolous subject. Often it serves as a silver foil for tragedy. Although the comic and tragic masks rest side by side in popular iconography, they seldom attain an equal eminence for philosophies of literature. Tragedy figuratively sits enthroned on high; ranged beneath it are poetic drama, problem plays, experiments, propaganda pieces, melodrama, and all the rest may be, somehow, comedy, prefaced by vague tags like romantic, drawing room, farcical, or dark. The feeling of its being essentially low prevails: whether as for Aristotle it depicts inferior people, or as in Greek productions it wears the sock, or as for Bergson it flatters audiences to become superior, or as in general usage it connotes insignificant entertainment. Behind these instances runs the moral prejudice of literary critics that at best it aims to instruct by showing creatures with slight dimensions and their errors. Furthermore, such characters, whether fools or knaves, must succumb to the attractions of virtue before the last curtain. Enid Welsford in her study of *The Fool* traces and evaluates the type. She departs consciously from the narrow view. After identifying roles of fools through the ages, she decides that their buoyancy when suffering any calamity rouses a sympathy and in this emotion the comic resides. The gentleness hardly fits Jonson, and she dismisses him; "when the mood of contempt is predominant—as for instance at the end of Jonson's *Volpone*—one feels at once that comedy is losing its character and turning into pure satire. . . ."[3]

The comic spirit impertinently will not keep its low station and refuses to be exorcised. Its inventions multiply until they threaten to become ubiquitous. Neither the distinctive garb of a buffoon's motley nor a Pierrot's white face satisfies it. Mockery seizes not just the dramatized fools but holds an uncomfortably polished mirror before audiences, which can scarcely sympathize when condescension to a clown verges on confronting themselves. Ultimately the implications of comedy may surpass those of tragedy. Chapman's title *All Fools* claims too much, but the relatives of Sir Amorous La Foole in *Epicene* fill every corner of England and beyond, "the LA-FOOLES o' the north, the LA-FOOLES of the west, the LA-FOOLES of the east, and south—we are as ancient a family, as any is in *Europe*—but I my selfe am descended lineally of the *french* LA-FOOLES. . . ." (I. iv. 37–41) Acknowledged or not, comedy depicts a grotesque summoning of every man in or out of his humour to a ship of fools, and his accumulated good deeds can only wave *bon voyage.*

To avoid contending with boundaries which refuse to stay put, one may succumb to the initially attractive temptation of calling a halt and declaring that a happy ending determines comedy. This expedient quickly bestows the greatest scope of all on it, far more than sanguine views will grant, as the translation of *La Divina Commedia* into *The Divine Vision* attests. This sort of euphemism belongs to the insular temperament which modified the stage direction "Enter a bloody sergeant" to "Enter a bleeding captain," but, a snobbish aversion to the word apart, considering just the consummation does reach meaningless proportions. If the ultimate happy ending is in heaven, then the theory that a Christian tragedy is impossible gains a certain cogency. When the Christian hero recognizes and repents his tragic flaw, redemption in most theologies must commence. With this view one rejoices that, although defeated by the world, the protagonist lives happily, in the broadest sense of the word, ever after. These arguments soon wax tediously academic because theatrically the embodiment of any eternity resembles the prolongation of a temporal scene: one big fish fry or a room in a provincial French hotel. Some tastes might elect the latter in preference to the former. Indeed, how peculiarly transitory pleasures translate into unending bores forms the substance of John Balderston's necessarily short sketch with the honest title, *A Morality Play for the Leisure Class.*

The real difficulty arises from suggesting what sort of world the characters can go on living in. Jonson's struggles with this detail increased throughout his career, and ostensibly seventeenth-century society could set a norm more convincingly than later ones. The whole theory that comedy upholds a golden mean which coincides with the mores of an ideal majority should be re-examined.[4] It sounds persuasive and theoretically ought to hold good, but few writers of English comedy practiced it in their mature works. Congreve comes closest, but he nearly broke with it in *The Way of the World*, his farewell to the genre. Wycherley flaunted it effectively in *The Country Wife; The Plain Dealer* reached an inevitable dead end. Shaw went out of his way to mock all standards, at least on the surface.[5] Molière provides in his bourgeois stories a satisfactory instance, but he exceeded it, perhaps unwittingly, at times. The other example, Menander, looks, finally, more like the exception than the rule. Jonson's preference for Aristophanes and the *vetus comoedia*, which led to the humour comedies, expresses his impatience with the domestic fables of Plautus and Terence. (And the Roman playwrights, in copying Menander, scarcely depicted their own day.) For lesser writers whether defense of the public arises from assent or defeat, whether it seeks truth or profits, poses an uninteresting problem.

If a critic regards the enduring in terms neither of the other world nor of this one's society, he may avoid some snags by reverting to a mythic, ritualistic pattern. Such a program satisfies the temporal prerequisites and likewise places them *sub specie aeternitatis*.

> Comedy is an art form that arises naturally wherever people are gathered to celebrate life, in spring festivals, triumphs, birthdays, weddings, or initiations. For it expresses the elementary strains and resolutions of animate nature, the animal drives that persist even in human nature, the delight man takes in his special mental gifts that make him the lord of creation; it is an image of human vitality holding its own in the world amid the surprises of unplanned coincidence. The most obvious occasions for the performance of comedies are thanks or challenges to fortune. What justifies the term "Comedy" is not that the ancient ritual procession, the Comus, honoring the god of that name, was the source of this great art form . . . but that the Comus was a fertility rite, and the god it celebrated a fertility god, a symbol of perpetual rebirth, eternal life.[6]

If one can trust anthropologists, these conditions do explain the origins of comedy in Greece, western culture, and throughout the world. The impulse may have persisted into the Elizabethan period, although reading deliberately ritualistic patterns into *Bartholomew Fair*, which pointedly alludes to the saint and his feast day, scarcely aids an appreciation. Mrs. Langer in her extended definition does not insist on an awareness of the initial tendencies. To deny that joy, as well as laughter, accompanies comedy would rob it of all its prime attributes. On the other hand, declaring it affirmative of man's triumphs in life disqualifies some brilliant works. Often man does not emerge as lord of creation, whatever trips him up. The sole consolation some valid examples supply promises him that he may avoid becoming lord of misrule.

In each of these four chief categories—laughter, characters (whether knaves or fools), the happy ending, and ritualistic rhythms —a likelihood exists but one which, pushed too far, in itself becomes ridiculous by swelling ambitiously or lacking applications. To regard the society from which situations grow and to which they lead isolates two kinds: those which celebrate or take for granted a continuum and those ignoring or denying it. The former might, for convenience, be tagged positive, the latter negative. Both draw upon infinite and indefinite attitudes in audiences. Its awareness of time and place reduces the chances which positive comedy has to survive because the atmosphere it invokes cannot reside entirely in the text. Negative comedy risks dullness or improbability from the outset. These two are not necessarily opposites, however, and they tend frequently to complement each other. Basically both capitalize on impulses which have been advanced to explain the nature of wit. For the dramatic conflict the positive commonly shows the workaday world with a factor altered (the familiar with an element changed) and the other tries to create a novel scene where one recognizable trait persists (the unknown with an element unchanged). Both may exhibit degrees of affirmation or denial, however; the emphasis makes the difference. As much may be claimed for some tragedy.

The difference here is that they look in opposite directions. Tragedy always surveys backward to plumb abiding mysteries, which assume new masks but stay one and the same dilemma. Wherever it ends, the ultimate temporal tragedy begins in the Garden of Eden; to nullify the fall as *O felix culpa* reiterates the elusiveness of a Christian tragedy. Comedy restricts itself to its own acting time; if it strays beyond those limits, it cautiously looks forward to test latent implications of present vices for coming years. The stock types forming so conspicuous a part of it embody no metaphysical mysteries but rather what seem almost irreducible human traits. The most satisfactory happy ending refers less often to heaven than Utopia. A true Utopia must by definition be incredible because its inhabitants and their world have left off being like audiences watching them. If it displays mankind as essentially unchanged and exploiting new gadgets, it merely intensifies the present. *Brave New World* no longer seems the book it once did.[7] To stay comic, the worship of mechanization had to look improbable. Now that many of its horrors occur in daily life, one makes little more of them. Tragedy mourns a fated doom; pity and terror recognize an awful inevitability extending from the past into the future. Comedy posits that a freedom exists beyond its own confines. What form it takes does not matter to the stage because free individuals must will their own lives. ". . . and they lived happily ever after" declares an end to questions which no one should be presumptuous enough to answer for another. Within their closed frame, the characters may arouse sympathy (a positive trait) or contempt (a negative one). Such attributes can vary with the production of the same play. Generally those who display the wits to continue improved but somewhat unchanged look positive; those incapable of reform or in need of a thorough overhauling, negative. In both these instances the enveloping society can figure as little more than a backdrop, which audiences take for granted. When it asserts itself with such force that the characters merge with it, after having been outstanding, the ritualistic pattern dominates. Or they may regard the group as unworthy and renounce it for a more satisfactory one. Such points represent absolutes, and some obvious refinements frequently mix the proportions.

These definitions do, however, include the main signposts pointing toward the comic. In every case, what ultimately binds them celebrates a degree of freedom, at least of the existence of choice. Mrs. Langer's insistence on a triumphant rite makes such an attitude prerequisite, as, to a lesser degree, does Miss Welsford's. Even when the stress hits only mechanical behavior, audiences rejoice that they need not fall victim to the same follies. At these times the buffoon may resemble a scapegoat. The meaning and practice of freedom remains, of course, an unresolved philosophic question, and nothing wrecks comedy more quickly than bare ideas bickering among themselves. Philosophy should be behind the comic façade, never part of it. Confronted with deterministic theories, especially, cheerfulness breaks through, and comedians go right on pretending freedom exists. A description of a famous instance in Chaplin's film *Limelight* makes the point.

> The difficulties that confront Calvero [Chaplin] and Keaton in their gentle attempt to give a concert are beyond satire. The universe stands in their way, and not because the universe is imperfect, either, but just because it exists; God himself could not conceive a universe in which these two could accomplish the simplest thing without mishap. It is not enough that the music will not stay on its rack, that the violin cannot be tuned, that the piano develops a kind of malignant disease—the violinist cannot even depend on a minimal consistency in the behavior of his own body. When, on top of all the other misfortunes that can possibly come upon a performer humbly anxious to make an impression, it can happen also that one or both of his legs may capriciously grow shorter while he is on the stage, then he is at the last extreme: nothing is left. Nothing except the deep, sweet patience with which the two unhappy musicians accept these difficulties, somehow confident—out of God knows what reservoir of awful experience—that the moment will come at last when they will be able to play their piece. When that moment does come, it is as happy a moment as one can hope for in the theater. And it comes to us out of that profundity where art, having become perfect, seems no longer to have any implications.[8]

Like a clown's pantomime, comedy mimics, but it knows what details heighten essentials. If, as rarely happens, readers or audiences assert their prerogatives and avoid a specific folly, then the satiric work in time sounds stale because no one believes in the practices it mocks. Particular comedies rarely survive very long, and Jonson's lasting achievements argue a deeper insight. In reviewing them, one may see how they obey and refine the given definitions.

Initially he shows a group of decent, likable people each dominated by a different *idée fixe* so that their perceptions of the obvious grow distorted. Both characters and their world are positive at the start and close. In between the figures yield to negative traits but always within the range of an audience's tolerance. Trifling confusions, close to farce, function best at this level. Justification of mistaken identity and disguise requires this position. At the end the deceived literally have their eyes opened and put off the follies which momentarily deluded them. *The Case Is Altered* and *Every Man in His Humour* belong in this category, whose moderately complicated plots amuse because they affirm that common sense will suffice to right the troubles. If, however, the author heeds Aristotle, or his own propensities, he may jettison plot to heighten character and its inevitable eccentricities in doing nothing. The attitude audiences are expected to adopt toward the whimsey—the title of one in this vein—is you can't take it with you. Everything twists askew, and upon leaving the theater, one may feel almost ashamed at having consented to the unmitigated frivolity. At this point comedy begins to enter its special realm. If the peculiarities attain grotesque and, consequently, quite negative dimensions, exaggeration may reach an outlandishness which a daily scene can no longer contain. The positive world exists at most as a bridge into and out of a nearly surrealistic one. The three humour comedies belong to this type. Whether nominally at home in the Fortunate Isles, Gargaphie, or Augustus' Rome, character, in the sense of mere ego, rules triumphant. If a playwright burns these initial and final bridges, he confronts a variety of difficult tasks.

One solution for treating a society and characters both negative contrasts them with the more nearly expected world by a double plot. An area for affirmation exists side-by-side with denial. Frequently, however, the halves pull apart, with the upper reaches stiffly idealized and the lower extravagant slapstick. In avoiding this pitfall the playwright may join their parallels so neatly that stylization makes them distorting mirrors without depth. The range which such intricacy requires seldom graces Jacobean drama or any other. (*The Case Is Altered* on both levels belongs entirely to comedy, of course.) The picture-frame stage finds itself hard pressed in balancing these opposite attitudes. Motion pictures provide a better medium for encompassing the variety. The somewhat inconclusive film by Jean Renoir, *La Règle du jeu*, almost succeeds as servants and masters cross lines. The game of love played by the wealthy becomes an earnest matter to those employed by them so that the two classes exchange the attitudes commonly assigned them. The *décor* brilliantly comments on the impulses of mechanization: the collection of bizarre toys, beaters chasing game to organized slaughter, an airport mob, and the masquerade. The outcome preserves a sardonic tone, and it remains a nearly unique performance.

Or the writer may resign his pen to the prerogatives of acrobats and mimes as the most worthy. In avoiding the problem of character, plot, scene, and imitation, he abandons the motto "the play's the thing," the title of a production which moved Joseph Wood Krutch to observe, "A condemned man might possibly spend his last night on earth reading 'Hamlet' or watching an exhibition of prestidigitation. He would not, I think, have much patience with a merely earnest play."[9] Comedy may not have engaged critics sufficiently, but acts now belonging to the circus have been wholly dismissed. One can hardly review them because they perish when their performers leave the tanbark. On the other hand, although every dramatic revival reinterprets an old work, Roman jugglers must have featured the same tricks now current. The professional clown who is no fool usually enters the theater not in a comedy but in sentimental or (to be charitable) tragic work. Such plays, operas, films, and pantomimes do not belong to this genre. They exploit the obviously ironic plight of the individual whose disciplined way of earning a living limits his experiences. To regard the clown as negative himself in a negative (or uncreated) world helps explain why his role lends itself to poignancy. Were war ever an impossibility, with armies still maintained, the professional soldier might serve as the symbol just as well. Whatever the agony of their performers, such troupes present the kind of comedy most enduring and widely appreciated throughout the world. Kleist, indeed, lavished encomiums on marionettes and performers who have eliminated imitation. ". . . so findet sich auch, wenn die Erkenntnis gleichsam durch ein Unendliches gegangen ist, die Grazie wieder ein; so, dass sie, zu gleicher Zeit, in demjenigen menschlichen Körperbau am reinsten erscheint, der entweder gar keins, oder ein unendliches Bewusstsein hat, d. h. in dem Gliedermann, oder in dem Gott."[10] This concept passes far beyond Jonson, who always cogently insisted upon content.

His solution in designing a negative comedy bestows on *Volpone*,

Epicene, and *The Alchemist* their unique greatness. They are by no extension of the term realistic. Each creates a special world and further hides most action in a secluded room. Freed of ordinary restraints, the characters' extravagance flourishes acceptably because it has few consequences and because it refers to general follies. Venice and London of the great comedies present singular dimensions. The forces which might ordinarily halt the drives are expelled, and one witnesses the unrestricted flourishing of delusions. The mirror it holds up to a limited life catches oblique reflections, but the partial truth it shows resembles a Medusa's head which can be contemplated in no other way. This description sounds far from the usual comedy, but so are Jonson's three plays. To consider them anything else distorts them. By their denials they still celebrate freedom. In them a character is chained by neither nemesis nor *hubris* but by a chimera which he has created and which, in turn, enslaves him. One cannot pity him because he sacrifices everything to a nonexistent idol. Bidding on a legacy, complete silence, or the philosophers' stone does not, with one individual, exceed probability in fact or fiction. That in all these plays groups compete with each other or among themselves forms the special sting. Moreover, no affection, much less love, survives this climate. In this aspect *The Rake's Progress,* although comparable with *Volpone,* adds an extra element; Anne Trulove cannot save Rakewell entirely from Nick Shadow, but her devotion contributes a value. Confronting negative characters in a negative world, what emotions does one feel? Jonson offers a practical answer. His 1616 folio collection, as has been seen, presents a co-ordinated body of work but one less programmatic from its outset than he pretends. Although no prologue introduces the quarto *Every Man in His Humour,* one heads the folio version. It recites Jonson's developed credo, and in a way heralds the whole volume. He proposes, more suitably for the great comedies than the first ones, that audiences acknowledge

> such errors, as you'll all confesse
> By laughing at them, they deserue no lesse:
> Which when you heartily doe, there's hope left, then,
> You, that haue so grac'd monsters, may like men.
>
> (Prologue, 27–30 b)

This rationale matches plays in which the expected world functions weakly or at a distance. Jonson's excepted, there have been few other respectable examples until the twentieth century. Views popularly associated with existentialism can capitalize on this denial most effectively, although the results resemble even less any comedy. *Huis clos* nominally places its characters in hell, but the location and action draw upon no supernatural attributes. It could be any room, anywhere, as the location of *Waiting for Godot* specifies, "A country road. A tree."[11] Estragon and Vladimir go through the tried music-hall routines to amuse themselves in a locale they do not understand and in waiting for any deliverance, which they cannot begin to identify. They, along with two other adults, Pozzo and Lucky, behave like the humour characters, but their play will have no end, and nothing can get them out of their enforced humour of waiting for Godot. Jonson could not yield to such extremes, and *The Alchemist*, unable to expel or contain external forces, nearly broke down. It is a step from waiting for a miracle called Godot to expecting the philosophers' stone, but Jonson had to account for his people and their environment in other guises. Again, not until the twentieth century has a whole society presented the totally negative and mechanical aspect to encase such comedies. Clément's film *Jeux interdits* terrifyingly adapts these same techniques. At the center two children play their one game of making a cemetery in an abandoned building. They go unnoticed by the blindly feuding families who will not stop their quarrels on this side of the grave. The warring world passes the small farms and exists as impersonal planes tracing a straight line of bullets across a bridge. Only the children, who have not yet developed capacities for adult stupidities, alleviate the fierceness of the ridicule, comparable with the boy (or boys) of *Waiting for Godot*. If such works belong to tragicomedies, they extend from the indignation of comedy rather than the awe of tragedy and expand the special attitudes behind Jonson's.

In more usual plays, including Jonson's late ones, when the enveloping action assumes its routine functions, the effect relies on a hero's and heroine's escaping from its limits when they have become more nearly positive, while other forces remain negative. The chief character must perceive a truth beyond anything the scene has to offer and go off in search of this gleam. Much sentimental writing starts here: adolescent poetry, stories in housewives' magazines, the bourgeois success novel, and television playlets. The widespread symbol for it shows Chaplin's tramp walking down a sunset road into, presumably, another world or, perhaps, a private garden. It presupposes a new life but one located neither on earth nor in literature. When fully realized, it celebrates deliverance, although the process may entail such suffering that it no longer sounds like comedy. To document the process of regeneration convincingly requires a long time, and few plays can sustain the portrayals. The novel, rather, seems congenial to this theme, and examples of it, all moderately vexing, come to mind: *The Idiot, Resurrection, Middlemarch, The Golden Bowl,* and, the climax of this genre, *Finnegans Wake.* In the majority of these a woman serves to redeem the inevitable; no laws can guide her because each situation bears its own uniqueness. Jonson's four late plays grope after the main aspects of this style. If he failed to dramatize it adequately, his trying argues a keen awareness. The praise of personal justice, the women's superior roles, invoking a transubstantial love, and contempt for commercial society mark *The Staple of News* and *The New Inn* particularly. In his day Jonson could not formulate the terms to define it theatrically. He could not concede that salvation is justified not by the worth of the person rescued but by the experience of a charity, bordering on agape, in a materialistic world. When, however, the leading character devotes himself to a value which is clearly wrong and which his misguided humility and veneration raise to dignity, criticism must lay down its arms: *Don Quixote* and Kafka's *Metamorphosis* or, in the theater, *Le Misanthrope* and *The Wild Duck.*

Both *Le Misanthrope* and *The Wild Duck* force special explanations from critics.[12] Until the twentieth century—not to be too severe now that the temptation of being sidetracked by digressions has almost passed—the only notably effective stage pieces in this vein have been Shakespeare's last plays, and a judicious admiration of these has come quite recently. Much of the recent vogue derives from Pirandello, particularly for technique. Giraudoux and Anouilh, especially, have exploited such sentiments. *La Folle de Chaillot* shows a woman who elects to view the same world each day through her nineteenth-century newspaper, but her repetition frees her from worse delusions. She opposes herself to all contemporary powers and destroys them for private reasons. At times, indeed, society presents so destructive a picture that the stage becomes a higher reality. Consequently, Anouilh's *L'Alouette* rescues Jeanne d'Arc from the stake at the last minute and locks her in a perpetual tableau of triumph: a contradiction, but not a repudiation, of history. Without joining society, denying it, or quitting it, these positive characters stand enshrined above it in artifacts which it honors grudgingly. Although such plays represent a small minority, their growing strength points out yet another area for comedy.

The only honest plays which today present positive characters in a positive setting must revert to a pastoral form with overtones of allegory. The conventions carry a hint of deceit. A broad continuity identifies the action, which, in turn, strives to enhance it. It celebrates things as they are, have been, and will continue to be. Such a program limits the characters' freedom because they must happily rest content in the best of all possible worlds. Unlimited freedom cannot exist even in comedy, however, and to recognize the boundaries honestly may prove desirable in the long run. The stage no longer mirrors, questions, or creates; it too becomes part of a cultural rhythm. Both *The Case Is Altered* and *A Tale of a Tub* imperfectly share traits with this impulse, although the first resembles the group into which it leads and the latter the one which it terminates. *The Sad Shepherd* illustrates the kind with amazing precision. The demands of a plot make certain conflicts inevitable, but a sustained affirmation gathers everything together. Death itself may join the pattern as a necessary concomitant to be accepted. The playwright rejoices in whatever happens, translated into legends or myths. Social customs prevailing at any point do not set the standards; the force of enduring rhythms continues unbroken. The cycle rounds out the denouement.

One can begin to discern within these limits the morality of these forms, a debated topic which has plagued Jonson and every critic of the genre. One may prefer to ignore all specific nostrums attributed the arts and see them as eternal. Most comedy, except for short passages, such as the Chaplin concert already described, adheres literally to immediate errors. When it invokes Perdix for its patron, it stays close to topics which audiences know. On the other hand, because it also tolerates extravagant follies, reading wholesome remedies into it looks equally disproportionate. When it praises social clichés, it is patently false; in exhibiting negatives, it may offend the public. By presenting characters who escape their limitations it often yields to sentimental phantasies, and a ceremony worships at forgotten shrines. By emphasizing specific errors, it has limited consequences and, as an extension of a game, none at all. This very fidelity to materials renews the marvels of acrobats and, in a larger sense, of all craftsmanship, even at its remote distance. Consequently, it remains true to itself, quite apart from its implications. "The question comes back thus, obviously, to the kind and the degree of the artist's prime sensibility, which is the soil out of which his subject springs. The quality and capacity of that soil, its ability to 'grow' with due freshness and straightness any vision of life, represents, strongly or weakly, the projected morality."[13] Comedy demands that the artist cultivate his special vision; whatever his inner anxieties, the work must display clarity. Lucidity bows before no illusions, and never cheats the laws it has created.

As an adjunct of this discipline, the writer's most valuable means is a conscious rhetoric. Granted its special world and characters, the language will soar to improbable heights because by definition it has lost contact with actualities. In tragedy language must investigate its subject intently because of the complex theme and its extensions. This gratuitous wealth in comedy makes any specific applications precarious. Save for paradoxes and anecdotes, almost none of its lines or speeches remains memorable out of context. The task of transposing the delusions underlined by this rhetoric to one's own position proves incongenial. Hazlitt's assertion, made with tongue partly in cheek, that the older satire had cured mankind's stupidities,[14] hardly bears a close examination. It may, however, unmask a foe who threatens all morality increasingly. "Gesellt sich dem Wirken und der Wirkung des Charlatans immer der Begriff des Geheimnisses, so sind nicht alle, sondern nur bestimmte Zeitperioden dadurch gekennzeichnet, dass sie die Wissenschaft mit dem Geheimnis paarten und so die Geheimwissenschaften erblühen liessen."[15] Grete de Francesco's formulation in a brilliant study *Die Macht des Charlatans* has enjoyed less recognition than it deserves. Although keeping to its topic with uncommon fidelity, it connects historical charlatans with this century when theory has fled before techniques. The clear implications are that the charlatan dominates almost all aspects of contemporary life. Although a reference to *The Alchemist* opens the book, and one occurs later, this study puts little hope in the power of comedy to dethrone the charlatan. Catherine II had Cagliostro expelled from Russia and commissioned satires about him. Yet "die kluge Katharina übersah genau so wie ihre aufklärerischen Freunde, dass diejenigen, die auf ⟨⟨der Höhe ihres gläubigen Dünkels⟩⟩ thronen, das Lachen längst verlernt haben und den Charlatanen gar nicht verfallen wären, wenn sie noch vermocht hätten, Witz su verstehen und Lächerlichkeit zu bemerken."[16] To a reader of Jonson, a surprise comes with the realization of how, in the course of his career, he anatomized almost every type of charlatan from those sincerely self-deluded to the consummate pretenders, those selling panaceas to those reclaiming waste lands, gossip mongers and advertising experts, dictators and worshipers of mediocrity, babblers in civil or ecclesiastical law, dilettantes in the arts and religious fanatics—but the list ends only in a catalogue of his entire gallery. Once again, this topic involves the ultimate morality of comedy, the insistence upon individual responsibilities for falling victim to delusions coupled with the assurance that cant will always snare some. The charlatan catches the ordinarily perceptive because they have the freedom to be fools. In the end reason may mock itself as a brand of charlatanism, but this very self-awareness becomes a tribute to reason. Only control and intelligence shape satires, which ultimately laugh at the restraints guiding them. Freedom, likewise, must be under the sway of reason, and both can exceed their limits to become humours or worse. This warning, however, suffices to keep comedy within bounds. Indeed, in laughing one affirms his consenting to the hard contradictions between the possible and the fantastic.

"In all the finer lights and shades of soul painting Jonson is not so much inferior to the rest as out of the competition altogether. Souls, as he understood them, or at least as they interested and engaged his art, have no chiaroscuro, and no perspective; no problematic possibilities, no dimly descried background, no conflicting moods. . . . We must not seek in the hard, categorical veracity of Jonson's art, the kind of truth by which supreme artists like Dante or Shakespeare in interpreting a country and an age interpret also universal humanity." With these words C. H. Herford and Percy Simpson conclude the penultimate section of what they term, without overt irony, "Final Appreciation." (I, p. 126) To point out the obvious irony, that the first man to declare Shakespeare "not of an age, but for all time!" (VIII, p. 391) has his own words reprimandingly turned against him, repeats a complaint made in the first chapter. By now, however, the significance of what unquestionably is Jonson's "hard, categorical veracity" needs no excuse. The comic truth must have such qualities: follies based on contemporary foibles, characters reduced to simplified drives, a neatly turned conclusion, and clarity throughout. The acrobat, similarly, asks only a carpet, two hooks in space, a rope, and an unfailing sense of balance. The content of comedy casts a supercilious look around its world at dangers, whether novelties or useless survivals. Less obvious tics, persistent and grounded in more than delusions, must remain mysteries. Whatever the characters' social status, dealers in junk or senators, or one become the other, they must remain, within this space, inconsequential. They claim no prerogatives beyond the acting time. In contrast, the language soars to any extreme because of these simplifications. Within such necessary restrictions comedy exhibits one special truth, and the most interesting examples can flaunt the unknowable truths which lie beyond it. The comic figure, then, lives only within the confines of whatever stage begets him. When he departs from these limits—to become quixotic, Gargantuan, or a benedict—he represents one aspect of life where comedy forms an incongruous part. Consequently, the comedian, as comedian, stirs mixed responses. In the film *La Strada*—a striking example for the middle of the twentieth century—a strong man, the gamin who assists him in his act, and a tightrope walker do not participate in a comedy at all. They represent almost allegorical aspects of human beings, comparable with the figures of hunchback, saint, and fool who dominate the final phases which Yeats describes in *A Vision*. The final scene, when the deserted strong man lies on the sand, might suggest by its configuration a

Picasso giant beside the sea or, at another level, merely A. B. Frost's "The Tennysonian Landscape" made to illustrate Lewis Carroll's parody "The Three Voices." Nevertheless, such forays into tragicomedy represent yet another aspect which may be eventually quite open to the truth of comedy.

These speculations, while scarcely doing violence to Jonson's plays, expand their boundaries beyond the scope he allotted them. Just as he took past rules and enlarged upon them,[17] so it seemed not an undue distortion to unite his into a code exceeding their immediate sources. Remembering his fondness for the circle to symbolize completeness, one might superimpose his plays on a rough diagram to sum up their progression. Jung has divided faculties on a circle, the quarter on the left belonging to sense perceptions, the top to rational processes, the right to intuitions, and the lower to emotions. Just as the four humours ought to be mixed, the four faculties ought to reinforce each other. For his masques, particularly, Jonson consulted many books similar to those from which Jung contrived his diagram. The comedies in their development exemplify this division; the tragedies and *Bartholomew Fair* assume a more nearly appropriate evaluation in this alignment, set forth on the facing diagram.

It seems less than fortuitous that Shaw, although always erratic, traced a career along roughly identical lines, and Shakespeare, as well, if congenitally incapable of staying within any limits, ordered his comedies in a similar fashion. To proceed through their works with the same points in mind might say new things about them without causing any of the compared titles to suffer. The truths which these plays take for granted do not bestow on them an inherent superiority. Whereas in Shaw the intuitions weaving through *Heartbreak House* make a richer fabric than rational debates give *Major Barbara*, Jonson took over the *données* for the great comedies more comfortably than those imperfectly realized in *The Devil Is an Ass*. The basis for judging lies not in how much the work includes but how much it successfully excludes.

The early plays recognize an open and apparent truth. No qualms deter the honest man from relying on his perceptions which refer to what society does. A segment of his better self may be be-

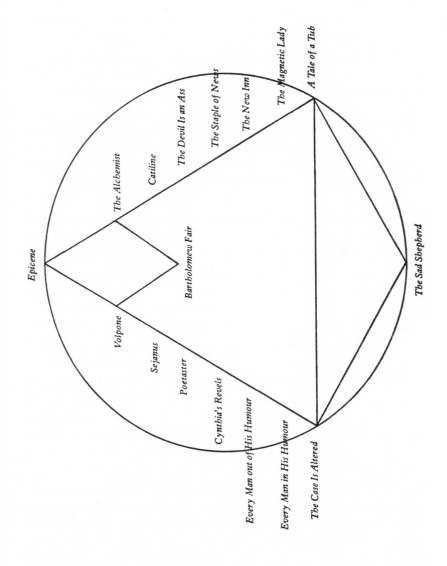

Epicene

The Alchemist

Catiline

The Devil Is an Ass

The Staple of News

The New Inn

The Magnetic Lady

A Tale of a Tub

Bartholomew Fair

The Sad Shepherd

Volpone

Sejanus

Poetaster

Cynthia's Revels

Every Man out of His Humour

Every Man in His Humour

The Case Is Altered

249

trayed when he misinterprets a trifling part of the public code. Such errors soon evaporate, and he can recover quickly. A gradual shrinking of internal and external virtues makes possible the progression through *Every Man out of His Humour* and *Poetaster* into *Sejanus*. The tragedy depends on a continuing uncertainty in all issues. Its reliance upon a blind Fortune links with medieval concepts, but the outlook derives more from Jonson's own observations than any return to historic modes. Awareness of all temporal limitations makes the suffering minority in Rome pitiable, but no power can deliver them from Sejanus' cruelty continuing in Macro. Sejanus, although a villain of proportions usually considered Senecan or Machiavellian, arouses fear because he manipulates others and no happiness accompanies a downfall promising disorder. Within these limits the play has a tragic force, which honestly keeps to its assumptions throughout. Three of the four great comedies draw upon a continuous celebration, and mockery, of intellectual qualities. Aspects of a game fit particularly with these. The protagonists amuse themselves on the brink of crime and violence, but other forces will detect them: "Mischiefes feed / Like beasts, till they be fat, and then they bleed" (V. xii. 150–51), as the conclusion of *Volpone* affirms. *Epicene*, a work unresolved at every point, relies upon the victories of a contemplative disbelief. Its prose suits the detached speculation for its own sake, another way of using and questioning reason. Love itself yields to every parody without, in the process, suffering any diminution outside these bounds. Viewed as the turning point of Jonson's career, *Epicene* deserves its freedom from commitments. *The Alchemist* lets language babble more extravagantly than ever, but both nature and society creep back into a rationale which cannot accommodate them under this dispensation.

    Catiline as a tragedy stands at the end of the great comedies, as *Sejanus* accounted for their inception. Catiline himself matches Sejanus. Cicero embodies the new elements and must rely on intuitions almost in the face of evidence. He should emerge the nominal hero. In Jonson's repertory this figure who overcomes odds because his heart is pure, though his mind may be simple, never quite convinces one. For *Catiline*, especially, Cicero's heroic love of an abstract State sounds in the orations like the last refuge of a charlatan. The heroines, rather, from *The Staple of News* onward help the men toward a new understanding and leave behind poseurs. Because Jonson could not dramatize, or express, convincingly a transcendent truth and because bad manners intrigued him to the end, the dotages must sound ineffectual. There remains, nevertheless, in a wonderfully "central" position *Bartholomew Fair*, which consents to whatever is merely because it is. It scrambles all faculties in a comedy which rejects nothing from Ursula to the puppets. If it never quite escapes the locale, it merely admits that men, all Adams like Overdo, never quite escape their flesh, blood, and folly. To insist on more demands, along with Zeal-of-the-Land Busy, the impossible or the tragic.

The two last plays share traits with *Bartholomew Fair* but stand remote, nearly pastoral. In stressing family relationships, a kind of romantic love, aspects of nature, and delicacy of feeling, they come close to the right emotions for this type. *The Sad Shepherd*, fragmentary though it is, belongs here with its consummate grace. Jonson's completed circle halves itself between perception and intuition rather than passion and reason, which reinforce one another. The latter two must bolster each other in comedy because the former lend themselves better to precise definitions for conflicts. This trait further explains why Jonson's works obey a classically thoroughgoing pattern in control and why they also violate what—assumed rightly or wrongly—the classical virtue of calm requires. If Jonson, like Perdix, worshiped in Minerva's temple, he did not, like Hippolytus, detest Venus' shrine.[18] Nevertheless, the absence of naked passions undoubtedly has contributed to his later neglect. Perhaps Venus took revenge on Jonson as surely as she did on Hippolytus. The fates suffered by the two have a figurative kinship.

After Jonson's death, a group of poets banded together to produce a volume of commemorative poems. Although these seventeenth-century memorials vary widely in quality, Jonson's seems unredeemable from the triviality which perfunctory exercises often entail.[19] Few of the more imposing names of the Caroline period appear in it: many contemporaries had died before Jonson, who started as one of the youngest Elizabethans; some of the rising generation had not yet attracted attention, and others, for unknown reasons, were unavailable.

Those who contributed produced a remarkably homogeneous group
of flat sentiments. Nothing rescues any of them entirely, although some
manage to rise for a few lines beyond the commonplace. Only the title
contains a happy augury; *Jonsonus Virbius* links him with the man
whom Virgil describes.

> The Son of fam'd *Hippolitus* was there;
> Fam'd as his Sire, and as his Mother fair.
> Whom in *Egerian* Groves *Aricia* bore,
> And nurs'd his Youth along the Marshy Shore:
> Where great *Diana's* peaceful Altars flame,
> In fruitful Fields, and *Virbius* was his Name.
> *Hippolitus*, as old Records have said,
> Was by his Stepdam sought to share her Bed:
> But when no Female Arts his Mind cou'd move,
> She turn'd to furious Hate her impious Love.
> Torn by Wild Horses on the sandy Shore,
> Another's Crimes th' unhappy Hunter bore;
> Glutting his Father's Eyes with guiltless gore.
> But chast *Diana*, who his death deplor'd,
> With *AEsculapian* Herbs his life restor'd.
> Then *Jove*, who saw from high, with just disdain,
> The dead inspir'd with Vital Breath again,
> Struck to the Center with his flaming Dart
> Th' unhappy Founder of the Godlike Art.
> But *Trivia* kept in secret Shades alone,
> Her care, *Hippolitus*, to Fate unknown;
> And call'd him *Virbius* in th' *Egerian* Grove:
> Where then he liv'd obscure, but safe from *Jove*.[20]

The patron suits Jonson, whose later fame, whether as Perdix or
Virbius, has endured overshadowing—a giant rather than a god. Nevertheless, remembering how often he celebrated Elizabeth as Diana,
one discerns a justice in placing him under the aegis of her shrine. Besides the usual boasts of Renaissance poetry for bestowing immortality,
a special suitability graces this niche. Probably Jonson, for the time
being, will retain his middle status in a minor genre, but this legend,
like any other, has varied uses. Although never quite the same from one
age to another, myths crop up repeatedly in new guises. It was, for
example, the story of Virbius as guardian of a dishonored altar which

started Frazer's pursuit of *The Golden Bough*,[21] the collection of folklore and speculations, some correct, some misapplied, which opened new approaches in diverse fields. No commentary ever exhausts a valid source; it should point toward a new interpretation. Hope for the rediscovery of Jonson's achievements in drama need not sound absurd. Meanwhile, acclaimed or not, the works themselves remain vital because they begin with solid materials of the actual, whether on earth or in books, and proceed by unfaltering craftsmanship to their defined ends, which transcend the literal. They endure in the sense that they become changing but indestructible artifacts. With the uncompromising assurances which Jonson bestowed on them, they will continue for a long time to record discoveries in the partly uncharted and constantly expanding, if sometimes elliptical, circle of the true and comic art.

Notes

Index

Notes

1 C. H. Herford, Percy and Evelyn Simpson, *Ben Jonson* (Oxford, 1925–1952; 11 vols.), I, p. 148. A note on these notes: I have held references down to an essential minimum. The text gives all necessary information. Here, however, I have recognized authorities to whom I am indebted and, now and then, disagreed with them on trifling points which have no place in the main discussion. All quotations from Jonson, except for a few indispensable quarto and folio citations, are in the Herford and Simpson edition. Hereafter, when the words are Jonson's, the documentation will follow in parentheses: for plays, acts and scenes in Roman numerals, lines in Arabic; for other references, volume number in Roman numerals, page references (designated by a "p.") in Arabic. The upright *s* and ligatures are not reproduced; otherwise, I have made no editorial changes. Titles and characters' names are given in their modern spelling.

2 Ovid, *Metamorphoses,* ed. Frank Justus Miller (London, 1928; 2 vols.), I, p. 422.

3 Joyce, of course, gave the Daedalus vogue a start with *A Portrait of the Artist as a Young Man* and *Ulysses.* The father of much "poet-as-craftsman" theory, Mallarmé, took a less enthusiastic view of the myth. See his *Oeuvres Complètes* (Paris, 1945), p. 1244.

4 Christopher Morley is responsible for the amusing conjecture that

"O Rare" might be read as Latin "orare," "pray for," in his pamphlet, *My One Contribution to Seventeenth-Century Scholarship* (New York, 1927).

5 M. C. Bradbrook, *The Growth and Structure of Elizabethan Comedy* (London, 1955), p. 8. At the risk òf turning Jonson and Shakespeare into Romulus and Remus building and jumping over improbable walls, see the note by T. S. Eliot, *Milton* (London, 1947), p. 8: "A little further on he [Dr. Tillyard] quotes another phrase of mine, of earlier date: 'The Chinese Wall of Milton's blank verse.' He comments: 'It must have been an ineffective wall, for *Venice Preserved, All for Love* and similar plays in blank verse were not confined by it; they owe nothing to Milton's versification.' Of course not—these were *plays*, and I have long maintained that dramatic blank verse and non-dramatic blank verse are not the same thing. The Chinese Wall there, if it existed, was erected by Shakespeare."

6 Two studies of Jonson's achievements in non-dramatic poetry should be mentioned: a book by George Burke Johnston, *Ben Jonson: Poet* (New York, 1945), and an article by Ralph S. Walker, "Ben Jonson's Lyric Poetry," *Criterion*, XIII (1934), pp. 430–48.

7 A satisfying general study of this genre remains Enid Welsford, *The Court Masque* (Cambridge, 1927).

8 However admirable its verse and elevated its philosophy, as a stage piece *Comus* moves clumsily. Performances in London at the Open Air Theatre, Queen Mary Gardens, carry a certain grace but remind one throughout of its quaintness.

9 See the conjecture advanced by C. J. Sisson, "Ben Jonson of Gresham College," *The Times Literary Supplement*, 21 December 1951, p. 604.

10 The term is G. Gregory Smith's in his introduction to *Elizabethan Critical Essays* (London, 1904; 2 vols.), I, p. xi. Recently, of course, scholars have drawn once again from these tracts; see especially Rosemond Tuve, *Elizabethan and Metaphysical Imagery* (Chicago, 1947), *passim.*

11 Ben Jonson, *Discoveries*, ed. Maurice Castelain (Paris, n.d.); this edition treats the many sources from which Jonson drew for these speculations. See also the notes by Herford and Simpson.

12 "Les dieux, gracieusement, nous donnent *pour rien* tel premier vers; mais c'est à nous de façonner le second, qui doit consonner avec l'autre, et ne pas être indigne de son aîné surnaturel."—Paul Valéry, *Variété I* (Paris, c. 1924), p. 66.

13 Herford and Simpson, I, p. 403.

14 Virgil, *Aeneid*, ed. H. Rushton Fairclough (London, 1932; 2 vols.), I, p. 406.

15 Volumes IX, X, and XI by Herford and Simpson list the main sources. An almost complete edition of Jonson's plays has come from Yale University, and these likewise treat sources. References to them appear in the appropriate chapters.

16 Virgil, *Aeneid*, II, p. 62.

17 Ovid, *The Art of Love and Other Poems*, ed. J. H. Mozley (London, 1929), p. 122.

18 The same, p. 122.

19 Robert M. Adams, "*Trompe-l'Oeil* in Shakespeare and Keats," *Sewanee Review*, LXI (1953), pp. 238–55, suggests a few possibilities of such a concept, but he stops short of a full investigation.

20 W. B. Yeats, *Collected Poems* (New York, 1951), pp. 184–85.

21 Algernon Charles Swinburne, *A Study of Ben Jonson* (London, 1889), p. 35. The phrase also occurs in John Addington Symonds, *Ben Jonson* (New York, 1886), p. 74.

22 See the thorough study by Gerald Eades Bentley, *Shakespeare and Jonson* (Chicago, 1945; 2 vols.).

23 T. S. Eliot, *Selected Essays, 1917–1932* (New York, 1932), pp. 127–39.

24 John Crowe Ransom, *The New Criticism* (Norfolk, Conn., 1941), pp. 158–75.

25 Ben Jonson, *Selected Works*, ed. Harry Levin (New York, 1938), pp. 1–36.

26 Elizabeth Bowen, *Collected Impressions* (New York, 1950), pp. 116–19.

27 Louis Kronenberger, *The Thread of Laughter* (New York, 1952), pp. 13–39.

28 *The Jonson Allusion-Book*, edd. Jesse Franklin Bradley and Joseph Quincy Adams (New Haven, 1922), *passim*.

29 A highly erratic account is Byron Steel, *O Rare Ben Jonson* (New York, 1927); more conservative is Marchette Chute, *Ben Jonson of Westminster* (New York, 1953).

30 The poem has been widely anthologized, so perhaps a reference is pedantic; see, however, Edwin Arlington Robinson, *Collected Poems* (New York, 1921), pp. 20–32.

31 "I told an American friend once that I intended to write a book called 'The Writer in Spite of Himself,' dealing with Joyce, Ben Jonson, Flaubert and. . . . Henry James."—Frank O'Connor quoted in *New York Times Book Review*, 24 June 1951, p. 14. O'Connor puts Jonson in the right company, although this attitude denies the artist a compass or wings and asks him to leap about through sheer inspiration.

32 H. de Vocht has attacked the folio as not receiving the benefit of Jonson's supervision. His tedious misreadings are effectively repudiated by Herford and Simpson, IX, pp. 74–84.

33 Erwin Panofsky, *Albrecht Dürer* (Princeton, 1943; 2 vols.), I, pp. 168–70.

CHAPTER II

1 *A Tale of a Tub* occupies a disputed position in the canon. It fits more suitably with the discussion in Chapter XI.

2 A question about the authenticity of parts of *The Case Is Altered* has been raised by J. M. Nosworthy, "*The Case Is Altered*," *Journal of English and Germanic Philology*, LI (1952), pp. 61–70. I find his argument less than convincing; the passages he cites do not touch the points here discussed.

3 A convenient summary of the materials available for discussing its production is supplied by E. K. Chambers, *The Elizabethan Stage* (Oxford, 1923; 4 vols.), III, pp. 357–58.

4 For data on the firm see R. B. McKerrow, *A Dictionary of Printers and Booksellers in England, Scotland and Ireland* (London, 1910), pp. 42–43.

5 W. W. Greg, *A Bibliography of the English Printed Drama to the Restoration* (London, 1939–1951; 2 vols.), I, pp. 417–18.

6 William Empson, *Some Versions of Pastoral* (London, 1935), pp. 27–86. His discussion of the implications of two social levels is perceptive and applies to many plays.

7 Some of the material in this section first appeared in a different form in my article, "*The Case Is Altered*: Initial Comedy of Humours," *Studies in Philology*, L (April, 1952), pp. 195–214.

8 Maurice Castelain, *Ben Jonson* (Paris, 1907), pp. 198–99.

9 See M. Channing Linthicum, *Costume in the Drama of Shakespeare and His Contemporaries* (Oxford, 1936), pp. 118–19, for a fuller explanation of the colors.

10 Ben Jonson, *The Case Is Altered*, ed. William Edward Selin (New Haven, 1917), p. 149.

11 *Plautus*, ed. Paul Nixon (London, 1937; 5 vols.), I, p. 280.

12 Mario Praz, *Studies in Seventeenth-Century Imagery* (London, 1939–1947; 2 vols.), I, p. 201.

13 For *Every Man in His Humour* a simplified system of citations has been adopted. The quarto is designated "a," the folio, "b." When a passage occurs substantially unchanged in both, the quarto reading is given, followed by "a" and "b." Convenient parallel texts are provided on facing pages in Ben Jonson, *Every Man in His Humour*, ed.

Henry Holland Carter (New Haven, 1921). A list of characters' names in the quarto and folio follows:

Quarto	*Folio*
Lorenzo Senior	Knowell
Giulliano	Downright
Prospero	Wellbred
Lorenzo Junior	Edward Knowell
Thorello	Kitely
Biancha	Dame Kitely
Stephano	Stephen
Hesperida	Bridget
Doctor Clement	Justice Clement
Peto	Roger Formall
Bobadilla	Captain Bobadill
Matheo	Matthew
Musco	Brainworm
Pizo	Cash
Cob	Cob
Tib	Tib

14 For further explanation of the terms see particularly I. A. Richards, *Interpretation in Teaching* (New York, 1938), pp. 120–44.

15 G. Gregory Smith, *Ben Jonson* (London, 1919), pp. 100–102.

16 Oscar James Campbell, *Comicall Satyre and Shakespeare's Troilus and Cressida* (San Marino, 1938), p. 55.

17 Ben Jonson, *Every Man in His Humour*, ed. Percy Simpson (Oxford, 1919), pp. xiii–xxv.

18 For a discussion of parallels between these plays and some of Jonson's, see *The Three Parnassus Plays*, ed. J. B. Leishman (London, 1949), pp. 41–60.

19 Carter expresses this view in his edition, p. 271.

20 Herford and Simpson favor this explanation, I, pp. 368–69.

CHAPTER III

1 Claims of this sort by publishers cannot be trusted, but this one must be quite reliable.

2 James G. McManaway, "Latin Title-Page Mottoes as a Clue to Dramatic Authorship," *The Library*, Fourth Series, XXVI (1946), pp. 28–36. For an attempt to make a little too much of this evidence see Robert Boies Sharpe, "Title-Page Mottoes in the Poetomachia," *Studies in Philology*, XXXII (1935), pp. 210–20.

3 Johnstone Parr, "Tamburlaine's Malady," *Publications of the Modern Language Association*, LIX (1944), pp. 696–714.

4 For a discussion of "humour" see James Bradstreet Greenough and George Lyman Kittredge, *Words and Their Ways in English Speech* (New York, 1901), pp. 30–31.

5 Edmund Wilson, *Note-books of Night* (San Francisco, 1942), p. 9.

6 Charles Read Baskervill, *English Elements in Jonson's Early Comedy* (Austin, Texas, 1911), pp. 107–43. This study continues to be useful; various insights that it puts forth have confirmed my generalizations.

7 George Chapman, *An Humorous Day's Mirth*, edd. David Nichol Smith and W. W. Greg (London, 1937), sig. A$_{2r}$.

8 This interpretation of the humours has been, in part, suggested by two articles: Henry L. Snuggs, "The Comic Humours: A New Interpretation," *Publications of the Modern Language Association*, LXII (1947), pp. 114–22; and John C. McGalliard, "Chaucerian Comedy: *The Merchant's Tale*, Jonson, and Molière," *Philological Quarterly*, XXV (1946), pp. 343–70.

9 W. W. Greg, "The First Edition of Ben Jonson's *Every Man out of His Humour*," *The Library*, Fourth Series, I (1920), pp. 153–60.

10 After all these years, there seems no point in connecting Joyce's evolution of the stream of consciousness with Jonson's style. Joyce apparently admired Jonson, but too many ancestors for the stream of consciousness have already been championed. See, for example, Leon Edel, *The Psychological Novel* (New York, 1955), pp. 22–35.

11 Episodes in the plot are borrowed from various sources; see especially Herford and Simpson, IX, pp. 455–57, 472–73.

12 For a study of the names see Allan H. Gilbert, "The Italian Names in *Every Man out of His Humour*," *Studies in Philology*, XLIV (1947), pp. 195–208.

13 Ben Jonson, *Every Man out of His Humor* (London, 1600), sig. A$_{1v}$. All citations of the quartos are from copies in the Houghton Library, Harvard University. The 1616 folio readings are from my copy.

14 George Kernodle, *From Art to Theatre* (Chicago, 1944). This discussion of the complex background of the Elizabethan stage seems essential for understanding it.

15 An illuminating study of certain aspects appears in the unpublished University of Wisconsin dissertation (1956) by David Laird, "The Inserted Masque in Jacobean Drama."

16 Erasmus, *Stultitiae Laus*, ed. I. B. Kan (The Hague, 1898), pp. 10–11.

17 The same, pp. 48–49.

18 Ben Jonson, *The Fovntaine of Selfe-Love* or *Cynthias Revels* (London, 1601), title page.

19 Elkin Calhoun Wilson, *England's Eliza* (Cambridge, 1939), pp. 273–320.

20 The quarto *Cynthia's Revels*, sig. A₁ᵥ.

21 Herford and Simpson, I, p. 406, modify this phrase in the introduction to *Cynthia's Revels*.

22 Edmund Wilson, *Classics and Commercials* (London, 1951), p. 284.

23 Ernest William Talbert, "The Classical Mythology and the Structure of *Cynthia's Revels*," *Philological Quarterly*, XXII (1943), pp. 193–210.

24 Ovid, *Metamorphoses*, I, p. 150.

25 John Webster, *Complete Works*, ed. F. L. Lucas (London, 1927; 4 vols.), II, pp. 195–96.

26 George Puttenham, *The Arte of English Poesie*, edd. Gladys Doidge Willcock and Alice Walker (Cambridge, 1936), p. 200.

27 See Clinton H. Collester, "*Narcissus* Plays Distinguished," *Modern Language Notes*, XX (1905), pp. 134–38, and *Narcissus*, ed. Margaret L. Lee (London, 1893).

28 Ben Jonson, *Cynthia's Revels*, ed. Alexander Corbin Judson (New York, 1912), pp. viii–ix, discusses some of these changes.

29 George Chapman, *An Humorous Day's Mirth*, sigs. A₃ᵣ–A₃ᵥ.

30 Allan H. Gilbert, "The Function of the Masques in *Cynthia's Revels*," *Philological Quarterly*, XXII (1943), pp. 211–30, points out the importance of this part of the play.

31 R. H. Tawney, *Religion and the Rise of Capitalism* (New York, 1926), p. 102.

CHAPTER IV

1 [Robert Cartwright], *Shakespeare and Jonson* (London, 1864), sets forth the most improbable identifications. His cheerful admission of his folly makes him almost preferable to sober historians. "However fanciful these opinions may appear, I hold them to be true, and have more delight in discovering these *imaginary* diamonds in the garden of Shakespeare, than picking up nuggets of gold in the fields of Australia" (p. 26).

2 Ben Jonson, *Poetaster*, ed. Herbert S. Mallory (New York, 1905), pp. xxiii–xxviii, lists the chief nineteenth-century contributions.

3 Roscoe Addison Small, *The Stage-Quarrel Between Ben Jonson and the So-Called Poetasters* (Breslau, 1899), gives one of the more temperate accounts, although it makes excessive identifications.

4 Ralph W. Berringer, "Jonson's *Cynthia's Revels* and the War of the Theatres," *Philological Quarterly*, XXII (1943), pp. 1–22.

5 Ernest William Talbert, "The Purpose and Technique of Jonson's *Poetaster*," *Studies in Philology*, XLII (1945), pp. 225–52. See also Oscar James Campbell's *Comicall Satyre*, pp. 109–34.

6 Arthur H. King, *The Language of Satirized Characters in Poëtaster* (Lund, 1941).

7 Henry David Gray, "The Chamberlain's Men and the *Poetaster*," *Modern Language Review*, XLII (1947), pp. 173–79.

8 Alfred Harbage, *Shakespeare and the Rival Traditions* (New York, 1952), pp. 104–19, sees *Poetaster* as one in a series of battles between two rival groups, those writing for the general public and those catering to a highbrow clique. With Jonson, surely, the explanation falls short. He was not the victim of such a system because, as the present study shows, he incorporated the talents of any performing company into the script. Furthermore, the theory tempts its inventor into wishful distortions, such as attributing *The Case Is Altered* to the Children in 1609, whereas, actually, they only revived it. Finally, the assumptions of such a division ignore history because they posit that no progress is possible and that all coteries in London whether under Elizabeth I or Elizabeth II must have identical, and disastrous, effects on literature.

9 Puttenham, *The Arte of English Poesie*, pp. 148–49.

10 A brief survey is in Eugene M. Waith, "The Poet's Morals in Jonson's *Poetaster*," *Modern Language Quarterly*, XII (1951), pp. 13–19.

11 Allan H. Gilbert, *The Symbolic Persons in the Masques of Ben Jonson* (Durham, North Carolina, 1948), p. 88.

12 Suetonius, *Divus Augustus*, ed. J. C. Rolfe (London, 1935), p. 82.

13 Horace, *Satires, Epistles, and Ars Poetica*, ed. H. Rushton Fairclough (London, 1942), pp. 105–11. Satire I, ix, contains the meeting with the Bore of the Sacred Way.

14 Chloe has not been reading Horace. At least, Crispinus' unkempt red hair (II. ii. 84–85) and beard (III. i. 29) would seem to come from *Ars Poetica*, which Jonson translated:

> a great sort will not pare
> Their nailes, nor shave their beards, but to by-paths
> Retire themselves, avoid the publike baths;
> For so, they shall not only gaine the worth,
> But fame of Poëts, they thinke, if they come forth,
> And from the Barber *Licinus* conceale
> Their heads. . . .   (VIII, p. 325)

The point is trifling in itself but indicates how vividly Jonson visualized what he read and put it to diverse uses.

15 T. S. Eliot, *Four Quartets* (New York, 1943), p. 35.

16 Vladimir Nabokov, *Nikolai Gogol* (Norfolk, Conn., c. 1944), pp. 54–55.

CHAPTER V

1 Ben Jonson, *Workes* (London, 1616), sig. 2G$_{4r}$.

2 Ben Jonson, *Sejanus*, ed. W. D. Briggs (Boston, 1911), contains helpful notes of the wide variety of sources; also Herford and Simpson, IX, pp. 585–633. To a degree Jonson obeyed the Roman authors, but in observing their multiplicity, one must concede that he had his design fully in mind. For a general commentary on Jonson's antiquarianism see Esther Cloudman Dunn, *Ben Jonson's Art* (Northampton, Mass., 1925), pp. 59–82.

3 Ernest William Talbert, "New Light on Ben Jonson's Workmanship," *Studies in Philology*, XL (1943), pp. 154–85; Ellen M. T. Duffy, "Ben Jonson's Debt to Renaissance Scholarship in *Sejanus* and *Catiline*," *Modern Language Review*, XLII (1947), pp. 24–30: both these works evaluate the intelligence with which Jonson utilized his sources.

4 My guess about the collaborator would favor Webster certainly over Shakespeare and probably Chapman; the point does not seem worth debating, however.

5 Dio, *Roman History*, ed. Earnest Cary (London, 1924; 9 vols.), VII, p. 200.

6 For the significant change between the two see the short but incisive definition by Harry Levin, *The Overreacher* (Cambridge, 1952), pp. 148–49.

7 Charles Baudelaire, *Oeuvres Complètes* (Paris, 1944), p. 18.

8 To draw once again on Oscar James Campbell's *Comicall Satyre*, on pages 87–88 he points out how closely the satire in passages of *Cynthia's Revels* parallels contemporary ridicule of effeminate courtiers.

9 Jonson's effective portrayal of locale begins here; the great comedies limit their settings with striking precision. In the late "domestic" plays the scene takes more for granted.

10 In all probability Jonson had Seneca rather than the Greek dramatists in mind.

11 Although Dryden has many references to Jonson as both *The Jonson Allusion-Book* and *Shakespeare and Jonson* prove, unless otherwise indicated, the source for Dryden's opinions when they are mentioned here is the essay *Of Dramatick Poesie*.

12 T. W. Baldwin, *Shakspere's Five-Act Structure* (Urbana, Ill., 1947), pp. 325–29, takes up the structure of *Sejanus* briefly.

13 In the quarto the speech which opens the meeting of the Senate is set entirely in capitals with a period between each word, another instance of how Jonson sought to have the book reinforce the play.

14 For a different interpretation of the tragedy see Edwin Honig, "*Sejanus* and *Coriolanus:* A Study in Alienation," *Modern Language Quarterly*, XII (1951), pp. 407–21.

CHAPTER VI

1 On the whole *Volpone* has received more fortunate criticism; see, for example, the introduction to Ben Jonson, *Volpone*, ed. Arthur Sale (London, 1951).

2 An account of a production appears in the *New York Times*, 5 July 1953, p. x5.

3 André Gide, *Journal, 1889–1939* (Paris, 1939), p. 911.

4 Ralph Nash, "The Comic Intent of *Volpone*," *Studies in Philology*, XLIV (1947), pp. 26–40, sees it as an essentially light comedy. This view overlooks far too much.

5 Jean-Louis Barrault, *Réflexions sur le théâtre* (Paris, 1949), pp. 23–24.

6 W. B. Yeats, *On the Boiler* (Dublin, n.d.), pp. 32–33.

7 Ben Jonson, *Volpone*, ed. John D. Rea (New Haven, 1919), pp. xi–xxx, gives an account of possible sources.

8 Werner Sombart, *Luxus und Kapitalismus* (Munich, 1913), p. 31.

9 Richard H. Perkinson, "*Volpone* and the Reputation of Venetian Justice," *Modern Language Review*, XXXV (1940), pp. 11–18.

10 For Jonson's earlier uncertainties with the unities see Martin Kallich, "Unity of Time in *Every Man in His Humor* and *Cynthia's Revels*," *Modern Language Notes*, LVII (1942), pp. 445–49.

11 Herford and Simpson, IX, p. 205.

12 Mary McCarthy, *Sights and Spectacles* (New York, 1956), pp. 136–37.

13 Wallace Stevens, *The Necessary Angel* (New York, 1951), p. 74.

14 Edmund Wilson, *The Triple Thinkers* (rev. ed., New York, 1948), p. 227, makes this point.

15 Attempts at an adequate appraisal are Joseph Kerman, "Opera à la Mode," *Hudson Review*, VI (1954), pp. 560–77, and George McFadden, "*The Rake's Progress:* A Note on the Libretto," *Hudson Review*, VIII (1955), pp. 105–12.

16 Jonas A. Barish, "The Double Plot in *Volpone*," *Modern Philology*, LI (1953), pp. 83–92, treats this topic thoroughly.

17 Harry Levin, "Jonson's Metempsychosis," *Philological Quarterly*, XXII (1943), pp. 231–39.

18 Mary McCarthy, *Venice Observed* (New York, 1956), p. 50.

CHAPTER VII

1 She appeared at court in Jonson's masques. John Owen, whom Jonson scorned, dedicated a volume of Latin epigrams, *Epigrammatum Liber Singularis* (London, 1607), to her. The complicated history of her disguises and flight has no bearing on this discussion.

2 W. W. Greg, "Was there a 1612 Quarto of *Epicene?*" *The Library,* Fourth Series, XV (1934), pp. 306–15.

3 Ben Jonson, *Epicoene,* ed. Aurelia Henry (New York, 1906), pp. xxviii–xli, discusses sources of the plot; see pp. xli–lv for origins of the dialogue.

4 Oscar James Campbell, "The Relation of *Epicoene* to Aretino's *Il Marescalco*," *Publications of the Modern Language Association,* XLVI (1931), pp. 752–62.

5 Daniel C. Boughner, "*Clizia* and *Epicoene*," *Philological Quarterly,* XIX (1940), pp. 89–91.

6 For a full discussion of Jonson's achievements in prose and a more complete analysis of *Epicene* than can be undertaken here, see the unpublished Harvard dissertation (1952) by Jonas A. Barish, "Ben Jonson's Dramatic Prose."

7 Ezra Pound, *Pavannes and Divisions* (New York, 1918), pp. 156–60. Some interesting parallels between the reputations of Jonson and Pound are drawn by Hugh Kenner, *The Poetry of Ezra Pound* (London, 1951), *passim.*

8 Miss Henry locates it in Ovid, *Ars Amatoria,* Bk. III. 11. 231–32.

9 As various editors have observed, one is reminded of Donne's "Elegie IX,"

> NO *Spring,* nor *Summer* Beauty hath such grace,
> As I have seen in one *Autumnal* face.

(John Donne, *Poetical Works,* ed. Herbert J. C. Grierson [London, 1951; 2 vols.], I, p. 92.) Jonson's tone falls close to contempt, Donne's to gentleness.

10 Effects such as this one contribute to what Robert M. Adams has called the *trompe-l'oeil,* (cf. note. 19, p. 259), but he fails to touch this aspect.

11 See, for example, his poem, "Why I write not of Love" (VIII, p. 93).

12 The discussion is to be found, of course, in George Lyman Kittredge, *Chaucer and His Poetry* (Cambridge, 1938), pp. 185–210.

13 Edward B. Partridge, "The Allusiveness of *Epicoene,*" *English Literary History,* XXII (1955), pp. 93–107, arrives at conclusions similar to mine, which I had reached independently, about the reversal of the sexes in *Epicene.* The first part of his article, which could be taken

farther, sets down these points. The second tries to read a moral into this conduct. "But, though the play offers no final answers, it suggests throughout that the various answers dramatized in the physical and verbal action of the play are comic in so far as they violate certain standards of what is masculine and what is feminine, as well as what is natural and what is artificial in dress, behavior, and beauty—standards which, presumably, the spectators brought to the theatre with them" (p. 106). The very qualifications of the assertion make it doubtful.

14 See page 753 of Oscar James Campbell's article referred to in note 4 of this chapter.

15 This play has attracted increasing attention. Jonas A. Barish, "Ovid, Juvenal, and *The Silent Woman*," *Publications of the Modern Language Association*, LXXI (1956), pp. 213–24, attempts to straighten out its indirections by looking at the sources. With Jonson this method always runs risks; for *Epicene* it becomes disastrous. Jonson expressed reservations about Montaigne and the essay as a form, but the style of the play shares affinities with the French speculations. Author is matched against author to support the weary resignation that there is no absolute truth but many engaging opinions. The article sums up the play as "a series of brilliant discords which . . . fail to fuse into a unified whole" (p. 224); rather, it seems a series of brilliant variations which consciously refuse to conclude their irresoluble theme.

16 Edmund Wilson, *The Triple Thinkers*, pp. 217–21, offers this explanation.

CHAPTER VIII

1 The observation is Coleridge's.—Herford and Simpson, II, p. 109.

2 Robert Gale Noyes, *Ben Jonson on the English Stage* (Cambridge, 1935), pp. 103–72.

3 Paul Goodman, *The Structure of Literature* (Chicago, 1954), has an analysis of *The Alchemist* (pp. 82–103) refreshingly apt and to the point. Because it forms part of a theory of literature it seemed unwise to wrench his observations out of context.

4 For a discussion of this subject see Bertil Johansson, *Religion and Superstition in the Plays of Ben Jonson and Thomas Middleton* (Upsala, 1950), pp. 195–271.

5 A general study of Jonson's language with special emphasis on "jargons" is Alexander H. Sackton, *Rhetoric as a Dramatic Language in Ben Jonson* (New York, 1948).

6 Edgar Hill Duncan, "Jonson's *Alchemist* and the Literature of Alchemy," *Publications of the Modern Language Association*, LXI (1946), pp. 699–710.

7 *Epicene* (II. ii. 91–123) and *The Alchemist* (III. iv. 54–99).

8 Helena Watts Baum, *The Satiric & the Didactic in Ben Jonson's Comedy* (Chapel Hill, North Carolina, 1947), p. 76, takes a more charitable view.

9 Some critics have felt the language goes too far: "Nimiety is a word which might have been invented to fit him [Jonson], and there can be too much even—as he might have said—of the gelastic."—Joseph Wood Krutch, "Drama," *Nation*, CLXVI (24 January 1948), p. 108.

10 *Grimm's Fairy Tales* (New York, 1944), p. 105.

11 Wallace Stevens, *Transport to Summer* (New York, 1947), p. 52.

12 Perhaps this sort of interpretation prompted the view that *The Alchemist* is "a play that is open to charges of sordidness in a way that *Volpone* is not."—D. J. Enright, "Poetic Satire and Satire in Verse: A Consideration of Jonson and Massinger," *Scrutiny*, XVIII (1951–52), pp. 211–23; see p. 217.

13 For discussion of backgrounds see Ben Jonson, *The Alchemist*, ed. Charles Montgomery Hathaway (New York, 1903), pp. 90–103.

14 A convenient discussion of applications of alchemical lore to psychology appears in Jolande Jacobi, *The Psychology of C. G. Jung* (New Haven, 1951), *passim*. Although Jung's theories lend themselves to criticism well, bringing many of them to literature may produce peculiar overstatements. For example, essays by Wylie Sypher in a volume called *Comedy*, containing "Laughter" by Henri Bergson and "An Essay on Comedy" by George Meredith (New York, 1956), trace myth and ritual through drama. In the process any awareness of the structure of comedy as a theatrical genre vanishes.

15 Paul Valéry, *Les divers Essais sur Léonard de Vinci* (Paris, 1931), p. 15.

CHAPTER IX

1 Samuel Johnson, *Lives of the English Poets* (Oxford, 1905; 3 vols.), III, p. 441.

2 T. S. Eliot, *Selected Essays*, p. 129.

3 Joseph Allen Bryant, Jr., "*Catiline* and the Nature of Jonson's Tragic Fable," *Publications of the Modern Language Association*, LXIX (1954), pp. 265–77, stresses Caesar's role especially. Although he does somewhat clarify this aspect, the play does not emerge as more effective.

4 Ben Jonson, *Catiline*, ed. Lynn Harold Harris (New Haven, 1916), pp. xvii–xxiii, cites sources.

5 Horace, *Odes and Epodes*, ed. C. E. Bennett (London, 1914), p. 4.

6 Their ambitions contain none of the rhetoric which Tamburlaine finds intoxicating; see the discussion in Harry Levin, *The Overreacher*, pp. 30–54.

7 There were exceptions, such as Nashe's satiric comments on Cicero's ghost in *The Unfortunate Traveller*.

8 D. J. Enright, "Crime and Punishment in Ben Jonson," *Scrutiny*, IX (1940), pp. 231–48.

CHAPTER X

1 Freda L. Townsend, *Apologie for Bartholmew Fayre* (New York, 1947), p. 71, regards this play as Jonson's outstanding achievement.

2 Ray L. Heffner, Jr., "Unifying Symbols in the Comedy of Ben Jonson" in *English Stage Comedy*, ed. W. K. Wimsatt (New York, 1955), pp. 74–95, discusses the mixture of fantasy and realism in this play, although within a limited scope.

3 Ben Jonson, *Bartholomew Fair*, ed. Carroll Storrs Alden (New York, 1904), p. 172.

4 T. C. Worsley, "Bartholomew Fair," *New Statesman and Nation*, XL (30 December 1950), p. 676.

5 Samuel Pepys, *Diary*, ed. Henry B. Wheatley (New York, n.d.; 2 vols.), I, pp. 314–15.

6 Jonas A. Barish, "Ben Jonson's Dramatic Prose," takes the style into detailed consideration.

7 Paul Valéry, *La Soirée avec M. Teste* (Paris, 1922), p. 17.

8 Julian Symons, "Ben Jonson as Social Realist: *Bartholomew Fair*," *Southern Review*, VI (1940), pp. 375–86. Although an intelligent article, it insists too strongly upon the "realistic" aspects.

9 Herford and Simpson make an attempt, II, pp. 37–46.

10 L. C. Knights, *Drama and Society in the Age of Jonson* (London, 1937), pp. 30–95.

11 W. B. Yeats, *Letters*, ed. Allan Wade (London, 1954), p. 671.

CHAPTER XI

1 Katherine Anne Porter, *The Days Before* (New York, 1952), p. 94.

2 John Palmer, *Ben Jonson* (London, 1934), p. 279.

3 For a more charitable view see the introduction to Ben Jonson, *The Devil Is an Ass*, ed. William Savage Johnson (New York, 1905).

4 The description appears on the title page of a typical collection: *The Pack of Autolycus*, ed. Hyder Edward Rollins (Cambridge, 1927).

5 The twentieth century cannot feel superior. Orson Welles staged a famous invasion from Mars, before the vogue of science fiction, which sent many radio listeners fleeing to open country. See Hadley Cantril, *The Invasion from Mars* (Princeton, 1940).

6 Ben Jonson, *The Staple of News*, ed. De Winter (New York, 1905), pp. xx–xxxiv.

7 L. C. Knights, *Drama and Society in the Age of Jonson*, makes these points reasonably.

8 *The New Inn* also appears in the Yale series: ed. George Bremer Tennant (New York, 1908).

9 Herford and Simpson, I, pp. 203–10, despair of *The Magnetic Lady*. The edition by Harvey Whitefield Peck (New York, 1914) attempts a mild but unconvincing defense.

10 Wallace A. Bacon, "The Magnetic Field: The Structure of Jonson's Comedies," *Huntington Library Quarterly*, XIX (1956), pp. 121–53; this article reads backwards from the structure of *The Magnetic Lady* into the earlier plays. As the progression of the chapters in this book should have shown, Jonson altered his structures constantly. Only in the broadest sense do they have one "Center attractive," and such a definition applies to almost all drama.

11 Herford and Simpson, IX, pp. 268–75, valiantly go on defending an earlier date. *A Tale of a Tub*, ed. Florence May Snell (London, 1915), pp. xiv–xxviii, favors the later one. Chambers in *The Elizabethan Stage*, III, p. 373, agrees in seeing it as wholly a late work. More recently Gerald Eades Bentley, *The Jacobean and Caroline Stage* (London, 1941–56; 5 vols.), IV, pp. 632–36, repeats Chambers' opinion. I favor this position myself. Simply how the old manuscript would have survived the fire which destroyed Jonson's library in 1623 poses one problem. Moreover in my unpublished dissertation "Ben Jonson's Imagery" (Harvard, 1951), pp. 456–58, I found that the metaphoric language of *A Tale of a Tub* likewise matches the later works. Bentley (p. 627) suggests, "I have sometimes thought that more could be made of the community of interest and attitude between *A Tale of a Tub* and *The Sad Shepherd* than I have seen suggested." I had arrived at this conclusion independently and develop it in the final chapter.

12 J. W. Fortescue, "Hunting," in *Shakespeare's England* (London, 1916; 2 vols.), II, pp. 335–40.

13 In connection with this work one should mention the ingenious survey, W. W. Greg, *Jonson's Masque of Gipsies* (London, 1952).

14 Lord Raglan, *The Hero* (New York, 1937), pp. 47–56.

15 Herford and Simpson, I, p. 261.
16 See the rearranged order in *Ben Jonson's Timber or Discoveries,* ed. Ralph S. Walker (Syracuse, 1953), especially the introduction, pp. 1–18.

CHAPTER XII

1   Søren Kierkegaard, *Either/Or,* trs. David F. Swenson and Lillian Marvin Swenson (Princeton, 1944; 2 vols.), I, p. 16.
2   Albert Camus, *Le Mythe de Sisyphe* (Paris, 1942), pp. 167–68.
3   Enid Welsford, *The Fool* (London, 1935), p. 321.
4   This view guides the elaborate survey by Albert Cook, *The Dark Voyage and the Golden Mean* (Cambridge, 1949).
5   An analysis of the difficulties of Shavian comedy appears in Francis Fergusson, *The Idea of a Theater* (Princeton, 1949), pp. 178–85.
6   Susanne K. Langer, *Feeling and Form* (New York, 1953), p. 331.
7   See the backward glance that Huxley throws over the novel after World War II: Aldous Huxley, *Brave New World* (New York, 1950), pp. xix–xxxii.
8   Robert Warshow, "Film Chronicle: A Feeling of Sad Dignity," *Partisan Review,* XXI (1954), pp. 674–75.
9   Joseph Wood Krutch, "Drama," *Nation,* CLXVI (1948), p. 558.
10 Heinrich von Kleist, "Über das Marionettentheater," *Werke* (Leipzig, n.d.; 7 vols.), IV, p. 141.
11 Samuel Beckett, *Waiting for Godot* (New York, 1954), p. 6.
12 For recent commentary see, for example, Molière, *The Misanthrope,* tr. Richard Wilbur (New York, 1955), p. ix, and Mary McCarthy, *Sights and Spectacles,* pp. 168–78.
13 Henry James, *The Art of the Novel,* ed. Richard P. Blackmur (New York, 1934), p. 45.
14 William Hazlitt, "On Modern Comedy," *Complete Works,* ed. P. P. Howe (London, 1931; 21 vols.), IV, pp. 10–14. Hazlitt, however, could hardly bring himself to consider Jonson. See, for example, "On Shakspeare and Ben Jonson" in Volume VI: "There are people who cannot taste olives—and I cannot much relish Ben Jonson, though I have taken some pains to do it, and went to the task with every sort of good will. . . . The comedy of this author is far from being 'lively, audible, and full of vent:' it is for the most part obtuse, obscure, forced, and tedious" (p. 39).
15 Grete de Francesco, *Die Macht des Charlatans* (Basel, 1937), p. 19.
16 The same, p. 200.
17 An excellent study of Jonson's artistic uses of sources appears in Madeleine Doran, *Endeavors of Art* (Madison, 1954), pp. 148–71.

18 Rule 4 of the Leges Convivales which he drew up for the Apollo room of the Devil Tavern is "Nec lectae foeminae repudiantor." (VIII, p. 656)
19 They need not, however, represent only dutiful exercises; see Ruth Wallerstein, *Studies in Seventeenth-Century Poetic* (Madison, 1950).
20 Virgil, *Works*, tr. John Dryden (London, 1698), pp. 481–82.
21 James Frazer, *The Golden Bough* (New York, 1947), pp. 1–9.

Index